Aim higher with Insights in Psychology

From phobias to research methods and relationships to sport psychology, our fantastic range of *Insights* titles take you on a tour of the field, providing a comprehensive, readable introduction to key areas of study within psychology.

Whether you're studying at A-level, university, or have a keen interest that you want to take further, you're sure to find what you need with our *Insights in Psychology* series.

Visit www.palgrave.com/Insights to explore our full range of books.

More titles in this series:

Forensic Psychology

Research Methods and Statistics

Psychology of Addictive Behaviour

Issues, Debates and Approaches in Psychology

9780230249424

PALGRAVE INSIGHTS IN PSYCHOLOGY
Series Editors: Nigel Holt and Rob Lewis

The Palgrave *Insights in Psychology* series provides short, readable introductions to a wide range of topics across the field of psychology. Accessible and affordable, each book offers clear, up-to-date coverage in a manageable format. Whether you're studying at A-level, university, or have a keen interest that you want to take further, you're sure to find what you need with our *Insights in Psychology* series.

Heather Buchanan, Neil Coulson *Phobias*

Graham Davey, Suzanne Dash, Frances Meeten *Obsessive Compulsive Disorder*

Ian Fairholm *Issues, Debates and Approaches in Psychology*

Leanne Franklin *Gender*

David Giles *Psychology of the Media*

Simon Green *Biological Rhythms, Sleep and Hypnosis*

Leo Hendry, Marion Kloep *Adolescence and Adulthood*

Nicola Holt, Christine Simmonds-Moore, David Luke, Christopher C. French *Anomalistic Psychology*

Chris Irons *Depression*

Amanda Ludlow, Roberto Gutierrez *Developmental Psychology*

Nick Lund *Intelligence and Learning*

Antony C. Moss, Kyle R. Dyer *Psychology of Addictive Behaviour*

Karen Rodham *Health Psychology*

Adrian J. Scott *Forensic Psychology*

Kevin Silber *Schizophrenia*

David Tod, Joanne Thatcher, Rachel Rahman *Sport Psychology*

Ian Walker *Research Methods and Statistics*

Julia Willerton *The Psychology of Relationships*

For more information, visit www.palgrave.com/insights

Depression

Chris Irons

PALGRAVE INSIGHTS IN PSYCHOLOGY

SERIES EDITORS:
NIGEL HOLT
& ROB LEWIS

palgrave
macmillan

First published 2014 by
PALGRAVE MACMILLAN

Palgrave Macmillan in the UK is an imprint of Macmillan Publishers Limited, registered in England, company number 785998, of Houndmills, Basingstoke, Hampshire RG21 6XS.

Palgrave Macmillan in the US is a division of St Martin's Press LLC, 175 Fifth Avenue, New York, NY 10010.

Palgrave Macmillan is the global academic imprint of the above companies and has companies and representatives throughout the world.

Palgrave® and Macmillan® are registered trademarks in the United States, the United Kingdom, Europe and other countries.

ISBN 978–1–137–31137–5

This book is printed on paper suitable for recycling and made from fully managed and sustained forest sources. Logging, pulping and manufacturing processes are expected to conform to the environmental regulations of the country of origin.

A catalogue record for this book is available from the British Library.

A catalog record for this book is available from the Library of Congress.

Typeset by MPS Limited, Chennai, India.

Printed in China

For my wonderful MFH

Contents

List of Figures

Note from Series Editors

It is not at all unusual for people to feel a little under the weather now and again, to feel a little run-down, a little 'flat'. It is also not unusual for people to describe themselves as feeling 'depressed' when this happens. Suffering with depression is something quite different. Unlike a low mood that passes when people encourage us to 'cheer up' or make us a nice cup of tea, or where having a good cry seems to make it all better, those who suffer with depression feel very low and flattened for extended periods of time. This can last for days, weeks, or even years. Chris Irons explains it as looking at the world through grey-tinted spectacles, and it is with this phrase that he sets the tone for this book.

Chris Irons is a busy man, and we asked him to engage with the series really as a long-shot but were delighted when he managed to fit his writing into his schedule. It is not easy to write about depression; we both have done so for various publications and are jealous of the clarity Chris has found here. This is a reflection of his professional under-standing of people and how they gather knowledge – skills that have helped him craft a book on an emotive and difficult-to-explain subject. Another great skill is speaking compassionately about the topic, with an awareness that many reading the book will be experiencing the problem he is writing about.

- *You may be reading this book in preparation for university.* Depression sits within a component of our subject that may be described as psychopathology, or abnormal psychology. It is one of a number of psychological problems people in society suffer with and is certain to feature on your course. Any time spent reading this book will not be wasted at all, and it will form a useful reference in your library during your time at university.

- *You may be reading this book while at university.* It is likely that depression will be part of your introductory and compulsory course in psychology. It may also be an advanced option. In either case, the book provides an introduction and an extended view of depression that will serve you very well in both cases.
- *You may be reading this as part of a pre-university course such as A-level.* Depression is studied as part of the psychology specification in a number of areas. The book has been skillfully written by Chris Irons to weave the components you require in amongst a more detailed narrative that will provide you with the very best chances of the top marks.

More than many of the books in this series, you may well be reading this book because you, a friend or someone in your family has been diagnosed with depression and you would like to learn more. Editing this book has been a learning experience for us, and we feel that it is the ideal place to find facts that will help you better understand depression from the perspective of a sufferer, a concerned friend, or an onlooker. Take the time to read it carefully and in your own time. We are very pleased to be able to make a text like this available as part of this very important series.

NIGEL HOLT AND ROB LEWIS
Series Editors

Reading Guide

This is one of the books in the *Insights in Psychology* series. There are a range of topics covered in the books, and these have been chosen to carefully reflect the subjects being studied in psychology at a number of levels.

Whether reading for interest, for your degree study or for pre-university courses, such as A-level or other courses where you may find psychology, the material in these books will help you reach the very best of your potential.

The authors of these books have written their books to include material from the specifications of all relevant A-level examination boards in the United Kingdom, these include:

- The Assessment and Qualifications Alliance (AQA)
- The Welsh Joint Education Committee (WJEC)
- Oxford, Cambridge and RSA (OCR)
- EDEXCEL

To keep the qualifications fresh and focussed on the workplace and further education destinations, and to respond to the very latest research and trends in our subject, the examination boards regularly update their curricula. To ensure you have the very latest information we have chosen to include a reading guide online at: www.palgrave.com/insights.

Acknowledgements

The publisher and authors would like to thank the organisations and people listed below for permission to reproduce material from their publications:

Figure 6.1 P. Gilbert, *The Compassionate Mind* (2009), reprinted with permission from Constable & Robinson Ltd.

Figure 6.2 Adapted from P. Gilbert, *The Compassionate Mind* (2009), reprinted with permission from Constable & Robinson.

Figure 6.3 Adapted from Gilbert and Choden, *Mindful Compassion* (2013), reprinted with permission from Constable & Robinson Ltd.

Figure 7.1 UK Antidepressant Prescribing between 1993 and 2012.

Many people helped with the writing of this book. Thank you to Jenny Hindley and Paul Stevens at Palgrave Macmillan for their guidance and support. I would like to extend my deep appreciation and gratitude to Paul Gilbert for his help, advice, mentorship and friendship. It is, and has been, greatly appreciated, but I don't get to voice this enough to him. Huge thanks also to my parents, brother and niece (Legs) – I feel lucky to have the love and care of such a wonderful family. Finally, a special thank you to my wife, Korina (BB). Your love, support, patience and wisdom have been a guiding light through this process. A deep heartfelt 'thank you' for everything.

Chapter 1

Introduction

At times, everyone feels low in mood, down in the dumps, unhappy or sad. In fact, these occasions are likely to be common for many of us, and can last a matter of minutes, hours, or sometimes, a day or two. At these times, if people ask how we are, we might even say 'I'm depressed'. These types of feelings could arise without any particular trigger – the type of 'getting out of the wrong side of the bed' day – or may follow a period of difficulty or **stress**, such as a having a lot on at work or following an argument with a friend. Indeed, it is very normal to experience changes in mood when difficult things happen to us, such as the break-up of a relationship or loss of job. Whilst these feelings are unpleasant, they are not the type that that we will be focusing on in this book.

When you speak to someone who is suffering from depression, they will tell you that it is very different from the type of low feelings described above. They are likely to tell you about feeling persistently low in mood, *over weeks, months or even years*. They will describe how it is difficult or impossible to get any pleasure or enjoyment out of things in the way they used to – as if looking at life through grey tinted spectacles. They may also describe a whole variety of other difficulties, including low energy, a lack of motivation, problems concentrating and many others (which we will explore later).

What is having depression like?

Depression is a very unpleasant experience and can affect many aspects of our day-to-day experience.

Motivation

Motivation – an organising and driving force towards a particular goal – is often impacted in a significant way during a depression. We can feel slowed down, lacking in energy and 'not bothered' to do anything. Things that we would normally do without thinking, like having a shower, getting dressed and eating breakfast, can suddenly become unimportant or overwhelming. Daily life can feel like an uphill battle, and people sometimes describe that they feel like they have a heavy weight on their shoulders or like they are walking through treacle, making each step or action difficult.

Emotions

Our emotions change in depression in two common ways – we experience a decrease in positive emotions and an increase in negative, unpleasant emotions. This combination is key. **Anhedonia** – derived from a Greek word meaning 'without pleasure' – is a core feature of life when depressed. Things that previously brought a joy and happiness, such as seeing friends, watching a film or playing football, now feel like they will be unfulfilling or unlikely to give us pleasure. As we will explore later, there can be problems here in both the anticipation of an activity (e.g. 'there's no point in trying, I won't enjoy it') and the actual engagement in the activity ('it's not enjoyable like it used to be').

Alongside a reduction in positive emotions, depression is also associated with an increase in negative emotions and feelings. For many depressed people, anxiety increases alongside depression, and things can feel threatening, scary or anxiety provoking in a way that they didn't used to be. In fact, over 50% of people diagnosed with depression will also meet diagnostic criteria for an anxiety disorder at the same time (Kessler et al., 2003). Anger may be another emotion that increases with depression; we may feel more irritable, frustrated and resentful, and take this out on people around us. We might even have intense feelings of rage and hatred that are difficult to express. Alongside these emotions, we may also experience an increase in sadness, shame and guilt, all of which can continue to feed our depressed feelings.

It is also worth mentioning here that there are some depressions in which people describe feeling numb or unemotional. This is often referred to as 'blunted' emotions, and here, both positive and negative emotions feel dulled; hence when a person would normally expect to feel excited or sad, they would experience minimal feelings or simply an absence of feelings.

Thoughts

A number of important changes occur in our thinking when we are depressed. The first relates to the content of our thoughts (the words or phrases that tend to go through our minds). When depressed, our thinking turns more negative, and in particular, many become self-critical, blaming themselves for feeling the way they do or focusing on perceived flaws about themselves. We may begin to dislike ourselves, feel that we are no good and inferior, and compare ourselves with others (and their lives) in a more negative way (known as negative social comparison).

Alongside the content of our thoughts changing, the process of our thinking can also change. For some people, this involves feeling that thoughts are slowed down, jumbled or fleeting. For other people, thinking becomes preoccupied and fixed on particular things, for example, how much of a failure they feel. Commonly in depression, we ruminate more (focusing on things that have happened in the past) or overly focus on the future in an unhelpful way (for example, by engaging in worry). This is often linked to feeling hopeless or the future being bleak.

Behaviour

Our behaviour can also change significantly in depression. Typically, people describe finding it difficult to get going, to have energy to do things, and often, there are reductions in the amount of things they do. They may find it difficult to get out of bed or engage in basic daily activities, such as showering, cleaning teeth, getting dressed or eating. As a result of these changes, but also in addition to them, people may withdraw from social interactions and become more isolated. When around others, people with depression can act in non-assertive or submissive ways, for example agreeing that they are wrong, even when they feel they are right.

◉ How common is depression?

Depression is a very common condition. It is estimated that between 12 and 18% of people will develop depression sometime in their lifetime, and it may well be that these are conservative estimates. The World Health Organization (WHO) has estimated that at least 350 million people world-wide are currently depressed (http://www.who.int/mediacentre/factsheet sfs369/en/). They also suggest that by 2020, depression will be the second most burdensome health disorder (following cardiovascular problems) in leading to disability-adjusted life years (DALYs – a measure of the amount of time someone suffers with a particular illness or disorder in their life). But it doesn't just stop there, as the WHO estimates that by 2030, depression will be the leading cause of DALYs worldwide. The apparent increasing commonality of depression is explored further in Box 1.1.

Box 1.1 The depressed generation: Are levels of depression increasing?

The World Health Organization (WHO), a United Nations organisation concerned with international healthcare, suggests that increasing levels of depression mean that by 2030, depression will affect more people than any other health issue. A number of studies have suggested that there are increasing levels of depression (prevalence rates). Moreover, there seems to be an increasing public and media awareness of depression as an illness, including greater publicity of well-known people, like actors, sportsmen and musicians, who have experienced depression.

Even though there is a popular perception that rates are increasing, is this backed up by scrutiny of the figures? Well, the research literature on this is quite mixed. For example, in a large study of 42,000 Americans, Compton et al. (2006) found a doubling of the prevalence rates of depression between 1991–1992 (3.3% of the population) and 2001–2002 (7.06% of the population). However, a number of other studies have reported no change. For example, in a study measuring depression prevalence in Canada between 1952 and 1992, Murphy et al. (2000) found that there were no significant changes during this 40-year period. In another study, Hawthorne et al. (2008) looked at rates of depression in Australia between 1998 and 2004. Although they found a slight increase in rates (0.6%), this was not statistically significant.

So, how are these two different findings – the WHO prediction of depression becoming the most burdensome illness by 2030, and recent studies showing no change in prevalence rates of depression – possible? There appear to be a number of factors related to this discrepancy:

- How rates of depression are measured – for example, whether this is via self-report questionnaire, semi-structured interview or professional diagnosis – as these can all lead to different rates being reported.
- Whether studies follow people over a set period of time, working out how many become depressed during that period, versus asking people to recall whether they have been depressed in the past. There are major concerns about the accuracy of peoples' memory when looking back on symptoms in the past, and this may distort the figures in studies that have used this methodology.
- Rates of depression might be increasing in some countries (i.e. developing countries) but staying stable in developed countries. This would then skew findings depending on what countries are included in any study.
- Although the use of illness 'burden' by the WHO is a helpful concept indicating how much a person's life is impacted by depression, it does not as such show how prevalent depression is, or that it is increasing in prevalence.
- Whilst depression will become the most burdensome illness by 2030, this may in part be due to the reducing burden of other health problems (due to better treatments, e.g. cardiovascular problems).

We will explore in later chapters about whether there are some people who are more likely to become depressed. However, the reality is that anyone can become depressed. Although stigma may still remain, there is now much greater awareness and appreciation of this condition and its consequences. In fact, many well-known people, including *Royalty* (Queen Victoria, Princess Diana), *Politicians* (Winston Churchill, Abraham Lincoln), *Sportsmen and women* (Frank Bruno, Marcus Trescothick, Dame Kelly Holmes), *Musicians* (Robbie Williams, Beyonce Knowles, Eminem, Mozart), *Actors* (Harrison Ford, Halle Berry, Angelina Jolie) and *Writers* (J.K. Rowling, Charles Dickens and Tolstoy), are known to have experienced depression.

> ## Box 1.2 Case study of depression – Princess Diana
>
> For many people, the idea of becoming a princess and the wife to the future King of England would be a dream come true, a fantasy held as a child but brought to reality as an adult. For Diana Spencer, this fantasy became a reality when she became Diana, Princess of Wales, after marrying Charles, Prince of Wales, in 1981. For many people, Diana had the perfect life, having been brought up in a rich family, with access to some of the finest education and opportunities anyone could imagine, before marrying into one of the most well-known, affluent and powerful families in the world. She was beautiful, seemed to be well liked by the press and public, and have everything going for her.
>
> However, despite all of the trappings of royalty, and unknown to many at the time, Diana was living anything but the fairytale life. Instead, she was lonely, miserable and following the birth of her first child (Prince William) experienced postnatal depression. She would later describe the difficulties she experienced adjusting to the pressures of life as a royal in the public spotlight, feeling alone and detached from her own family and struggling to deal with difficulties in her marriage, knowing that her husband was still in love with a previous girlfriend, Camilla Parker Bowles.

What is the impact of depression?

Depression can have significant consequences in many different aspects of a person's life. In a large survey based in the United States, Kessler and colleagues (2003) found that almost 97% of people questioned who had suffered from a depressive episode that year had experienced impairment in at least one of four roles – home, work, relationship and social. Moreover, they found that almost 60% of people felt that this impairment was either severe or very severe. Research has shown that depression may have a negative effect on a number of different areas in life:

Education

Depression appears to have a negative effect upon academic attainment. Rothon et al. (2009) found that higher depression self-report scores in adolescent boys (aged 13–14) were associated with decreased academic exam achievement (GCSE) results at age 16. Similar findings hold for students at university, where higher levels of symptomology on a common self-report depression questionnaire were associated with lower levels of academic achievement in end-of-year exams, and increased likelihood of dropping out of university (Andrews and Wilding, 2004; Eisenberg, Golberstein and Hunt, 2009).

Employment

Merikangas et al. (2007) found that depression is the second most common reason for people taking days off work, besides only neck and back pain. It may be a little surprising, but people in this survey took more time off work because of depression than for suffering with cancer, having had a heart attack, or a stroke. It is estimated that people suffering from depression are likely to take more than twice as many days off work sick than people who are not depressed (Adler et al., 2006), with some studies placing this as three times more likely, equivalent to 15 days per year (Almond and Healey, 2003). Moreover, it appears that the more severely depressed you are, the greater number of days off work you will take. It has been estimated that in England alone, an astonishing 109 million working days were lost due to depression in the year 2000 (Thomas and Morris, 2003). It is likely that this figure is far higher today. Due to the type of symptomatic difficulties experienced when depressed (including reduced concentration and energy), on average depressed individuals will lose over five hours of 'work productivity' a week compared to when they are not suffering an episode of depression (Stewart, 2003). It is also likely that they will struggle to perform to the standard they usually would, and performance becomes increasingly impaired if they suffer from more severe levels of depression symptomology (e.g. Lerner et al., 2010).

Relationships

Depression appears to have a negative effect on interpersonal relationships. Research looking at this has found that an individual who is depressed is more likely to experience reduced relationship quality, increased romantic relationship dissatisfaction and increased relationship break-up and divorce. It also seems that this is the case over time, so that people with a history of depression, but not currently depressed, are also likely to experience greater difficulty in their relationships. In a group of

13 to 18-year-old teenagers, Jaycox and colleagues (Jaycox et al., 2009) found that in comparison with non-depressed individuals, those teenagers who had experienced depression were significantly more likely to report problems in social and familial functioning (e.g. reduced sense of support in these relationships). Moreover, the researchers also asked the parents of those teenagers involved in the study to rate their relationship with their child. Parents of teenagers who had been depressed rated themselves as having higher levels of negative emotions, and greater relationship strain with their child, than those parents of non-depressed teenagers.

Physical health

A number of studies have found that people who are depressed are more likely to suffer from another mental or physical health problem. However, the causal relationship here is complex – that is, does depression lead to the increased likelihood of physical health problems, or do physical health problems lead to increased likelihood of depression? There is evidence that the former might be true. For example, in a longitudinal study, Raikkonen, Matthews and Kuller (2007) found that depression symptoms measured 15 years previously predicted a significant increase in future diagnosis of metabolic syndrome (coronary heart disease, diabetes type 2) in women. Moreover, depression has been found to increase mortality rate when suffering from a variety of other health problems (including heart attack and stroke) and reduced survival time following a diagnosis of cancer (see Freedland and Carney, 2010, for a good review).

Suicide

For some people, the impact of depression is as serious as can be imagined – death. Suicide is perhaps the single most tragic consequence of depression for some people. As we will see in the next chapter, suicidal feelings are one of the symptoms that can lead to a diagnosis of depression under both of the major diagnostic systems used by health professionals. Thomas and Morris (2003) measured, amongst other things, mortality rate in people over the age of 15 in England in 2000 due to depression. They estimated that 2615 people died from suicide, self-inflicted injury, accidental poisoning or accidental poisoning with anti-depressants. Whilst women in this study were found to be more than twice as likely to be suffering from depression, there were three times as many deaths due to depression in men compared to women. Research has consistently shown that whilst women are between two and three times more likely to attempt suicide than men (Weissman et al, 1999), over 75% of completed suicides are by men (Berman, 2010). Given that suicidal ideation (thinking about suicide) broadly appears to be as common amongst depressed men as depressed women (Weissman et al., 1999), this finding suggests that men may be more likely to *act* on these thoughts and may use more lethal methods to kill themselves than women.

Economic costs of depression

In recent years, researchers, healthcare professionals, economists and politicians have become increasingly aware of the impact depression has on a nation's economy. Recent research by the UK Government (House of Commons Report, 2009) estimates that the total loss of income to the UK economy in 2009 due to depression was £8.97billion a year, a figure that had increased by almost £4billion in ten years from the estimated cost to the economy in 1999. For a comparison, that is almost the same amount that the UK Government spends on its transport budget each year, and represented approximately 1% of the country's gross domestic product (GDP) that year. It is further likely that this is an underestimate of the true amount, as it does not take into account the loss of productivity of other work colleagues who have to provide cover for the absence or underperformance of the depressed individual.

For depressed individuals themselves, the economic costs appear to be significant. For example, a study in the United States suggested that over the course of their lifetime, people who suffer from depression will earn 35% less money than if they had not been depressed, and that by the age of 50, they would be earning $10,000 (roughly £6,000) less a year (Smith and Smith, 2010).

◉ Chapter summary

This chapter has introduced some ideas about how depression affects people, their education, employment, health and relationships, and society more generally.

👁 Overview of this book

The following chapters will set out to:

- explain how depression is diagnosed and outline the different types of depression that one can experience,
- identify how common depression is, what impacts on its development and course, and whether some people are more susceptible to developing a depressive disorder, and
- explore how depression is treated, including biological, psychological and social approaches.

Chapter 2

Depression: Diagnosis and Classification

In this chapter we will:
- outline how depression is diagnosed and classified
- consider what symptoms are common in depression
- consider how prevalent depression is
- consider whether certain factors (e.g. age, gender, ethnicity) affect how common depression is
- discuss the different methods that are used to diagnose and classify depression

Introduction: what is depression?

Whilst you might expect depression to be a relatively easy thing to describe, it turns out that this is not necessarily the case. This book focuses on the type of depression that medical professionals sometimes refer to as 'clinical depression'. Many people who work professionally with depressed individuals have discussed and argued over many years about the relationship between unhappiness, misery and general despondency with life, and a so-called 'clinical' condition that is called 'depression', and that may require intervention. To some extent these have been driven by medical concerns to identify specific classes of 'diseases', with particular causes and identifiable physiological markers. In addition, drug companies need to have specific diseases in order for people to be given a drug. In reality, however, these distinctions are very complicated, and it is difficult to pinpoint where normal reactions to

Box 2.1 History of depression

The origin of the word depression comes from the Latin word *deprimere* which means 'to press down, depress'. Over two thousand years ago, the Greeks and Romans were using the labels of 'melancholia' and 'mania' to describe variations in mood state. In approximately the year 400 B.C., Hippocrates – a famous Greek doctor who is sometimes known as the 'father of Western medicine' – made reference to melancholia in which he described it as an aversion to food, feeling despondent and irritable, and sleeplessness. As we will explore later in this chapter, these are all symptoms seen as common in depression today.

It was not until the late 19th and early 20th centuries that the term 'depression' started to be used in the place of melancholia, and this came in the wake of the attempts of psychiatrists such as Emil Krapelin, Kurt Schneider and Adolf Meyer to more systematically study and define the nature and symptoms of psychiatric problems. But we had to wait until 1951 for depression to be 'officially' recognised as a mental health condition in the first edition of the Diagnostic and Statistical Manual of Mental Disorders (DSM), which went on to be viewed by many as the 'bible' of the diagnosis and classification of mental disorders.

difficult life events begin, and more autonomous 'illness process' takes over, and this is still a source of great debate.

Defining and describing depression is also difficult because combinations of quite different symptoms and causes can result in the same diagnosis of depression. For example, in some depressions people can lose their appetite, whilst in others they eat more; in some depressions people find it difficult to sleep (insomnia), whereas in others, they sleep much more than normal (hypersomnia). Whilst some depressions appear to be linked to the loss of something (e.g. of a close relationship), others appear to be linked to the presence of something unpleasant (e.g. a bullying boss or an abusive partner). We will explore the diagnosis of depression later in the chapter, but for now, there are two key points to make. The first is that depression is a highly heterogeneous disorder, that is, it includes a mix of different types of symptoms. In fact, using one of the classification symptoms used for diagnosing depression, one may diagnose depression in 227 different people without them sharing exactly the same symptoms! The second point is that amongst these different symptom combinations and seemingly contradictory symptoms of depression (i.e. sleeping more or less both being a potential feature), the important thing to hold in mind is that **two symptoms** are usually seen as key to the experience and diagnosis of depression:

- Persistently low mood and/or sadness
- Loss of, or a reduction in, the ability to experience pleasure

The reason why these symptoms are salient is that they point towards two key processes in depression – an *increase* in negative emotions and feelings and a *reduction* in positive emotions and feelings. This combination - the double impact of **increasing negative emotions** and **decreasing positive emotions** – is why depression is such an unpleasant experience. Some people reading this book will have experienced depression and therefore have a firsthand experience of just how unpleasant it can be. However, for many others, it can be helpful to understand what depression feels like by hearing about the experiences of those who have suffered from it. For example, Elizabeth, a woman in her 40s who I once treated for depression, described the experience to me as:

> Imagine waking every day where, for the first second or two, you experience the only sense of feeling 'ok' for the rest of the day, before reality slams home until you next fall asleep – deep, unwavering sadness in the pit of your heart and stomach; loneliness and isolation that is so strong that it doesn't change whether you're with people or not; and, to add to everything, a lack of motivation or energy to do anything ... anything at all, whether that's getting out of bed and cleaning my teeth, or spending time doing things that I know I used to enjoy. I just want the day to end so that I can crawl into bed and sleep once again ...

When you spend time with people who have experienced depression – as a friend or family member looking after someone you love or as a health professional caring for your patients – these types of descriptions are common. However, if any of you reading this book haven't spent time with someone who is depressed and want to learn more about what this is like, there are a number of good books describing the firsthand experience of depression and its impact on life (e.g. see *Shoot the Damn Dog: A Memoir of Depression* by Sally Brampton).

Diagnosis and classification of depression

Internationally, there are two main approaches used for diagnosing depression, and more generally, mental health problems. The **Diagnostic and Statistical Manual of Mental Disorders (DSM)** is published and developed by the American Psychiatric Association (APA). It has recently been updated and is now in its fifth incarnation as the DSM-5. It was developed to provide a common way of classifying mental health disorders, and whilst primarily used in the United States, it is also used in a variety of other countries around the world. In comparison, the 10th revision of the **International Statistical Classification of Diseases and Related Health Problems (ICD-10)** is used by many countries across the world – including the UK – and was developed by the World Health Organization (WHO). It is now in its 10th edition and is due to be updated to edition 11 in 2015. An overview of the criteria for the diagnosis of depression for both manuals is displayed in Box 2.2.

Box 2.2 DSM and ICD criteria for diagnosis and classification of depression

The DSM-5 suggests that to diagnose depression, someone would need to have five or more symptoms from the list below. At least one of the five symptoms needs to be either (i) depressed mood or (ii) loss of pleasure. Moreover, symptoms need to have been present in the past two-week period and represent a change to how the person previously functioned. The nine potential symptoms are:

(i)   Depressed mood, reported by individual or others, that is present most of the day and nearly every day
(ii) Clear loss of interest or pleasure in most, if not all, activities
(iii) Decreased or increased appetite or significant weight loss or gain (e.g. at least 5% of total body weight in the past month)
(iv) Insomnia or hypersomnia most days
(v)   Psychomotor agitation or retardation
(vi) Loss of energy or feeling fatigued nearly every day

(vii) Feeling worthless or (inappropriately) guilty most days

(viii) Decreased ability to concentrate or think or difficulties making decisions

(ix) Repeated thoughts of death, suicidal ideation, suicidal attempts or making of specific plans to commit suicide

There are various other conditions that are specified for diagnosis, including certain exclusions (e.g. not being the result of an illicit drug or medication, or the result of a physical health problem) and that the symptoms have to be associated with impaired functioning or significant distress.

The ICD-10 suggests that a diagnosis of depression requires at least two of the following symptoms, most of the time, for at least two weeks:

- Persistent sadness or low mood
- Loss of interests or pleasure
- Fatigue or low energy

If any of the above symptoms are present, then the clinician assesses whether any of the following are present:

- Disturbed sleep
- Poor concentration or indecisiveness
- Low self-confidence
- Poor or increased appetite
- Suicidal thoughts or acts
- Agitation or slowing of movements
- Guilt or self-blame

Although reference to both the DSM-5 and ICD-10 will be made in this book, we will mostly refer to the DSM-5 as the most up-to-date, revised diagnostic criteria.

The criteria for diagnosing depression are very similar between the DSM and ICD, and both agree on eight common items. However, there are some small differences; the ICD-10 lists loss of confidence or self-esteem and excessive guilt as two separate symptoms, whereas DSM-5 has one item of inappropriate or excessive guilt with feelings of worthlessness. With regard to the process of diagnosing depression, the ICD-10 suggests that a diagnosis of depression can only be concluded if two out of three key symptoms (low mood, lack of pleasure and low energy) are met, along with a minimum of four other symptoms. In comparison, the DSM-5 requires one of two symptoms – low mood and lack of pleasure – as essential but a minimum of five symptoms to meet threshold for diagnosis.

◉ Different types of depression

Rather than there being one type of depression, clinicians and researchers have attempted to classify different *subtypes* of the disorder. Broadly, classification of these types has been linked to severity of symptoms, course of the illness and the different features (clusters of symptoms) of the illness. Whilst there is some overlap between these different types, the broad categories are explored in more detail below.

Symptom severity

There are different ways of classifying the severity of depression symptoms, but commonly these are referred to as:

Subthreshold Depressive symptoms – Here, there are not enough symptoms to meet criteria for a full diagnosis of depression (i.e. less than five symptoms), but the person does experience some of the common signs of depression.

Mild Depression – This involves a reduction in mood, with an additional five or six symptoms of depression which are likely to cause relatively minor difficulties or impairments in daily functioning.

Moderate Depression – This involves a greater number of symptoms than in mild depression, with an associated greater impact on impairment of functioning.

Severe Depression (without psychotic features) – Here, depression is associated with significant distress and functional impairment, with most, if not all, of the nine depressive symptoms outlined in Box 2.2 present. Severe depression usually requires professional support and treatment, and can lead to an increased risk of self-harm and suicide.

Severe Depression with Psychotic Features (also known as Psychotic Depression) – Psychotic depression is a form of severe depression in which the person also experiences psychotic symptoms. Psychotic symptoms – or psychosis, more generally – refers to experiences in which there is some form of loss of contact with reality. In psychotic depression, an individual may experience a variety of different psychotic symptoms, including delusions and hallucinations. Delusions are particular strongly held beliefs that lack strong or clear evidence to the contrary. In psychotic depression, delusions can involve a sense that one is being persecuted or targeted unfairly, or excessive beliefs of guilt and responsibility for something. Hallucinations are when someone has a perceptual experience (via any of the senses, e.g. hearing, vision or touch) in the absence of a direct or observable stimulus for this experience. In psychotic depression, hallucinations sometimes involve hearing a derogatory voice making comments about the self.

There have been very few comprehensive studies looking at differences between levels of depression severity. However, Kessler and colleagues (2003) analysed results from the National Comorbidity Survey Replication (NCS-R) study, carried out across the United States between 2001 and 2003. The authors found that the average duration of depressive symptoms was longer for those rated as *very severely* depressed in comparison to those rated as mildly, moderately or severely depressed. Moreover, they also highlight that increased severity of symptoms was associated with greater levels of role impairment (with the greatest impact being on levels of social impairment) and a higher level of comorbidity with other mental health problems.

Box 2.3 Controversies with the classification and diagnosis of depression

Whilst depression is a widely accepted and acknowledged disorder, there are a number of issues in defining, measuring and diagnosing it. The DSM-5 and ICD-10 suggest that this should be done based on number of symptoms present, rather than particular constellations of symptoms that might represent different types of depressions. Thus, there are huge varieties of symptom combinations that could lead to a diagnosis of depression, often with the assumption that regardless of which symptoms are present, as long as there are enough of them, the same, underlying condition is present. For example, for the DSM-5, out of nine possible symptoms, five are needed to diagnose depression. This means that two people diagnosed with depression may only share one symptom, whilst their experience of this symptom (in terms of its frequency, severity, persistence, etc.) may vary hugely. In total, there are 227 different combinations of symptoms that would still lead to a diagnosis of major depression using the DSM-5. Given this, some people question whether it makes sense to use the term 'depression' to describe such a broad array of symptoms.

There also appear to be problems with whether to use categorical methods to classify depression (i.e. making a diagnosis based on a certain number of symptoms) or to use dimensional constructs to describe severity of symptoms (e.g. non-depressed, subthreshold depression, mild depression, moderate depression and severe depression), or a mixture of the two. Ingram and Siegle (2010) suggest that it may be more appropriate to look to a *symptom*-based approach (where diagnosis is around how symptoms cluster or constellation of symptoms) to understand and classify depression, rather than a *syndrome*-based approach (where diagnosis requires the presence of a number of symptoms).

Some people also criticise the notion of the diagnosis of depression – and mental health problems, in general – for a lack of clear, consistent aetiological (causal) factors. In other words, unlike a physical health problem like cancer or TB, there are no objective and consistent physical markers of depression (e.g. blood tests, brain scans) that show categorically that someone is depressed. Rather, for depression we have to rely on clinical assessments and subjective descriptions to help us diagnose. For some people, the term 'depression' is a non-scientific entity, lacking clear, coherent or consistent ways of accurate measurement and therefore should not to be used to refer to an illness or a disorder.

Finally, a very specific and recent controversy arose when the DSM-5 was removed from its criteria the 'bereavement specifier'. In the previous version of the DSM (the DSM-IV), clinicians were directed not to diagnose someone with depression following a bereavement unless the symptoms have persisted for over two months following the loss. However, in the DSM-5 this has been removed. There are now great concerns that this will lead to the over-medicalisation of normal human grieving, and that people will be given treatments – such as antidepressant medications – for an experience that would naturally pass on its own. For those of you who have suffered from a bereavement and then experienced some of the symptoms as outlined in Box 2.2, it might be worth considering how, if you were living in America or many other countries in the world that use the DSM-5, you might be told that you are suffering from a mental health problem and advised to take medications for this.

⊙ Course of depression

Up until the later part of the twentieth century, many researchers and health professionals held the belief that depression was an episodic illness, and that it followed a presenting pattern of onset, illness, remission and, finally, recovery. However, increasingly, the course and prognosis of depression is recognised to be highly variable, idiosyncratic and complex. This shift in understanding has in large part been the result of epidemiological studies. **Epidemiology** is the study of illness and disease in a population and, in particular, their presentation (e.g. how common, how evenly distributed, how long lasting), along with their causes and how they impact people. In a large epidemiological study of people in the Netherlands, Jan Spijker and colleagues (2002) found that the median length of a single depressive episode was three months, and that between 63% and 76% of people had recovered within 12 months. However, Spijker and colleagues also found that 20% of the sample had not recovered by 24 months, suggesting a large proportion of people suffered from a chronic course of depression. In summarising some of the longitudinal studies investigating course of depression, Boland and Keller (2010) estimate that approximately 10% of depressed individuals will remain depressed for at least five years.

To differentiate the various types of depression course, the following terms are sometimes used by scientists and health professionals:

Single episode depression

A single episode of depression is just that – a period of time (the first one) in which an individual meets criteria for a diagnosis to be made by DSM or ICD criteria. A single episode of depression may vary in terms of the number, type and severity of symptoms experienced.

Remission

Remission from depression is the point of time when an individual no longer suffers from depression, the point that they no longer meet diagnostic criteria for a depressive episode. There can be two forms of remission – partial or full. In partial remission, the symptoms of depression are still present but are reduced in number so that the person does not meet diagnostic criteria anymore (e.g. having four or fewer depressive symptoms specified by DSM-5). In comparison, full remission involves at least two months in which the individual has not experienced significant symptoms of depression – although this does not mean that they are completely free of any symptoms of depression.

Recovery

Recovery from depression is usually thought as recovery from an episode of depression but not necessarily recovery from the condition itself (i.e. it does not imply that the person will never become depressed again). Recovery is specified by a set period of time in which someone has been in full remission, usually seen as at least four months (Rush et al., 2006).

Recurrence

This refers to the beginning of a new episode of depression following a period of recovery. *Recurrent depressive disorder* describes a clinical picture in which an individual experiences at least one recurrence of depression following a period of recovery. It has been estimated that approximately 60% of individuals who experience a depression for the first time will go on to experience another episode of depression in the future. Interestingly, for those experiencing a second episode of depression, there is a 70% likelihood of experiencing a third depression, and for those in their third period of depression a 90% chance of going on to have a fourth episode (see the American Psychiatric Association, 2000). In fact, in a 10-year longitudinal study of 318 people with depression, Solomon et al. (2000) found that risk of a reoccurrence of depression rose by 16% with each successive recurrence, but that the risk of reoccurrence decreased as the amount of time in recovery increased.

Persistent (chronic) depression

For many years, there existed a prevailing belief that depression was an episodic disorder, in which someone experienced a depressed episode, and after a period of time, this alleviated and they would feel well again, even if they went on to experience further episodes of depression in the future. However, during the past 20 years our understanding of the course of depression has increased greatly, and we now know that a significant number of people can continue to meet diagnostic criteria for depression for many years after they initially started feeling depressed. There are a number of different types of persistent depression:

- Dysthymia, also known as subthreshold depression, is a type of mild depression that continues for over two years. Although not currently specified in ICD-10 criteria, there is growing research suggesting that dysthymia can have a significant impact upon an individual's well-being and functioning.
- Double depression – this involves an underlying dysthymic disorder (see above) but with an episode of major depression at the same time.
- Depression with residual features – this involves the persistence of debilitating depressive symptoms but which no longer fulfil diagnostic criteria for a major depressive episode.

⊙ Factors influencing the course of depression

There are a number of factors that impact on the course or presentation of depression:

- Early onset – whilst there are relatively high levels of remission following an episode of depression in adolescence, emerging evidence suggests that individuals who first develop depression in childhood or adolescence are at increased risk for future adverse outcomes. For example, early onset depression is associated with greater likelihood of future depressive episodes (Rao, Hammen and Daley, 1999). Moreover, Fergusson and Woodward (2002) also found that early onset depression was associated with a variety of negative future psychosocial outcomes, including increased nicotine and alcohol dependence, poor education attainment and unemployment. It is, however, unclear at this stage whether there are differences in future outcomes based on how *early* the first episode of depression was experienced (e.g. developing depression pre- or post-puberty).

- Late onset – whilst research suggests that individuals experiencing their first episode of depression later in life have similar remission and treatment rates as those with a first experience in middle life, it appears that a later age of onset is associated with a poorer prognosis (e.g. in terms of quicker relapse; Mueller et al., 2004; Mitchel and Santiago, 2009). It may be that this is linked to comorbid, physical health difficulties that are more prevalent in older age or with greater frequency of certain types of life events (e.g. death of one's spouse).

- Type of symptoms – as described above, depression is a heterogeneous syndrome, in which two rather different constellations of symptoms may lead to the same diagnosis of depression. Moore and Garland (2004) suggest that common psychological symptoms such as hopelessness, low self-esteem and lack of pleasure may be a core feature of poorer recovery from depression than biological symptoms. Other researchers have suggested that certain comorbid problems (e.g. physical pain, comorbid physical illness) may represent risk factors for a more persistent depressive presentation. In contrast, in following a group of depressed people for ten years, Moos and Cronkite (1999) found that difficulties socialising, tendencies to deal with stress with avoidance, suicidal thoughts, problems with sleep, high levels of fatigue and anhedonia were symptoms predictive of a more persistent, chronic course of depression. In particular, they found that fatigue was the strongest predictor of progression to a chronic course of depression.

- Comorbid medical illness – In a thorough review of the literature, Freedland and Carney (2010) highlight how depression and medical illness tend to co-occur more frequently than would be expected by change alone. They discuss studies highlighting how medical illness may be a predictor and cause of depression, and vice-versa. Research has shown links between depression and a broad range of medical illnesses, including metabolic syndrome, diabetes, coronary heart disease and cancer (Freedland and Carney, 2010; Katon, 2011).

Depression with comorbid medical illness has been found to be more chronic in its presentation, more recurrent, less likely to be in full remission and take longer to achieve remission than non-comorbid depressions (Muskin, 2010). Moreover, the presence of depression appears to have an adverse effect on the outcome of the medical condition, with poorer prognosis and higher mortality levels.

- Early life experiences – for many years, researchers have been interested in how different experiences that we have in life may be associated with the development and maintenance of depression. There is now a large research base highlighting how life experiences may affect the course of depression. For example, difficult early experiences, including abuse or neglect, have been associated with a more persistent presentation of depression (Brown and Moran, 1994; Lara et al., 2000). We will explore environmental explanations of depression in more detail in Chapter 5.
- Current stress – there has been a lot of research looking at the role of stress in depression, including its potential causal and maintaining role (Monroe, Slavich and Georgiades, 2010). There have been a variety of biological, psychological and social and evolutionary explanations for how stress impacts upon depression, and we will explore some of these in Chapter 3–6.

◉ Other subtypes of depression

Alongside the severity and course of depression described above, there are a variety of other types of depression. Some of these subtypes are outlined in the DSM-5 as 'specifiers', others are terms that were commonly used in the past but are rarely used today. These include:

Depression with catatonic features

This refers to a depression in which there is marked psychomotor change, including physical immobility, mutism (inability to speak), odd bodily, voluntary movements, repetitive copying of words/phrases another person has uttered (echolalia), or repetitive copying of another person's actions (echopraxia).

Depression with melancholic features

This refers to a feature of a major depressive episode in which the primary feature is loss of interest/pleasure in all – or nearly all – activities, to the extent to which a person's mood is no longer reactive (even momentarily) to a positive event or experience (i.e. something that previously would have brought interest or pleasure). Alongside these primary features, the person must also meet three of the following symptoms: distinct quality of depressed mood, lower mood in the morning, early morning waking, increased psychomotor retardation or agitation, weight loss, excessive or inappropriate guilt.

Depression with atypical features

This refers to primary presenting features of mood reactivity (mood improving due to positive events/experiences) and two of the following: increased appetite or weight gain, hypersomnia, leaden paralysis (heavy feelings in arms and legs) and persistent sensitivity to interpersonal rejection.

Seasonal–affective disorder

In 1984, Dr. Norman Rosenthal, a South African psychiatrist working in the United States, along with a group of researchers, published a paper outlining a form of recurrent depression with seasonal fluctuations, commonly known as Seasonal Affective Disorder (SAD). Although commonly mis- and/or under-diagnosed, it appears to be a relatively common disorder, with **prevalence** estimates ranging from 1–3% of the population (Magnusson, 2009) but with some studies finding much higher levels in some groups. In comparison with non-seasonal depression, SAD appears to involve similar cognitive and emotional features but with increased symptoms relating to sleep, appetite, weight gain and decreased activity (Magnusson, 2009). Although more common in winter months, for some people depression has been found to correspond with the summer months, and although somewhat mixed, there are some indications that SAD is more common at more northerly latitudes (Magnusson, 2000; Mersh et al., 1999).

Postpartum depression

Postpartum (literally, 'following birth') depression, more often referred to as postnatal depression or 'the baby blues', is a depression experienced by women following childbirth. Most postpartum depressions occur within the first month following childbirth, but for some women this can occur anytime within the first year post-delivery. Symptoms experienced include sadness and hopelessness, feeling overwhelmed and irritable, and problems with sleep and low energy. For some women, postpartum depression can be associated with feeling distant, unemotional or even negative about their babies, and in a minority, there can be thoughts of hurting the baby. Tragically, in very rare cases where postnatal depression has not been identified or treated successfully, mothers have gone on to murder their babies.

Neurotic depression

This is not a commonly used description for depression anymore, and although it appeared in the DSM-II and ICD-9, it was removed from later, updated versions. Previously, a common distinction used by health professionals was between psychotic depression (i.e. a severe depression with experiences of delusions or hallucinations – see above for more details) and neurotic depression, which was often taken as any other depression as long as it was not psychotic. In recent years, neurotic depression has been replaced conceptually with milder forms of depression and, in particular, the term **'dysthymia'**.

Endogenous versus reactive depression

Endogenous and reactive depressions were terms initially used to describe types of depression which were seen to have different causes. Whereas a reactive depression was seen as an understandable result of an adverse or traumatic life event, endogenous depression (from the Greek prefix endo- 'within' and the English suffix -genous 'producing') was seen as having no external trigger but instead being related to an internal, biological cause. In terms of treatment, it was thought that whilst endogenous depressions were most effectively treated with medication, reactive types would be more suitably and effectively treated with talking therapies.

Bipolar depression (bipolar affective disorder)

Bipolar affective disorder – known previously as manic depression – involves periods of sustained low mood and depression but with episodes of high mood and increased energy (mania). The word 'bipolar' means to have or experience two poles or extremities; in this case, the two poles are different types of mood, depression and mania. The periods of high mood or mania often involve feelings of elation, excitement and optimal well-being, along with reduced sleep and desire for food. Many people experiencing highs appear to have a lot of energy, can speak very quickly and sometimes seem to jump from one theme to another when talking. For some people, having a 'high' is associated with periods of creativity and productivity. For others, it can include impaired decision-making and choice selection, which may be accompanied by non-normal behaviours (for the individual), including spending a lot of money on items that one normally would not or engaging in certain types of risky behaviour (e.g. sexual promiscuity).

Although manic episodes are usually experienced as pleasurable, some manias are associated with increased irritability and anger. For a small number of people, highs in mood are associated with psychotic experiences, including delusions and hallucinations, where the person may feel that they are special or have been selected or chosen for greatness. In recent years a number of well-known people – such as Stephen Fry – have described their experience of bipolar disorder, and in particular, what it is like to experience hypomanic and manic phases. For further reading on biploar disorder, Dr Kay Jamison's book *An Unquiet Mind: A Memoir of Moods and Madness* offers a helpful and insightful perspective. Dr Jamison is a clinical psychologist and professor in the United States, and has professional experience treating people with bipolar affective disorder, but has also been diagnosed with bipolar disorder herself.

In DSM-5, three major forms of the bipolar affective disorder are:

- <u>Bipolar I</u>: This involves one or more period of mania and usually (although not necessary for diagnosis) an episode of depression.
- <u>Bipolar II</u>: This involves one or more depressive episodes and an episode of hypomania rather than mania. The 'hypo' in 'hypomania' derives from the Greek word 'below'. So, in hypomania the individual experiences shifts in mood that are less extreme than mania, such that he/she is not as socially or occupationally impaired and does not experience psychotic experiences.

- Cyclothymia: This involves a cycling of mood, from depressive episodes (but which do not meet criteria for major depression) to hypomania, which can interfere significantly with an individual's ability to function well on a day-to-day basis.

◉ Section summary

This section has looked at different terms used to describe depression. Some of these terms – like endogenous, reactive or neurotic – are not commonly used anymore. This is partly because they acquired negative, pejorative meanings, but also as a result of advances in research suggesting that such terms may not be clinically distinctive or evidence based. This section has also highlighted that whilst depression is often seen or talked about as a homogenous, single disorder, there may be a number of different subtypes, which involve variations in severity of symptomology, length of episode and how prominent certain symptoms are. It is clear therefore that depression is a highly *heterogeneous* disorder.

◉ How common is depression?

As noted in Chapter 1, the WHO has estimated that at least 350 million people are currently suffering with depression worldwide. This means that approximately 5% of the people living on this earth are currently depressed. So, it is clear that by sheer numbers alone, depression affects a significant number of people at any one time.

Box 2.4 How do we measure how common depression is?

- **Point prevalence** – This refers to the proportion of people with depression at any one period of time (usually by asking people to recall depressive symptoms during a period of the previous one week or month).
- **12 month prevalence** – This refers to the number (percentage) of people included in a survey who report having had an episode of depression within the previous 12 months.
- **Lifetime prevalence** – This refers to the proportion of a population who will have depression at some stage in their lifetime.

In a large epidemiology study in the US, Sociologist Ronald Kessler and colleagues (Kessler et al., 2005b) found that in a 12-month period, 6.7% of Americans experienced depression. Kessler (Kessler et al., 2003) also found a lifetime prevalence of 16.6 % for **major depressive disorder** and 20.8% for mood disorders on the whole (including bipolar affective disorder and dysthymia). In other words, it is estimated that *one in five* of us will likely experience an episode of mood disorder at some point in our life. As we will explore below, it may be that for some groups of people, this number is significantly higher.

⊙ Do the rates of depression vary across different groups of people?

Whilst depression occurs in all populations of people, it appears to be more common in some people than others:

Gender

Research has consistently shown that depression is more prevalent in women than men, with most estimates suggesting that women are approximately *twice* as likely to develop depression than men (Kessler et al., 2003). This degree of difference between genders appears to be relatively stable across different countries and cultures, even though there is evidence that there are varying rates of depression between countries and cultures (Andrade et al., 2003). There have been a number of suggestions for why this gender difference may exist, including:

Biological

- Rates of depression are similar between pre-pubescent boys and girls. At the onset of puberty, rates in both boys and girls begin to rise, but in girls this rise is greater. Therefore, relatively quickly, the difference in prevalence observed between the two genders becomes clear in post-pubertal adolescents. This suggests that there may be a hormonal component that predisposes women to greater risk of depression than men.
- It has been postulated that hormonal changes specific to women, including those involved in menstruation, childbirth (and the

period just after this – called the postpartum phase) and the menopause may make women more susceptible to depression than men (see Nolen-Hoeksema and Hilt, 2010, for a helpful review).

Psychological and social

- There are some suggestions that women may be more vulnerable than men to certain types of thinking style, such as *rumination, worry* and *self-criticism*, which are all, in turn, significantly related to the onset and maintenance of depression. We will explore these types of thinking style more in Chapter 4.
- Some people suggest that men and women cope with their emotions and feelings, and with experiences of shame and stigma, in different ways, such that women are more likely to report depressive symptoms than men. From this perspective, differing rates of depression are not biologically determined, but they are merely a reflection of gender role differences.
- Women continue to experience a variety of inequalities in comparison with men, including status, economic mobility and gender stereotyped roles. Moreover, women appear to experience more frequent life traumas (e.g. rapes, sexual abuse, physical abuse), which have been hypothesised to be potential triggers to the development of depression.

Whilst all of these factors (along with others) may contribute to the increased prevalence of depression in women, it is likely that *complex interactions* between these factors lead to women being more likely to suffer from depression than men.

Age

Until the later part of the twentieth century, the prevailing clinical belief was that depression was a disorder of adulthood, and in particular, that 'children do not get depressed'. Over the past 30 years or so, our understanding of age variations in the picture of depression has increased substantially:

- Infants – infants are very rarely assessed for depression, and therefore evidence for whether infants can be depressed is limited.

However, some estimates suggest very low levels (e.g. 0.3%; Egger and Angold, 2006).

- Childhood – in young and middle-aged children (below the age of five years old) rates of depression appear to be relatively low – approximately 3% – and tend to remain at lower levels until puberty (Garber, Gallerani and Frankel, 2010).
- Adolescents – in a large US study, Kessler and Walters (1998) found a lifetime prevalence of 14% for major depressive disorder, but they estimated that 10–20% adolescents would meet criteria for subthreshold depression.
- Adults – as mentioned above, Kessler and colleagues (Kessler et al., 2003) found a lifetime prevalence of 16.6 % for major depressive disorder and 20.8% for mood disorders on the whole (including bipolar affective disorder and dysthymia) in a large sample of residents in the United States.
- Older Adults – in a large sample of more than 2,000 older adults (65 years old and above) living in England and Wales, McDougall et al. (2007) found the prevalence of depression to be 9.3% for people living at home but a massive 27.1% for those living in institutions (residential or long-stay nursing homes, or a long-stay hospital). Interestingly, they found that depression was more prevalent in 'younger' older adults, rather than 'older' older adults.

Country

Epidemiological data suggest that rates of depression vary to a large extent across different countries. Reviewing a variety of epidemiological studies, Chentsove-Dutton and Tsai (2009) point out that in any 12-month period, approximately one in ten Canadians is likely to experience major depression, whereas only one in 50 Chinese or Koreans will during the same period. In a large epidemiological study, Bromet et al. (2011) measured rates of major depressive episode in 18 low-, middle- and high-income countries by interviewing over 89,000 people using the World Health Organization Composite International Diagnostic Interview (CIDI). High-, middle- and low-income countries were determined by guidelines used by the World Bank. They found that the lifetime prevalence of depression in the ten 'high income' countries (including the United States and Germany) was 14.6%, in comparison with just

11.1% in the eight 'low-medium income' countries (e.g. Brazil, China and India). Bromet et al. (2011) did not look at causes or explanations for these differences; however, as others have also highlighted, it might be that factors related to affluence, or in particular, large stratifications in wealth commonly found in high-income countries contribute to greater lifetime risk of depression in high-income countries (for a review, see Wilkinson and Pickett, 2006).

Socioeconomic status (SES)

In a study looking at the rates of depression and **socioeconomic status (SES)** in New York, USA, Galea et al. (2007) recruited a sample of 820 participants who had no history of depression. When they followed up these participants 18 months later, they found that 113 had experienced a depressive episode during this time, which represented an incidence rate of 14.6 per 100 people. However, when they separated these people into two groups – those from high and those from low SES neighbourhoods – they found an interesting difference. Those coming from the lower SES neighbourhood – who were seen to have experienced greater poverty – had a cumulative incidence of depression of 19.4 per 100 people. This was significantly higher than the incidence rate of 10.5 per 100 people from the high SES neighbourhood. This represented a 2.19 odds ratio of developing depression from a poor neighbourhood relative to a well-off one.

Similar data were found by Kosidou et al. (2011) in a large (n=23,794) five-year longitudinal study in Stockholm, Sweden. Here, participants were coded in terms of socioeconomic and income levels at baseline and followed up five years later to determine levels of psychological distress or depression. Amongst other findings, the researchers discovered that higher disposable household income was associated with lower levels of depression, particularly in women.

Where you live – Urban or rural areas

Most of us can appreciate that where we live can have a significant effect on the way we feel. Researchers have explored this experience on a broader level, and investigated whether living in urbanised or rural areas has an impact on the prevalence of mental health, including depression. Although the evidence is somewhat mixed, researchers have found that urbanised living may be associated with higher levels of depression prevalence than living in rural areas (Wang, 2004; Peen, Schoevers, Beekman and Dekker, 2010). There may be a variety of explanations for these differences, including demographic (e.g. ethnicity, age) and social (e.g. socioeconomic and employment status) factors. Some theorists have suggested that the nature of urban living, linked to cramped housing conditions, proximity to high numbers of strangers and the increased likelihood of threatening experiences (e.g. interpersonal violence, theft, etc.), may produce a chronic stress response in people and that this may translate to higher rates of depression.

Ethnicity

Collecting accurate data on whether there are variations in the prevalence of depression amongst different ethnic groups is actually more difficult than it might initially seem. There are a number of reasons for this. To start with, looking for differences between ethnic groups has often been a very sensitive topic. For some people, even looking at these types of differences represents a type of implicit prejudice. Others cite criticisms about classification – in particular, that race is socially constructed rather than biological entity. There are also further problems with defining different ethnic groups, particularly whether this is based on culture or country, or genetic background.

Ahmed and Bhurga (2006) describe the findings from the literature as lacking consistency and hard to explain, with some studies suggesting higher levels of depression in ethnic minority populations, whilst other suggesting higher levels in the ethnic majority population. For example, in the United States, Gonzalez, Tarraf, Whitfield and Vega (2010) found that Black Americans and Mexican Americans had higher rates of major depressive disorder and lower levels of seeking healthcare for this, in comparison with White Americans. They also found that overall, native-born Americans had higher levels of depression than foreign-born responders. However, in comparison, Riolo et al. (2005) found that rates of major depression in the United States were significantly *higher* in Whites in comparison with Black or Mexican Americans.

There may be a variety of reasons for the differences found between rates of depression in different ethnic groups. These could represent *biological* (e.g. genetic), *psychological* (e.g. the way in which different groups of people describe thoughts, emotions and behaviours) or *environmental factors* (that certain ethnic groups, through stressful experiences like racism, discrimination and poverty, might be more prone to depression – see also socioeconomic factors described above). In fact, there is evidence that once you statistically control for the effect of social factors that are related to increased levels of depression, inter-ethnic differences in rates of depression may no longer be statistically significant (e.g. Diala et al., 2001; Dunlop et al., 2003). Moreover, inter-ethnic differences might also reflect differences in how depression manifests and gets communicated. For example, Ahmed and Bhurga (2006) suggest that some ethnic groups may experience, and report, depression with more somatic symptoms (e.g. pain in certain parts of the body) than cognitive and emotional symptoms, which may in turn lead to medical professionals overlooking the possibility of depression, instead ascribing the difficulties to physical health problems. Ahmed and Bhurga (2006) also suggest that in some communities, levels of shame and stigma about discussing mental health problems might be higher, which in turn may lead to reductions in help-seeking and attendance at health clinics. If this is the case, it is likely that our current prevalence rates of depression for some ethnic groups are a gross underestimation of actual levels in the community.

To make the picture more complicated, it is likely that differences in depression rates between ethnic groups are fluid and changing over time. This would mean that any current differences in rates of depression between one group and another may not be the same in 10, 20 or 30 years' time, as the shifting sands of various social factors (such as social economic status, reductions in prejudice and greater integration into mainstream society) may reduce the risk of depression in groups currently experiencing some of these risk factors.

◉ How is depression assessed and measured?

There are a variety of ways in which depression is assessed and measured, the most common being clinical interviews conducted by trained professionals, and/or the administration of self-report measures.

Clinical interviews

The typical method for assessing and diagnosing depression is via a clinical interview, conducted by a trained health professional assessing the difficulties an individual is currently experiencing. In primary care (e.g. G.P. practices) or mental health settings, this clinical assessment is often very broad, and includes information related to the condition, such as current mental state, symptoms experienced, history of difficulties, as well as personal information, such as early life history, occupation and home life. For depression, the clinician will have in mind DSM-5 or ICD-10 diagnostic criteria, and spend time finding out about the type of symptoms experienced, their frequency, duration, and so forth. The clinician may also use his/her observations regarding the way in which the person is describing their difficulties to help diagnosis. For example, if someone were to be responding in a slow, monotone voice, with little emotional reactivity (even when talking about distressing or pleasurable events), and had poor eye contact, this might add to the content of the individual's response to suggest they might be depressed.

Clinician ratings

Clinical ratings of depression involve the use of interview schedules or rating scales which help researchers or health professionals decide whether someone is depressed, what types of symptoms they are experiencing and how severe these symptoms are. There are a number of common clinician ratings. The Diagnostic Interview Schedule (DIS-IV) and The Structured Clinical Interview for DSM-IV Axis I Disorders (SCID) are both linked conceptually to DSM-IV criteria. Whereas the above interview schedules can take over an hour to complete, the Hamilton Rating Scale for Depression (HAMD) is the most commonly used rating scale for depression, and can be completed in less than ten minutes.

Box 2.5 How accurate is the measurement of depression?

Whilst there are a number of different ways of measuring and diagnosing depression, are these systems accurate and reliable? There are two key methods of statistically testing the accuracy of clinician-administered and self-report scales. *Sensitivity* measures the percentage of people with depression based on correct identification of the disorder using a particular measure or questionnaire. *Specificity* is the percentage of non-depressed people who the measure identifies as not having depression. A perfectly accurate depression measure would have both 100% sensitivity and 100% specificity, so that it would detect every single depressed person as depressed and every non-depressed person as not depressed.

A statistical review of published studies (called a meta analysis) looking at the sensitivity and specificity of the Patient Health Questionnaire (PHQ-9) in predicting major depression in a variety of health settings (e.g. primary and community care, hospital wards) found that it had good diagnostic power. The PHQ-9 had 92% sensitivity in predicting depression in those diagnosed with depression and 80% specificity in correctly identifying non-depressed individuals. In other words, for every 100 depressed people (as diagnosed by clinical interview), scores on the PHQ-9 correctly identified 92 as depressed. In comparison, the PHQ-9 was slightly less specific in that, out of every 100 people classified by clinical interview as non-depressed, it correctly identified 80 as not depressed. In reality, the consequence of this might be that eight actually depressed people may not have been given treatment for depression, whereas 20 people who were non-depressed may have been given treatment.

So, how well can healthcare professionals detect depression in the absence of rating measures? Well, interestingly, in a UK study looking at GPs' level of sensitivity and specificity in primary care, Henkel et al. (2003) found rates of 67% and 75%, respectively. In comparison, when aided by the use of the PHQ-9, GPs' rates of sensitivity rose to 78% and specificity to 85%, which represented statistically significant improved detection rates. It seems likely therefore that the use of brief screening measures, whilst not perfect, may help busy health professional like GPs to make more accurate diagnoses of depression.

Self-report

There are a variety of self-report measures which provide information about the presence, frequency and/or severity of depressive symptoms, or indicate whether someone might be depressed or not. The most well-known is the Beck Depression Inventory (BDI-II; Beck, Steer and Brown, 1996). The BDI-II is a 21-item measure in which responders rate the intensity of each of the 21 symptoms on a 0–3 scale. Various other self-report scales commonly used have items derived from the BDI and/or

Box 2.6 Comparison between two common depression self-report measures

Kung et al. (2013) compared the performance of two of the most frequently used patient self-report measures – the Personal Health Questionnaire 9 (PHQ-9) and the Beck Depression Inventory II (BDI-II). In total, the researchers compared 625 patients attending different mood disorder clinical settings. They found that scores on the two scales were significantly correlated (r=.77); in other words, if you reported lots of depression symptoms on one questionnaire, you were also likely to report lots on the other. The authors noted that whilst the BDI-II was previously used as the 'gold standard' measurement of depression, the PHQ-9 might have a number of strengths over the BDI-II, partly because it is free to use but also because it is shorter to administer making a significant difference in busy clinical settings. They also noted greater diagnostic coherence with the PHQ-9, as it directly reflects DSM-IV criteria.

diagnostic criteria from the DSM or other diagnostic frameworks. A commonly used measure in the UK, particularly in GP surgeries, is the Patient Health Questionnaire Depression Scale (PHQ-9; Kroenke, Spitzer and Williams, 2001), taken from the larger Patient Health Questionnaire. The PHQ-9 is a nine-item scale which asks questions that map directly onto the nine symptoms of depression described by DSM-IV, based on a 0–3 rating scale referring to rates symptom frequency. The PHQ-9 has been found to have good statistical properties and appears to be a reliable measure of depression. If interested, readers can find this scale online at www.patient.co.uk/doctor/Patient-Health-Questionnaire-(PHQ-9).htm. The scale generally takes five minutes to complete, and scores are calculated and placed in different categories of non–depressed, mild, moderate, moderately severe and severe categories.

Comorbidity

Comorbidity in mental health relates to the presence of more than one diagnosis in an individual at any point of time. It turns out that depression is a highly comorbid condition, meaning that when someone is depressed, there is a high likelihood that they may also be suffering from another mental health condition at the same time. Research has suggested that within a 12-month period, approximately two-thirds of people meeting criteria for major depressive disorder also meet criteria for another diagnosable mental health problem, with anxiety disorders as the most common comorbid disorder.

It is unclear at this stage exactly what this high level of comorbidity reflects; some researchers suggest an underlying causative factor that gives rise to both depression and anxiety, such as genes or certain types of personality factors, like neuroticism, common in both depressive and anxiety disorders. Others suggest that the breadth of diagnostic criteria results in people being able to reach criteria for multiple diagnoses.

Interestingly, it is not just other mental health problems that people with depression are likely to experience, as there is an increased risk of comorbid medical illnesses, including cardiovascular problems, obesity and diabetes (Freeland and Carney, 2010). It seems likely that depression may increase the likelihood of a health disorder developing, but the opposite route is also possible – that is, having a pre-existing medical illness may increase one's chances of becoming depressed. There have been a variety of explanations for this association, including common underlying problems with the *immune system* (i.e. chronic activation of the immunological response) and in the **stress response** (e.g. the role of certain stress hormones such as cortisol). The relationship between physical health problems and depression may actually be rather complex, depending on factors, including the type of physical health problem, its severity, the potential impact on life quality, functioning and mortality and whether it has an acute or chronic course.

Box 2.7 Is it just humans who get depressed?

It might be somewhat surprising, but researchers have found evidence of certain behaviours in animals that closely match how humans react when they are depressed. A number of studies have focused on behaviours that might indicate an animal is anhedonic. As we discussed above, anhedonia describes a lack or absence of pleasure from activities, and is seen as a key symptom of depression. For example, anhedonic-like behaviour has been observed in a variety of animals, including rodents (Rygula et al., 2005) and primates (Ferdowsian et al., 2011), where the animal appears no longer interested in food, sexual activity or interacting with members of their group. Researchers in these types of studies will spend a lot of time observing specific types of behaviour in animal groups – for example, the amount of time depressed chimpanzees spend engaging in play activities – and will then notice if the amount changes. Changes in this, and in particular, reductions in time spent in 'play', have been used by researchers as an indicator for 'depression'. In a review of published case studies that focused on chimps who had experienced stressful life events (such as social isolation or maternal deprivation), Ferdowsian et al. (2011) found that a small number met criteria for DSM-IV depression. When they adapted these diagnostic criteria by using ethnograms (i.e. by focusing on particular types of chimp behaviour), the authors found high numbers of chimpanzees meeting criteria for depression. In particular, amongst those animals that had lived in sanctuaries where there was evidence of experimentation, separation from parents/social group and violent human contact, the rate of depression-like symptoms was significantly higher than in those raised in the wild (58% of sample versus 3% of sample, respectively). This points towards the role of stress in depression, an idea we will return to in the following chapters.

Of course, we have to be careful when studying animals not to fall into the trap of inferring a particular conclusion based on our observations. Whilst we might think that a reduction of time spent engaging in play as an indicator of anhedonia, we cannot know this for sure, as animals are not able to tell us how they are feeling. At times, we are guilty of anthropomorphism, or in other words, the ascribing of human characteristics (e.g. emotions, feelings, actions) to animals. However, as we will explore in Chapter 6, many of the evolutionary-informed explanations of depression were developed from animal observations and models. Moreover, we share many of our genes, biological structure and physiological responses with other animals. Many of the biological correlates of depression identified in humans are also present in animals which display behavioural signs of depression. It may be that we will never know if animals experience depression in the same way that we do, but it appears likely that at least some of the causes, both biologically and environmentally, may be similar.

Whilst we might not know yet the exact cause of this overlap between depression and a range of other mental and physical health problems, the evidence is clear that having depression is associated with higher than chance occurrences of experiencing other health problems. Clearly this has significant implications on the burden of distress for the individual suffering with comorbid disorders, and presents challenges in terms of providing effective treatments.

Chapter summary

This chapter has highlighted that, whilst depression is the most common mental health problem and one of the most common health problems generally, it is not a simple, singular entity. We have looked at how depression:

- is a very common problem, affecting up to one in five people at some stage of life
- is a highly complex disorder, with different subtypes, levels of severity and length of course
- appears to be more prevalent in certain groups of people than other (differentiated by gender, age, sociocultural factors, and physical health variables)
- can be diagnosed and measured in a variety of ways

With all of the above in mind, Chapters 3, 4, 5 and 6 will explore some of the different explanations for the causes of depression.

Further reading

Gotlib, I. H. and Hammen, C. L. (2010) *Handbook of Depression.*

Chapter 3

Biological Explanations

Biological explanations seek to understand how a variety of factors – including genes, anatomical brain structures and neurotransmitters – may be involved in depression. As we will find out in this chapter, there is no single biological profile or signature of depression but rather a variety of processes that may play an important role. Whilst reading this chapter, it is also worth holding in mind an important point: Depression, like all other human experience, is biological in nature; without a particular set of physiological changes in the brain and body, we would not 'feel' depressed. However, whilst this is very important, it is difficult to say whether, in simple terms, depression is 'caused' by biological factors or whether certain types of experience (e.g. environmental stress) affect our biology in a way that leaves us feeling depressed. This of course relates to 'nature–nurture' and 'cause and effect' debates. It is therefore important to hold in mind that these biological factors are related to depression through a complex biopsychosocial interplay, in which an individual's unique biological, psychological and social characteristics *interact* to lead to depression.

◉ Neurobiological factors

For many, the brain is the starting point for exploration of mental health problems, including depression. For a long time, scientists and health professionals have been interested in whether there are particular changes in the brains of depressed people, in comparison with those who are not depressed. It turns out that there are a variety of neurophysiological and biological changes in depression, including changes in certain brain structures, neurotransmitters and neurohormones.

Neurotransmitters

A neuron is a type of nerve cell that helps to form our nervous system. It is similar in many ways to other cells in the human body but has a special ability to transmit information to other cells and thus communicate information throughout the body. Neurons can communicate this information in both electrical and chemical forms. When they communicate in chemical form, they do this via **neurotransmitters**. Neurotransmitters are chemicals that operate between neurons, facilitating the transmission of a message or signal from one neuron to another. Neurotransmitters are released at part of a neuron called the axon terminal, and travel across the synaptic gap (the gap between neurons) before reaching the 'receptor site' of another neuron. They are then 'taken up' by the same neuron – a process known as *reuptake*. This process is displayed in Figure 3.1.

Because neurotransmitters communicate information between neurons, they are partly responsible for how we think, feel and behave. So, when we feel good – happy, elected, excited or joyful – on a molecular level this corresponds to certain types of neurotransmitters (e.g. endorphins) being

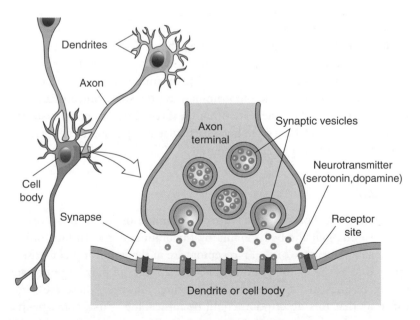

Figure 3.1   Picture of a neuron and neurotransmission between neurons

released by particular neurons and acting on others. Given that depression is associated with a reduction of positive affect and increase in negative affect, and changes to a variety of cognitive, motivational and somatic processes, it makes sense that scientists would be interested in looking at whether certain types of neurotransmitter may function in a different way in someone with depression, in comparison with someone without depression. Whilst there are over 60 different neurotransmitters, it turns out that a specific group, known as the *monoamines*, seem to play an important role in depression.

The role of monoamines in depression was first discovered by accident in the 1950s, when scientists trialling a drug called reserpine for hypertension (high blood pressure) found that this caused a side effect, in that it left some people feeling depressed. As this drug affected the brain by depleting a type of neurotransmitter called monoamines, scientists began to wonder whether this meant that a reduction, or depletion, in monoamines could be responsible for causing depression. This theory – known as the *monoamine hypothesis of depression* – was given further support when another drug used to treat tuberculosis (called iproniazid), which blocked the breakdown (depletion) of monoamines (thus increasing them in the brain), was found to improve mood for some of the people taking it. These serendipitous findings led to the development of the first types of antidepressants – known as **monoamine oxidase inhibitors (MAOIs)**. Therefore, the monoamine hypothesis of depression suggests that depression is caused by the altered production, release, reuptake and/or function of monoamine transmitters, or the altered functionality of the monoamine receptor sites. Since the 1950s, scientists have focused their attention on three subtypes of monoamine neurotransmitters which seem to be particularly important in depression: serotonin, noradrenaline and dopamine.

Serotonin

Serotonin, also known as 5-Hydroxytryptamine or 5-HT for short, is found throughout the body, including the brain and gut. In fact, only a very small percentage of 5-HT receptors are in the brain. It is sometimes referred to as the 'happy transmitter', as it appears to play an important role in feelings of happiness and well-being. However, there are some concerns that this description could be misleading. First, some people have pointed out that use of the term 'happy transmitter' was encouraged by drug companies to sell more of their **antidepressants**! Second, it has not been clearly established that serotonin levels are necessarily linked to positive emotions and moods. For example, serotonin plays an important role in the regulation of sleep, appetite and sexual desire which, and as discussed in Chapter 2, can all be affected when people get depressed. Moreover, it may be that serotonin is associated with the regulation of negative emotion and mood, more than positive emotion. For example, we know that serotonin also plays an important role in the regulation of anxiety, and as we will see in Chapter 9, antidepressant medications targeting serotonin are prescribed for both depression and anxiety problems.

Scientists have suggested a number of ways that serotonin may be associated with depression, including:

- the low production of serotonin in brain cells (potentially linked to a lack of tryptophan, a chemical involved in the making of serotonin),
- a reduction in the amount of serotonin reaching the receptor sites or cells,
- a lack of serotonin receptor sites themselves.

Noradrenaline

Noradrenaline plays a crucial role in the body and brain's ability to become activated for action, and therefore, are associated with the brain's response to stress. In response to a **stressor**, there is a rapid increase in noradrenaline activity, stemming from a number of brain areas, including the Locus Coeruleus (which contains the majority of noradrenaline cells in the brain). Noradrenaline is involved in the 'fight or flight' response by increasing heart rate, blood pressure, muscle tone and the release of glucose, allowing the body to get ready to deal with stress. However, whilst this system is very useful in dealing with short-term stressors, problems can occur when it is under *prolonged activity*. Sustained or non-resolved stress may lead to depletion of brain levels of noradrenaline, which may in turn lead to, or be associated with, decreased motivation, exploratory and consummatory behaviour (Thase, 2010). The difference between acute and chronic stress is discussed further in Box 3.1.

Box 3.1 What is stress?

The term 'stress' is such a ubiquitously used phrase, that it is easy to forget and that it only entered everyday language relatively recently. The word has its origins in the Latin stingere, which means 'to draw tight'. Current definitions of stress suggest it is a nonspecific bodily response to a stimulus that threatens to overwhelm the body's ability to keep homeostasis (e.g. Torres and Nowson, 2007). However, it was in the 1920s and 1930s, and with the work of American physiologist Walter Cannon and Hungarian endocrinologist Hans Selye that modern concepts of stress, and the stress response, began to develop.

Of particular importance is Selye's idea of the General Adaptation Syndrome (GAS) (Selye, 1965), which refers to three different phases of response to the presence of a stressor: alarm, resistance and exhaustion.

1) An initial <u>alarm</u> phase in which the body's resources are mobilised to deal with the stressor
2) A <u>resistance</u> phase in which the body attempts to cope with the stressor and switch off the alarm phase
3) If stage 2 (resistance) is not successful – maybe because the initial stressor remains or is too powerful to resist – the organism '<u>exhausts</u>' its coping capacity

Selye's theory is seminal as it relates to the idea of a triphasic (three phase) response to stress. The first phase involves the body's activating response to the presence of a stressor. This involves the triggering of the sympathetic nervous system and the 'fight or flight' response (a phrase initially coined by Cannon), activation of the hypothalamic–pituitary–adrenal (HPA) system and, ultimately, the release of the hormones cortisol and adrenaline from the adrenal cortex and adrenal medulla, respectively. Following this initial phase, the body shifts into a second phase in which the parasympathetic nervous system 'turns on'. This helps many of the body's physiological systems to return to normal levels of functioning, although the body is still on alert, with higher heart rate and blood pressure. If these first two phases of response are successful the organism returns to homeostatic balance and normal levels of functioning. However, in the face of sustained chronic stressors in which our attempts to cope are overwhelmed or the stressor cannot be escaped from, the body shifts into another response, involving demobilisation of energy and a reduction of activity. This phase of demobilisation or exhaustion in the face of a continued stressor relates to evolutionary psychology informed explanations of depression (see Chapter 6).

The different phases of stress response also relate to the important area of acute versus chronic stress. Interestingly, recent research has found that exposure to acute stress may actually have a positive impact on our physical health by enhancing our immunological response, whereas chronic stress inhibits healthy immunological responses (e.g. Dhabhar, 2009). Moreover, as we will see in this chapter and in Chapter 6, stress that feels uncontrollable or inescapable has been found to be associated with depression.

Dopamine

Increasingly, scientists are looking at the potential role of **dopamine** in depression, and in particular, its link to anhedonia (Argyropoulos and Nutt, 2013). Short-term release of dopamine is generally associated with the experience of positive emotions and pleasurable feelings, such as happiness, joy and elation. Considerable research has previously highlighted the important role of dopamine in pleasure, reward and addictions. Dopamine is also associated with psychomotor activity, motivation, goal-directed tasks and consummatory behaviour (Thase, 2010). In rats displaying 'learned helplessness' (see Chapter 6 for a discussion of this) scientists have found lower levels of dopamine in a number of brain areas, and in humans, there have been a number of findings showing indirect evidence for decreased dopaminergic activity in people with depression (Meyer et al., 2006). As with noradrenaline, under chronic stress levels of dopamine may be reduced. It is thought that reduced levels of dopamine may underpin some of the common symptoms of depression, such as lack of energy and interest, and anhedonia.

As we discussed in Chapter 2, there is increasing evidence that we need to consider different components of anhedonia – one linked to problems with motivation and drive to engage in goal-related behaviour and another linked to the ability to experience pleasure once engaged in an activity (Argyropoulos and Nutt, 2013; Gilbert, 2013). It may be that both of these components are compromised in depression, although there is some evidence that the difficulty with motivation, energy and drive to engage in goal-related activity may be a particular problem in depression (Argyropoulos and Nutt, 2013). It is likely that in time we will have a greater understanding of different neurophysiological processes in these components of anhedonia.

Non-monoamine neurotransmitters

Although the monoamines have received the greatest amount of attention in depression, scientists are increasingly looking at the role of GABA (gamma amino butyric acid). GABA has an important role in regulating and fine tuning our mood, thinking and behaviour. It appears to play an important inhibitory, 'balancing' role on other neurotransmitters – such as the monoamines described above. In a review, Luscher et al. (2011) found that people with depression have lower levels of GABA than non-depressed people, with those more severely or chronically depressed having the lowest levels of GABA.

Neurotransmitters in depression: summary

The above section has discussed the role of different neurotransmitters in depression. Research has highlighted that both monoamine (serotonin, noradrenaline and dopamine) and non-monoamine (e.g. GABA) neurotransmitters may play a role in some of the common symptoms of depression. Interestingly, it may be that different subtypes of depression (i.e. depressions with differing symptom profiles) are associated with different patterns of neurotransmitter functioning or imbalances. For example, depressions with clear anhedonic features, involving the loss of positive emotion, motivation and energy, may be primarily underpinned by dopaminergic changes, whereas depression characterised by low mood/negative emotion and dysregulation of sleep/appetite may be associated with serotonergic problems (e.g. Nutt et al., 2007; Argyropoulos and Nutt, 2013). Further research is needed here to understand these relationships further.

There are also difficulties of a 'chicken and the egg' nature here. Whilst the monoamine hypothesis of depression suggests that a depletion of monoamine may cause (or be involved in the cause of) depression, it is still unclear whether changes in these neurotransmitters do this, or that the changes are a consequence of someone being depressed. Scientists have attempted to investigate this using a variety of methodologies.

For example, in a type of research methodology known as a 'depletion studies', scientists try to reduce the level of some of the monoamine neurotransmitters and then see whether this leads to reductions of mood. Although there have been various, and at times, contradictory findings from these studies, in a large meta-analytic review, Ruhé et al. (2007) found that whilst depletion of monoamines led to a reduction in mood in people with depression (who were not taking antidepressants) and in people with a familial history of depression (that is, close relatives had experienced depression), they did not find consistent evidence that depletion led to a reduction of mood in healthy, non-depressed people. Ruhé et al. (2007) conclude that, based on the findings in healthy adults, depression is not caused by reductions in monoamine neurotransmitters. However, they suggest that the reduction in monoamines may play a role, maybe in combination with other factors (e.g. genetic vulnerability), or represent a common 'final pathway' of changes that occur in depression. Clearly, future research will help scientists to better understand how these neurotransmitters are involved in depression.

◉ Neurohormones

A neurohormone is a hormone produced by cells in the brain and released into the blood stream. Much of the research on the role of neurohormones in depression has focused on the functioning of the **hypothalamic–pituitary–adrenal (HPA) axis.** The HPA axis has sometimes been referred to as the body's 'stress axis'. It involves a complex set of interactions between the hypothalamus (H), pituitary (P) and adrenal (A) glands, and plays a key role in a number of bodily process (e.g. digestion and immune system function), as well as the regulation of mood and emotions, and the physiological response to threat and stress.

In a stressful encounter, the HPA axis operates in three stages:

(1) The first stage involves the release of Corticotropin Releasing Hormone (CRH) and Vasopressin in the hypothalamus following the presence of a stressor.

(2) The release of these hormones triggers the second stage of the process – the stimulation of a part of the pituitary gland, which as a consequence, secretes adrenocorticotropic hormone (ACTH) into the blood stream.

(3) In the third stage, ACTH, travelling in the blood stream, stimulates the adrenal glands (located above your kidneys), which produce glucocorticoid hormones, such as cortisol. Cortisol is often referred to as the 'stress hormone'. It has a variety of functions, which include suppressing the immune response (inflammation), increasing blood sugar (gluconeogenesis) and helping the metabolism of fat, protein and carbohydrates. Cortisol is released into the large muscle groups, which are important for short-term threat response and survival.

Once the stress has passed or has been dealt with, the presence of cortisol in the blood stream plays a final important role in signalling to the hypothalamus and pituitary gland to stop firing and producing CRH and ACTH, respectively (so, steps one and two above terminate). A simplified depiction of the HPA process is shown in Figure 3.2.

However, problems can occur when cortisol levels remain elevated over an extended period of time, and this has been found to be associated with a variety of physical health problems, such as obesity, heart disease and autoimmune disorders. Some researchers feel that cortisol is one of the most reliable biological signs of depression (e.g. Thase, 2010), particularly in the context of *chronic or persistent stress*, rather than in the transitory process described above. In the face of apparently ongoing or

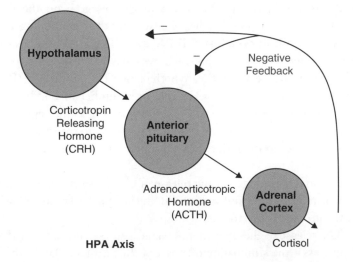

Figure 3.2   Visual depiction of HPA axis

indefinite stress, cortisol is continually produced which can have a negative impact on other neurotransmitters and neurohormones and a damaging effect upon anatomical structures in the brain, such as the **amygdala** and the **hippocampus** (see section below for further discussion of these brain areas in depression). Interestingly, Thase (2013) suggests that the association between depression and elevated levels of cortisol may be partly linked to the severity of depression symptoms. He suggests that only 20–40% of outpatients with depression (more likely to be suffering mild to moderate depression) had elevated levels of cortisol, in comparison with 60–80% of inpatients suffering from depression (inpatients are assumed to be suffering from more severe depression, therefore needing more specialised care in hospital). However, fitting with the complex nature of depression, not all depressions are associated with increased cortisol; in fact, some depressions (including those associated with trauma) may be associated with lower levels of cortisol (e.g. Oquendo et al., 2003). It may be that early life stress may compromise HPA regulation and functioning (Thase, 2013).

Finally, a neurohormone that has recently emerged as playing an important role in mood, emotion, behaviour and relationships is oxytocin. Oxytocin has been referred to in the popular press as 'the hormone of love' or the 'cuddle hormone', as it seems to be secreted when we are in close contact with people we love or feel close to. Oxytocin is linked to the experience of caring for others and being cared for by others, and seems to play an important role in the process of bonding, trust and attachment. As we will see in Chapters 5 and 6, depression may be associated with difficult interpersonal experiences (e.g. the lack of care and nurturance) or loss (e.g. a marital separation, the death of a loved one), so there are reasons for us to consider the potential role of oxytocin here. Although there has not been much research to date, a few studies have found that oxytocin levels are associated with depression severity (Scantamburlo et al., 2007; Ozsoy, Esel and Kula, 2009) and may be present at increased levels in depressed than non-depressed people (Parker et al., 2010). Interestingly, there is evidence that oxytocin helps to regulate or attenuate activation of the HPA system (e.g. Parker et al., 2010); thus, it may be that an interaction effect occurs in depression, whereby problems in the production of oxytocin may impact upon depression partly through continued HPA activation.

◉ Immunological inflammatory response

Increasingly, researchers are recognising the role of the immune system and inflammatory response in depression. The immune system and inflammatory response are one of our body's key protective systems; in the presence of an identified harmful or noxious stimulus (e.g. bacteria, injury), affected cells 'signal' to the body (via a variety of substances, e.g. cytokines) that there is a problem. This triggers a variety of responses, including increased blood flow to the area of the body that has experienced the harmful stimulus. The body also mobilises a response in the form of plasma and white blood cells (e.g. lymphocytes), directing these in the blood to the site or part of the body in which the harmful stimulus is present. Although complicated and diverse, these responses are designed to protect the body from further damage (e.g. via spreading of a bacteria) and in dealing with the actual harmful stimulus itself. In reviewing the literature, Raison and Miller (2013) highlight how a variety of inflammatory markers have been found to correlate with symptoms common in depression, such as fatigue, sleep problems and poor concentration. Moreover, the administration of cytokines (a substance secreted by cells in the immune system to communicate information to other cells and trigger inflammation in response to infection) can induce depressive-like responses (e.g. depressed mood, fatigue and anhedonia) in people who previously did not show any such symptoms.

The 'cytokines hypothesis of depression' is gathering increasing evidence and awareness as a potentially important way of understanding the development of depression. Some early evidence suggests that pro-inflammatory cytokines are raised, and anti-inflammatory cytokines reduced, in depressed rather than non-depressed people, although this difference is rather modest, at best. There are a number of ideas on how the cytokine response may impact upon depression, including through degrading serotonin production and decreasing the process of neurogenesis (the 'birth' or generation of new neurons). It is likely that the link between depression and immunological functioning may also help us understand why depressed people are more likely to suffer from higher levels of physical health problems.

◉ Section summary

Whilst some of the above description of neurotransmitters and neuro-hormones might seem rather complicated, the key point to remember is that our thoughts, emotions, moods and behaviours, all have physiological correlates in the brain and our body. In depression, it seems that a complex picture emerges whereby some of the neurotransmitters and neurohormones that help to keep our thoughts, feelings, emotions, behaviour and motivation in balance stop functioning in the way they normally would. In addition, more recent interest and research into the immunological response in depression has suggested that in some people, inflammatory responses may play an important role in the development and maintenance of depression. As we explored in Chapter 2, this idea appears to fit with the concept of depression as a highly heterogenous disorder, with multiple neurophysiological causes and pathways.

◉ Neuronal anatomical structures

With the increasing sensitivity of research tools, such as brain scanning equipment, scientists are increasingly able to look at how certain anatomical areas of the brain might be related to mental health disorders, including depression. We shall briefly examine below some of the key brain structures that have been implicated in depression.

Amygdala

The amygdala are small, almond-shaped groups of neurons found bi-laterally (both hemispheres of the brain), deep in the temporal lobes. In fact, the word 'amygdala' comes from the Greek word meaning 'almonds'. Following the extensive work of Joseph LeDoux (2000) and others, we now have a good understanding of the amygdala's role in threat detection, emotion (anxiety, anger, disgust and joy), initiation of the stress response, and in learning and memory. Given that depression is often associated with an increased sense of threat, changes in emotions (increased negative emotions like anxiety and anger, and reduced positive emotions like joy), stress, and problems with learning and memory, the amygdala have been the focus of considerable research in trying to understand these difficulties.

In terms of the structure of the amygdala, there appear to be a number of anatomical changes in depression, although the literature here is somewhat mixed for what these changes are. Whilst some studies have found increased amygdala volume in depressed versus non-depressed people, others have shown either no difference or smaller amygdala volume in depression. Other studies looking at activation of the amygdala by scanning peoples' brains have found altered (increased or decreased) amygdala activation in response to emotional stimuli in people with depression in comparison with a group of non-depressed people. It may be that some of the difficulties in getting consistent results are linked to which area of the amygdala is being scanned/focused on, and a lack of sufficient control for the different types of depression participants are suffering from. Either way, given their prominent role in threat detection and emotion regulation, it is likely that the amygdala will continue to be a focus for neuroscientists in the years to come.

Hippocampus

The hippocampus is also located in the medial temporal lobe, and has a close relationship with the amygdala. It plays an important role in learning and memory, in linking emotion to memory, and the regulation of the body's stress response, including the adrenocorticotropic hormone (ACTH; see above for a discussion of the role of ACTH in depression). These functions would appear to have close overlaps in some of the experiences people with depression describe – such as poor memory and capacity to learn new information. Clinically, many people with depression describe difficulties in experiencing certain types of emotional memories, with positive memories far more difficult to recall than negative ones.

So, is there any evidence that the hippocampus plays a role in depression? Well, **fMRI** studies (Sapolsky, 2004; Campbell, Marriott, Nahmias and MacQueen, 2004) have consistently shown hippocampal atrophy (wasting away or size reduction) in depression, whilst other studies have estimated the reduction in volume to be around 8–10% in people who are depressed (Videbec and Ravnkilde, 2004). It may be that this atrophy is a result of activation of the HPA axis, and in particular, excessive levels of cortisol which can cause cell damage in the hippocampus. Moreover, because the hippocampus is involved in the regulation of the HPA axis, any damage to it via excess cortisol would then inhibit its ability to regulate the HPA axis, thus potentially exacerbating the problem.

What scientists are unsure of is whether decreased volume in the hippocampus precedes, or follows, a depressive disorder. Currently, it appears that the latter is more likely, and there is some tentative evidence that decreased hippocampal volume is related to recurrent depressive episodes rather than first episode depression.

Nucleus accumbens (NAcc)

The nucleus accumbens (NAcc) plays an important role in pleasure, motivation and reward. There is now growing evidence that the NAcc may have an important role in depression, and in particular, the loss of positive affect in depression. Pizzagalli et al. (2009) found reduced NAcc response to reward in people with depression. Nestler and Carlezon (2005) and Shirayama and Chaki (2006) suggest that the NAcc has been an area of the brain overlooked with regard to depression. They both conclude that based upon animal and human studies, dopaminergic activity within the NAcc may play a role in the aetiology and experience of depression, and in particular, reduced motivation and energy, and anhedonia.

Anterior cingulate cortex (ACC)

The anterior cingulate cortex (ACC) is found behind the prefrontal cortex (PFC – one of the more recently evolved brain areas, which is found under the forehead) - and appears to act as a type of bridge between phylogenetically (i.e. in terms of our evolutionary history as humans) older emotional areas of the brain (sometimes referred to as the limbic system), and newer cognitive and attentional areas (Bush, Luu and Posner, 2000). Like all neuroanatomical structures, the ACC can be divided into different subareas. Research has found that one part of the ACC seems to be connected with newer areas of our brain associated with cognitive functioning. Research has found this part of the ACC is hypoactive (inactive or under active) during a depressive episode. In comparison, when in remission and recovery from depression, activity in this part of the ACC increases. Some have suggested that in depression, the ACC does not 'communicate' well with the PFC, and is unable to 'recruit' this area of the brain to help process a particular conflict or difficulty (Davidson et al., 2010).

Researchers have found that another part of the ACC has greater connections with older areas of the brain that are associated with our emotions. Interestingly, in depression it might be that different things happen to this area of the ACC, depending on the type of depression experienced (e.g. the specific symptoms experienced). For example, Davidson et al. (2010) postulate that hypoactivation (under activity) in this part of the ACC is related to blunted emotions and anhedonia. However, others have pointed out that there may be hyperactivation (over activity) of this area in some depressions which feature high levels of anxiety or sadness. Finally, there is increasing evidence that an area of the ACC known as the 'subgenual' or sgACC is significantly reduced in people diagnosed with depression (e.g. Drevets, Savitz and Trimble, 2008).

Prefrontal cortex (PFC)

The prefrontal cortex (PFC) is located at the front of the brain in a small area just above the eye socket, behind the mid-to-lower part of the forehead. It is associated with a variety of complex tasks relating to cognition, planning and decision-making. These functions are sometimes also known as 'executive functions', invoking ideas of an executive having to make the most important decisions/actions from a myriad of options for the best of the company.

The PFC, and particularly the left PFC, is associated with approach-related, goal-based behaviours, and has been found to be under-activated in people with depression (Davidson et al., 2010). A number of studies have highlighted that changes in PFC neuronal structure, with reduced grey matter, number of cells, along with generalised under-activation of this area in depressed compared to non-depressed controls.

Summary of the role of brain anatomical structures in depression

The above overview of anatomical brain structures involved in depression is not an exhaustive description of all of the brain areas involved in depression. Rather, it outlines some of the key areas that appear to have a significant role in the experience and regulation of emotion, in attention, concentration and memory and in task- and goal-related behaviour. These structures are all interconnected, and it is likely that different subtypes of depression are related to differential patterning of responses in these areas.

Genetic explanations – can we inherit a vulnerability to depression?

Is it possible that our genes can cause us to suffer from depression? In other words, can some of us be more vulnerable to depression because of the genes we inherit from our parents? Many researchers have spent time over the years investigating this question, and the current evidence seems to lead to the answer: partially.

Some of the initial work looking at the heritability of depression stemmed from the observation that depression, like other mental health problems, seemed to run in families; that is, if one member of a family were depressed, *it was more likely* that another close genetic relative would also be depressed. Studies looking into this found interesting results. For example, in a review of published studies on the familial links to depression (known as 'family studies' – see Box 3.2), Sullivan, Neale and Kendler (2000) found a two- to four-fold increase in the likelihood of depression if a first-degree relative also had depression, in comparison with non-depressed controls. In reviewing studies investigating the prevalence of depression in twins (known as 'twin studies' – see Box 3.2), the authors found genetic heritability to be in the range of 31–42%. These findings are interesting to scientists for a number of reasons. Clearly, given that we share a certain percentage of our genes with familial relatives, the increased ratio of depression within different family members suggests that there may be certain genes that are related to depression.

Box 3.2 Different types of genetic studies

Epidemiological researchers use a variety of studies to investigate the potential role of genes in depression. These studies include:

Family Studies

In family studies, researchers look at rates of depression – or symptoms of depression such as anhedonia – in families of blood (genetic) relations. If depression is heritable, it would be expected that other family members – particularly close family relatives who have a higher percentage of shared genes – also have depression. Although this is a powerful way of investigating whether particular genes shared by different family members may be associated with depression, it is not conclusive proof that any particular 'gene' caused the depression. For example, as family members are also likely to share the same environment, there is a high possibility of 'confounding effects' – that is, it becomes difficult to separate out whether the depression is caused by a particular gene(s) or by the type of environment family members share (e.g. poverty or a city caught up in a war), or even some mix of the two.

Twin Studies

In twin studies, researchers compare identical twins with non-identical twins, to assess the role of genes and environment in leading to the development of certain traits, illnesses or diseases. Identical twins, or monozygotic (MZ) twins, are assumed to share 100% of the same genes with each other. They are the result of a single ovum, fertilized by a single sperm, which then 'splits' into two, so that the same genes are divided in two. Alternatively, non-identical, or dizygotic (DZ) twins, on average share 50% of their genes. Twin study methodology is helpful, as it examines the degree to which genetic factors account for health variables, over and above environmental factors.

Whilst twin studies have been an invaluable way of looking at gene versus environmental influences, there are problems with this methodology. Firstly, although initially researchers assumed that MZ twins share exactly the same genes, research on twins has recently shown that this is unlikely to be true. Due to mutations and changes to genes over time (in interaction with the environment), small differences in genes begin to arise over time. In fact, as MZ twins get older, it is likely that their genetic code increasingly differs, although this only impacts on a relatively small number of genes.

Secondly, the assumption that both identical and non-identical twins share the same environments has not been fully supported. For example, people often treat non-identical twins as if they are identical, whilst sometimes, both types of twins will have different school and peer group relationships. This creates problems for twin studies, as the environment begins to become dissimilar, limiting how much results can be said to be down to the influence of genes.

Researchers have attempted to adapt twin study methodology to overcome such problems. One variation involves studying identical twins separated at birth and reared apart. The hope here is that if both twins are found to be depressed later in life, then this would point towards a genetic cause, as the environments they would have been exposed to are assumed to be different. However, it is still likely that there are various, shared experiences (e.g. shared uterus environment, shared early environment before separated).

Adoption Studies

In a further attempt to separate the influence of environment from genes, researchers have studied individuals who have been adopted, and compared their rates of depression with that of their biological parents and their adopted parents. In these studies, if the child and biological parent are depressed, a common genetic link is suggested. This is drawn from the assumption that the child shares part of their genetic makeup, but no common environment, with their biological parent, whilst the reverse is true with their adoptive parent.

◉ Which genes are associated with depression?

Whilst studies seem to show at least some genetic underpinnings to depression, have scientists been able to identify the specific gene(s) responsible? Well, simply put, no. But this is likely to be partly due to depression being a highly complex disorder in which multiple genes might be involved in predisposing one to developing depression. Scientists often refer to the genes that might be related to depression as *candidate genes*, and currently, there appear to be a number of key 'front runners', that research has shown to potentially play a role. We will briefly look at these below:

Genes involved in the synthesis, degradation or neurotransmission of serotonin

Thase (2010) points out that, so far, scientists have found 15 subtypes of serotonin receptor, all of which are linked to the way that genes express themselves (in other words, the way they work). The most frequently studied serotonin gene in depression (and in general) is 5-HTTLPR. This gene is involved in the 'coding' (or the controlling) of the serotonin transporter, which impacts on the 'reuptake' or reabsorption of serotonin by the neuron that initially produced and secreted it. This gene has been studied as it is involved in processes targeted by many antidepressant medications.

So far, studies have suggested that variations in 5-HTTLPR may be important in depression. In particular, scientists have focused upon whether an individual has either long or short versions of an allele. An allele is one of two or more variations of a gene, and we all have one allele passed to us from one parent, and one allele from another. Short variations of the 5-HTTLPR gene have been found to be involved in the reduced capacity of serotonin reuptake, and some studies have found that people with this gene are more likely to become depressed in comparison with people with the longer version of this gene. Interestingly, as Levinson (2010) points out, although some studies have shown a link between short and long variations of 5-HTTLPR and depression, this has not been replicated consistently. However, some of the most exciting research in this area is concerned with the interaction between the types of genes we have and the types of experiences we have in life. In a way, this research is interested in *biosocial interactions*. A well-known study here was conducted by Caspi et al. (2003), who found that the risk of depression was greater for people with two copies of the short 5-HTTLPR gene, rather than those with two copies of the long version of this gene, but only if they had experienced a high number of stressful life events. At low levels of stressful life events, these different versions of the 5-HTTLPR gene did not make a difference in how likely one is to experience depression. These studies are important as they suggest a diathesis-stress model of depression, in which the genes we inherit interact with life experiences to make us more vulnerable or protected to depression.

A number of studies have also looked at other genes involved in serotonin, for example, another gene linked to 5-HT (5HTR2A), but also genes linked to tryptophan hydoxylase (TPH1, THP2). Although somewhat mixed, Levinson's (2010) review of the literature suggests that as yet, there are not enough good data to clearly support these as genes involved in depression.

Genes involved in the synthesis, storage, release, degradation and neurotransmission of dopamine

Scientists have looked at the potential role of a number of gene variations linked to dopamine, including those that relate to Tyrosine Hydroxylase (TH), Catechol-O-methyltranserase (COMT) and one of the dopamine receptors (DRD4). In a large meta-analysis of the existing data, Lopez-Leon et al. (2005) found that a polymorphism of the DRD4 gene was significantly associated with greater risk of depression. A polymorphism refers to a variation – or different form – of something – in this case a gene. Unfortunately, even though this was a meta-analysis of other studies (the pooling of data looking at DRD4 and depression) there were a relatively small number of people with depression in the analysis (n=318), which makes it difficult to extrapolate how reliable these findings are.

Genes related to Brain Derived Neurotrophic Factor (BDNF)

BDNF is likely to have a role in 'protecting' neurons – maybe in the hippocampus along with other areas of the brain – from the deleterious effect of the brain's and body's response to prolonged stress. There have been a number of studies suggesting an association between a polymorphism of BDNF (in particular, a gene known as Val66Met) and depression. However, a number of large-scale recent studies have not found a significant association between Val66Met gene and depression (e.g. Surtees et al., 2007; Chen et al., 2008).

Genomewide association studies (GWAS)

GWA studies use gene sequencing technology to scan the human genome more comprehensively for gene polymorphisms that are associated with depression or depression-related traits, such as neuroticism. They have the advantage over candidate gene studies in that rather than looking at the potential effect of one gene they can look at any potential link between approximately a million different genes and depression (Lohoff, 2010). In reviewing five GWA studies, Lohoff (2010) found that overall, there were no genome-wide significant findings. However, these studies did suggest a number of potential new, candidate genes for further study.

Summary of the role of genetics in depression

The above section highlights a number of plausible areas for investigation of the role of genes in leading to depression, such as candidate gene studies looking at those genes that control certain neurotransmitters implicated in the cause of depression. However, to date there seems to be little consistent evidence of specific genes implicated in depression. It is important to remember that lack of evidence does not mean that there is no link, but rather, may reflect the complexity of conducting such research (e.g. recruiting large enough samples to detect a significant finding). Moreover, it is further likely that the heterogeneous nature of depression makes it hard to isolate particular genes to study their potential involvement in the various forms of depression.

⊙ Chapter summary

This chapter has reviewed a variety of explanations for biological causes of depression, including those relating to:

- Neurotransmitters – for example, serotonin, dopamine and noradrenaline
- Neurohormones – such as cortisol and oxytocin
- Neuroanatomical areas – such as the amygdala, hippocampus and prefrontal cortex
- Genes – including those that regulate the neurotransmitters serotonin and dopamine

Whilst there are a number of studies showing evidence for potential roles of all of these biological factors in depression, there is no single causal explanation that can account for depression. It may be that this is because, as discussed in Chapter 2, depression is not a 'single' disorder, but rather, a complex heterogeneous disorder in which some forms of depression are related to one biological underpinning (e.g. serotonin) whereas others are linked to neuroanatomical structures (e.g. problems with functioning in the prefrontal cortex). It seems most likely that the biological factors discussed above interact in complex ways, and that this may best help to explain the biological basis of different depressions.

However, although there are some tentative suggestions in the literature about the exact way this might happen, research is yet to find a way to demonstrate this conclusively. Moreover, it is likely that different types of depression need to be understood in terms of complex biopsychosocial interactions, in which aspects of an individual's psychology and social/environmental experiences interact with underlying biological mechanisms, the result of which can lead to depression. Here, ideas that we have discussed in the previous chapters on social/environmental and psychological explanations of depression are likely to play important roles in impacting upon the development and functioning of key biological substrates of depression discussed in this chapter.

It is also important to note that, although scientists have been looking at biological explanations for depression for a long time, we may actually be in the infancy of our understanding here. For example, the influential American Psychiatrist and Neuroscientist Thomas Insel, current Director of the National Institute of Mental Health (a prominent US organisation researching mental health), suggests that due to new technological advances, we are on the cusp of important new understandings of the brain and mental health problems. If this is the case, the coming years should provide us with greater nuanced understandings of the different biological profiles (genes, neural circuits, neurotransmitters and hormones) of depression, and saliently, the complex process of biopsychosocial interaction in the cause and maintenance of this disorder.

Further reading

Nunn, K., Hanstock, T. and Lask, B. (2008) *The Who's Who of the Brain: A Guide to Its Inhabitants, Where They Live, and What They Do.* London: Jessica Kingsley Publishers.

Chapter 4

Psychological Explanations

👁 Psychological explanations

In the previous chapter, we explored biological explanations of depression, and discovered that these were rooted in an understanding of how certain changes to *brain* functioning are central to the development and maintenance of this disorder. In this chapter, we will explore psychological explanations of depression. Here, we will look at understanding how the way in which the *mind* functions may affect our vulnerability to depression. The distinction between *brain* and *mind* is not a purely semantic one, although it is somewhat arbitrary. Whilst most psychological explanations acknowledge the importance of biological underpinnings to psychological processes, the focus here is on understanding the *processes of mind*. With regard to psychological explanations of depression, psychiatrists, psychologists and researchers have focussed on motivations, desires, impulses, thoughts, feelings and behaviours as ways of explaining the occurrence of depression. There are a number of key psychological explanations that we will consider in this section:

- Psychodynamic perspective
- Behavioural (conditioning and learning) theory
- Cognitive approaches

Psychodynamic explanations

One of psychology's most famous – and infamous – figures is Dr Sigmund Freud. Freud, who was actually a neurologist by training, became interested in the functioning of the human mind, and his great legacy is in bringing the ideas of psychoanalytic and psychodynamic approaches to understanding the mind and mental health problems. Psychodynamic approaches to mental health were the primary model for understanding the mind throughout the later nineteenth and early to mid-twentieth century, and continue to play an important role in understanding mental health problems today. Whilst some of Freud's ideas are sometimes best understood through the lens of history and within the socio-political context of the time they were developed (over 125 years ago), they continue to provide a useful perspective on understanding depression.

Although there is not space to go into much detail on psychoanalytic theory here, certain basic elements of classic psychoanalytic theory are helpful in terms of our understanding of depression. Psychoanalytic approaches suggest that human behaviour is heavily influenced by certain drives, most of which are unconscious and shaped by early childhood experiences and their influence on our personality.

Box 4.1 Psychoanalytic and psychodynamic – A question of apples and pears?

The terms 'psychoanalytic' and 'psychodynamic' are often used inter-changeably, when referring to theoretical models. Whilst the two are underpinned by similarities – for example, an acknowledgement of the importance of unconscious mental processes in influencing moti-vation, emotions, thinking and behaviour – there are some differ-ences. Psychoanalysis was developed originally by Freud and is the 'original' psychodynamic theory, but not the only one. Psychodynamic refers to a broader umbrella of theory and approaches that were inspired by Freud but were developed further by a number of his students and contemporaries. Some of these, like his daughter, Anna Freud, remained close in position to Freud's initial ideas and theo-ries. Others, however, such as Carl Jung and Alfred Adler, developed ideas about the mind that diverged from Freud's and led to fractures and divisions within the psychoanalytic movement. So, whilst psycho-analysis could be seen as a type of psychodynamic therapy, other psychodynamic therapies include self-psychology, ego psychology and object relations. Moreover, there are differences between how psychoanalytic therapy is practised (traditionally, the client lies on the couch and faces away from the therapist) and other, more contemporary psychodynamic therapies.

Some of the early psychodynamic and analytic perspectives considered anger as key in understanding depression. Along with Freud, Karl Abraham (a German psychoanalyst and pupil of Freud) suggested that the experience of anger, rage and hatred can evoke anxiety when such experience is felt to be at odds with what is acceptable and appropriate within one's immediate environment, and/or the wider society. Anger can therefore become repressed, through a process known as 'ego defence', where angry feelings towards another person/a situation become inverted or turned inwards. These, in turn, serve as a form of self-punishment or self-criticism, evident in states of depression.

There have been numerous studies exploring the association between anger and depression. Some of these have found that depression is associated with inhibited anger. For example, in a comparison between people with depression, people with post traumatic stress disorder (PTSD) and 'healthy' people, Riley et al. (1989) found that anger levels were higher in the depressed group than the healthy group (but lower than the PTSD group), but that the depressed group had the highest level of anger suppression. Similarly, Goldman and Haaga (1995) found that in comparison with a group of non-depressed people, people with depression had significantly higher levels of anger and anger suppression but were no different in the amount of anger expression. Whilst both these studies are limited by the small numbers of participants involved, they support the potential role of anger, and in particular, anger suppression, in depression.

In a study that I was involved in along with Paul Gilbert, a British psychologist (Gilbert, Gilbert and Irons, 2004), we explored, amongst other things, how anger was related to participants' experiences of their depression. Although not coming from a psychoanalytic approach, we found that 82% of participants answered 'yes' to the question 'Have there ever been any occasions when you felt angry with someone but were unable to tell them?'. Of these people, over half (56%) felt that their inhibited anger preceded their depression, and 22% 'about the same time'. We also found that whilst people described feeling angry, and wanting to express their anger, there were a number of reasons for why they did not do this. These included a number of fears, such as 'I worry that I may be rejected by those I love' or 'I worry that I may lose control'. These types of worries and concerns about expressing anger were significantly associated with severity of depression; in other words, the more concerned, worried and fearful people were about expressing their anger, the more severe their depression symptomology tended to be. Whilst the findings of this study have a number of important limitations (e.g. lack of a non-depressed control group) they again suggest that there might exist an important relationship between anger, anger inhibition and depression.

Other psychoanalytic explanations link depression to the experience of loss. This arose out of Freud's work in the early 1900s, and in particular, was addressed in his seminal 1917 text *Mourning and Melancholia*. In drawing attention between such similarities, Freud and Abraham later postulated that depression may represent a state of unresolved grief in the face of a real or imagined loss of a loved one (or an ideal). In this, Freud reflected on his clinical experience of the similarities between how people felt when they were depressed and when they had suffered a loss or bereavement (e.g. tearfulness, loss of pleasure, withdrawal). There is an interesting recent parallel to this (as discussed in Chapter 2) with the **DSM-5** allowing for some forms of bereavement to be reclassified as depression, whereas in previous versions of the DSM, those who had experienced a bereavement were excluded from the diagnosis.

⊚ Behavioural theories of depression

Unlike their psychoanalytic counterparts, the behaviourists viewed the human mind – and consequentially depression – very differently. The behaviourists were steeped in scientific enquiry, and in particular, focussed on things that were *measurable*. Rather than speculating about or exploring how the recesses of the mind controlled impulses, drives, thoughts, feelings and behaviour, the behaviourists were instead interested in how the environment influenced the way we behave. One of the pioneers of **behaviourism** was an American Psychologist called John Watson, who borrowed findings of researchers studying animals, and began to apply some of these ideas to humans. Watson viewed many psychoanalytic ideas with scorn and at times, contempt, as he felt these could not be measured in any way. In fact, in his famous 1913 paper introducing the ideas of behaviourism, Watson said:

> Psychology, as the behaviourist views it, is a purely objective experimental branch of natural science. Its theoretical goal is the

prediction and control of behaviour. Introspection forms no essential part of its methods, nor is the scientific value of its data dependent upon the readiness with which they lend themselves to interpretation in terms of consciousness. (p. 158)

The behaviourists were particularly interested in how environmental stimuli impact upon *learning*. Whilst behaviourism is an overarching term that incorporates a number of different perspectives and views, it can be helpful to hold in mind that, in general, it is interested in the link between a *stimulus* (commonly referred to as 'S') and the *response* to this stimulus (referred to as 'R'). A stimulus is taken as any environmental input – (a situation, event or occurrence) that is measurable and may affect behaviour in some way. A response is taken to be a particular, defined behaviour. A response may include either reflex or voluntary behaviours, and for behaviourists, quantification of the observed behaviour (e.g. its quality, frequency, length and so forth) is key.

Behaviourists were particularly interested in how S-R relationships influenced learning. There are two key behavioural theories regarding this that we will explore in greater detail: *Classical Conditioning* and *Operant Conditioning*.

Classical conditioning

Classical conditioning emerged from the work of Ivan Pavlov, a famous Russian physiologist. Actually, the origins of classical conditioning were serendipitous; Pavlov was originally studying the salivatory response of dogs, which involved inserting tubes into their stomachs and observing how much they salivated when they were given food. However, during the experiment, Pavlov became frustrated when the dogs began to salivate before they had the food. Pavlov also noticed that over time the dogs started to salivate in the presence of the lab technician who would usually feed them, even in the absence of food itself. This got Pavlov thinking about how an automatic reflex like salivation may become *associated* with something that previously did not trigger that response (in this case, the lab assistant).

This curiosity led Pavlov to develop one of the most well-known psychological experiments. In the first stage of the experiment (also described in Figure 4.1) Pavlov presented two unrelated stimuli (food and the sounding of the bell) to a dog at different times. The presence of

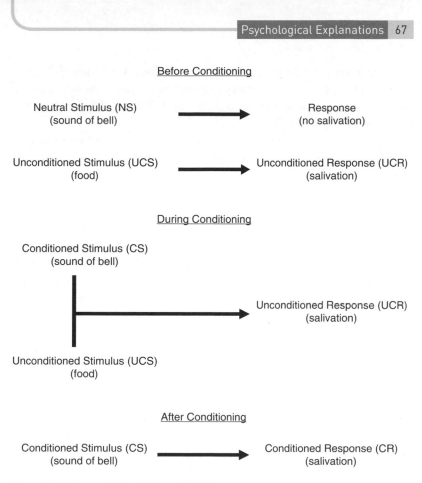

Figure 4.1   Stages of classical conditioning

food (described as the unconditioned stimulus – or UCS) triggered a salivatory response in the dog. Salivation here is referred to as the unconditioned response (UCR) as it is the reflexive (biological) response to seeing food, as opposed to a learnt response. In comparison, the sounding of the bell (known as the neutral stimulus – NS) was not met with salivation but merely with the dog turning towards it or twitching its ears. In the second stage, the *conditioning phase* of the experiment, the food (UCS) was presented to the dog shortly (one or two seconds) after the bell (NS) was rung. During this stage, the dog salivated again in response to the presentation of food (UCR). However, Pavlov discovered that, following several repeated presentations of this bell-food sequence, at the sound of the bell alone (in the absence of food), the dog salivated.

In other words, the sound of the bell was no longer a neutral stimulus, but instead triggered the salivatory response in the dog. The sound of the bell thus became the conditioned stimulus (CS), and the salivation the conditioned response (CR).

Pavlov's research earned him a Nobel prize in 1904, but interestingly, this was not for his discovery of classical conditioning, but rather for his work on the physiology of digestion! However, he is now remembered throughout psychology and science as the person who discovered the process of associative conditioning.

Classical conditioning therefore involves learning via *association* and operates on a non-conscious level. Whilst Pavlov continued his research on animals and humans, it was the work of John Watson and his colleagues that brought classical conditioning into focus in understanding human learning. Watson's most famous experience involved 'Little Albert', an 11-month-old infant who was to become the figurehead of one of the most infamous of psychological experiments. Watson and his colleague Rayner (Watson and Raynor, 1920) presented Albert with a white rat (neutral stimulus – NS), with which he interacted without any fear. Unsurprisingly, when a loud noise was made behind his head by the banging of an iron rod with a hammer (unconditioned stimulus; UCS), Albert responded with showing fear and by crying (unconditioned response; UCR). Following this, Albert was presented the rat again, but at the same time, a loud noise was made behind his head (unconditioned stimulus; UCS) to which he again responded with fear and distress/crying (unconditioned response; UCR). This combination – the presentation of the rat and the loud sound – was repeated a number of times. Subsequently, Watson and Rayner presented the rat to Albert in the absence of the loud noise (conditioned stimulus; CS), and found that Albert displayed a fear response (conditioned response; CR) upon seeing the rat. Watson and Rayner described this as a classically conditioned response, in that they were able to change Albert's emotional response to the rat by associating it (the rat) with an aversive stimulus (the loud noise). You can watch an explanation of this process, along with some video footage of the experiment with Albert, here: www.youtube.com/watch?v=FMnhyGozLyE&noredirect=1.

Classical conditioning has been observed experimentally in a number of species, including humans, primates, birds and even worms! It appears to be a very helpful mechanism in which an organism can learn about the environment and crucially be prepared for potential threats. From this perspective, it appears likely that classical conditioning is a highly adaptive protective mechanism for animals. For behaviourists, it was initial proof that supported one of their general principles – that is, all behaviour could be learnt and unlearnt.

How is classical conditioning related to depression?

Whilst classical conditioning has often been used to explain how anxiety and fear develop, in terms of depression, behavioural understandings have focused on Wolpe's (1971, 1979) ideas about neurotic depression. Wolpe suggested that the 'neurosis' of neurotic depression (also known as reactive depression) is fuelled by anxiety, which, along with a number of unhelpful behaviours developed to deal with it, is learnt via classical conditioning processes. In essence, Wolpe was suggesting that the depression was secondary to a severe and/or prolonged conditioned anxiety. He suggested that therapists needed to take a detailed assessment of a depressed person's history, to try and identify the situations in which anxiety had been conditioned. An example to illustrate this might be helpful. A number of years ago, Paul, a 20-year-old student at university, came to see me for help after becoming depressed. Although in many ways a confident, popular young man, he had been feeling increasingly stressed about his university work. Over a number of weeks, he started avoiding going to lectures and had also stopped attending social events. As we spent more time focusing on this, Paul was able to identify that prior to these changes, he had become preoccupied and stressed about doing a series of assessed presentations in front of his year group as part of a module he was taking. Initially, he found it difficult to understand why he was struggling with this so much, as in his words, 'I'm a confident guy – I'm chatty and people often tell me I'm funny'. However, when we looked at some of his early experiences, a long forgotten memory emerged that appeared to offer a helpful explanatory framework for his difficulties. As a 10-year-old boy, Paul had given a presentation to his year group, almost 100 people. He recalled – in vivid detail – feeling 'scared sick' before getting up to talk, and highly self-conscious. One of his teachers told him to drink lots of water as his mouth was dry. Whilst giving the presentation, he was unable to control the urge to urinate, and unfortunately, in front of everyone, he 'wet' himself on stage, and the children in the audience started laughing. In terms of classical conditioning, at this moment the act of public speaking/social exposure (previously the neutral stimulus) became associated (conditioned) with being laughed at (the unconditioned stimulus), which resulted and now conditioned response of anxiety and shame. Whilst this type of situation could be avoided for much of his remaining childhood and adolescence, Paul was now required to face this as part of his university course. The mere thought of facing a crowd (the conditioned stimulus) was sufficient to elicit the conditioned response of anxiety and shame, to the extent to which Paul began to avoid going to his lectures and attending social events.

Wolpe's ideas then would suggest that the early conditioning of anxiety here can subsequently lead to patterns of behaviour later in life (e.g. avoidance of public speaking, and the avoidance of large social gatherings) and interfere with a person's life by reducing opportunities for positive reinforcement, thus contributing to the experience of depression (we will return to the concept of positive reinforcement in the below section on operant conditioning).

Another way that classical conditioning has been used to understand depression is through a process known as higher-order conditioning (or second or third order conditioning). Here, following the establishment of conditioning, higher-order conditioning involves the 'transfer' or association from the conditioned stimulus (e.g. the sound of the bell) to a neutral stimulus. Pavlov trialled this concept in his experiments with dogs, in which once he had produced a conditioned response (e.g. salivation in response to the ringing of a bell alone), he then repeatedly presented to the dog a black square at the same time as ringing the bell. After a number of trials of this pairing, the dog was just shown the black square on its own. He found that following this process, the black square alone could produce salivation in the dog, although this was not as consistent or as strong a response as to hearing the bell. So, how might higher-order conditioning relate to depression? Well, let's take an example of a young boy, who each winter was sent away from his parents to live with an elderly aunt because his parents had specific work commitments at that time of year. Each year the boy was sent to his aunt's, he became low in mood and less active, struggling to engage in activities and complaining that he did not find anything of interest. Now an adult, and long after having stopped going to see his aunt, he still experiences depressed-like feelings every winter, although he struggles to understand why that might be. This might be an example of higher-order conditioning – the association of a time of year with negative feelings still has a powerful impact even though the specific original cause (visiting the aunt) no longer happens.

Another classical conditioning-informed approach to depression arose from the work of Ferster (1973). Ferster developed a number of important behavioural theories about depression, but with regard to classical conditioning, he highlighted how some emotions or desires could become inhibited due to classical conditioning processes. He pointed out that if a child looking for affection from their mother was repeatedly punished for this, this would result in the child experiencing anxiety and developing fears of being punished again. Ferster suggested that, over time of experiencing parental punishment, the desire for affection itself (the inner experience of it) triggers a conditioned anxiety response. If this experience continues, then the child may lose awareness of the desire for affection and inhibit seeking it, even in situations where affection may be needed (e.g. when in distress). Such learning experience can thus create the conditions whereby an individual gradually becomes withdrawn from interpersonal connection and increasingly vulnerable to feeling alone, isolated and potentially depressed, particularly in times of difficulty and stress. This same process of gradually learning to inhibit emotional expression and needs could also occur with other emotions, such as sadness or anger. If we take the example of anger, this may help us understand the process of inhibited anger described earlier in the section of psychoanalytic explanations of depression. If we imagine a child repeatedly being punished for showing anger, it is likely that they will experience anxiety and fear in response to punishment. Over time, and repeated experiences whereby the expression of anger is met with punishment and fear, feelings of anger themselves will be associated with the conditioned fear response, so much so that anger may become repressed or inhibited. Given that anger can be an adaptive emotion in standing up for ourselves and other people, its inhibition may lead to difficulties navigating challenging social situations or circumstances (e.g. relationships where one is being treated badly) and, over time, potential vulnerability to depression.

Finally, Ferster's ideas might apply to positive emotions, in that if someone is punished for showing certain types of positive feelings (e.g. happiness, joy or contentment), these two could, over time, become associated with a conditioned fear response, to the extent to which they become feared or inhibited. Thus, an individual may develop chronic difficulties experiencing or expressing positive emotions. Given that anhedonia (the lack of feelings of pleasure and enjoyment) is a core symptom of depression, it is not hard to see that people with histories of having positive feelings punished, may be particularly vulnerable to depression. Interestingly, research conducted by a colleague of mine, Professor Paul Gilbert, has found that people can fear positive emotions, and that the more they fear positive emotions, the higher they tend to score on symptom measures of depression, anxiety and stress (Gilbert et al., 2012).

Operant conditioning

In comparison with classical conditioning, which is interested in the *association between a stimulus and a response*, **operant conditioning** is interested instead in how behaviour is affected by the consequences that follow it. It initially arose from the work of an American psychologist, Edward Thorndike (1898) who was investigating learning in animals. His most famous experiment involved the 'puzzle box', in which he placed a cat inside a cage, and observed its attempts to escape from it. Thorndike had designed his puzzle box with a lever inside, so when the cat pressed the lever, the box opened and the cat was then rewarded with food. Thorndike found that following an accidental pressing and escaping, and repeated trials of being placed in the box, the time taken for a cat to press this lever (and therefore escape from the box) reduced. It appeared that the cat quickly learnt to *deliberately* press the trigger lever, unlock the cage and escape. This experiment led Thorndike to propose the law of effect, which posits that:

- Any behaviour that is followed by a pleasant experience will be repeated again.
- Any behaviour that is following by an unpleasant or aversive experience or consequence will be reduced in frequency.

Thorndike's early work was notably built upon by another American psychologist, B.F. Skinner, who introduced the idea of **reinforcement** to the law of effect and coined the term 'operant conditioning'. Using an adapted version of Thorndike's puzzle box, Skinner initially studied the behaviour of rats in a box (known as the Skinner Box) in which, when they pressed into a lever, they received a food pellet. Over time, as a result of receiving food upon (initially accidentally) pressing the lever (i.e. positive reinforcement), the rat's behaviour became more specific (goal-orientated) and, as long as the reward continued, the number of lever presses increased over time. However, when Skinner ceased giving the rat the reward (i.e. the food pellets were stopped), the reinforced behaviour (lever pressing) also quickly stopped (or *extinguished*). Skinner postulated that humans learned behaviour in similar ways, and that what was learnt was dependent on the consequences that followed the initial behaviour. The different types of consequences to behaviour are outlined in Box 4.2.

Box 4.2 Different types of reinforcement

There are a number of common terms used when describing operant conditioning:

Positive Reinforcement – This involves the addition of a stimulus after a behaviour that makes the behaviour more likely to occur in the future. For example, being given money by your teacher or tutor for handing in an essay on time is likely to increase the likelihood of handing in the next essay on time.

Negative Reinforcement – This is when a stimulus is removed following a behaviour, which makes the behaviour more likely to occur in the future. For example, cleaning your room to avoid being nagged at by mum. Here, mum's nagging is a negative reinforcer for cleaning your room.

Positive Punishment – Although seemingly contradictory at first (how can a punishment be positive?) this term actually refers to an aversive stimulus being added following a behaviour, thus making the behaviour less likely to occur again. For example, being caught by the police for speeding and given a warning and three points on your driver's licence. Here, the positive punishment is being caught by the police and given a warning and three points on your driver's licence, which leaves you less likely to speed again in the future.

Extinction – This occurs when a particular behaviour decreases after the previous consequences (reinforcers) of that behaviour are removed or withdrawn. An example of this might be when a parent, who would usually respond to their child's attention-seeking tantrums by giving them sweets (which would lead to an increase in the likelihood of the child having a tantrum), change their response and, instead, ignore the child's behaviour. By withholding of reinforcement, this is likely to eventually lead to the reduction of the behaviour (tantrums).

How do operant conditioning principles explain depression?

Much of the application of operant principles to depression emerged from Ferster's (1973) paper, which were then developed further by Lewinsohn (1974). Ferster (1973) highlighted the importance of functional analysis of depressive behaviours, whereby one examines how contextual features of a person's environment influence individual behaviour. Key here was identifying 'depressive contingencies' – those factors that caused the depression and also the consequences of the depressive behaviours themselves. Ferster's idea was that in depression, opportunities for positive reinforcement are reduced, whilst those for negative reinforcement increased. Lewinsohn (1974; Lewinsohn et al., 1976) built upon Ferster's ideas, and suggested a variety of factors that inhibit contact with events, which were previously sources of positive reinforcement. This could include a change in one's *environmental circumstances*. For example, moving to a lovely home in the countryside, but which limits or removes contact with close, supportive and loving friends and family which acted as positive reinforcers of behaviour in the past. Alternatively, it may be that a positive reinforcer is still available, but the individual cannot access it. An example would be having no energy to engage in previously enjoyable activities, after falling ill with ME (Myalgic Encephalomyelitis).

For traditional behaviourists, there was less interest in the depressed mood state itself (as this cannot be clearly observed or measured), and more on the consequences of this (i.e. behavioural output). One way of understanding depression from an operant perspective is that depression is the result of an ongoing schedule of 'extinction' (see Box 4.3), in which the individual receives diminishing experiences of, or opportunities for, reinforcement. For example, Lewinsohn (1974) suggested that the low physical movement in depression is the result of low levels of reinforcement in a person's environment – he suggested that with reducing levels of reinforcement, a person would respond with decreased behavioural output, which in turn would lead to reduced reinforcement (e.g. from others), which in turn, would lead to reduced physical output. He suggested that this process would eventually lead to the physical symptoms – for example, lethargy and low energy – commonly seen in depression.

Another way that operant conditioning ideas can be helpful in understanding depression is in considering factors that *maintain* the condition.

For example, some depressed people may experience others' response to their depression – for example, extra care or kindness – as rewarding (positive reinforcement), thus increasing the likelihood that the depressed behaviour continues. For other people, it may be that whilst depressed, others may take over undesired activities (e.g. chores around the home), thus leaving the person more likely to remain depressed in order to avoid such activities (an example of negative reinforcement).

Evaluation of behavioural theories of depression

Behavioural theories have provided important insights into the triggers and maintaining factors in depression. These understandings have been developed via in-depth laboratory study of classical and operant conditioning (with animals and humans), but also via clinical insights of working with people who are depressed. In this regard, there is well-tested and established evidence base for classical and operant-conditioning processes. As we will discuss in greater detail in Chapter 8, research in conditioning processes has also led to effective interventions for treating depression, particularly in terms of behavioural activation (i.e. changing patterns of reinforcement in a person's life).

However, there have also been a number of criticisms about behaviourism, and its application to depression. One of the broad criticisms of behavioural approaches is that its impact on 'real life' is difficult to observe; that is, whilst there have been lots of important findings in the laboratory, it has not been so easy to empirically show that these processes – such as changing patterns of reinforcement or classical conditioning – lead to depression. In fact, Lewinsohn et al. (1988) in a longitudinal study of 562 non-depressed individuals did not find evidence that reductions in positive reinforcement predicted the development of depression at a later point. Rather, they found that elevated stress, previous experience of depression and some sociodemographic variables (e.g. gender and age) predicted depression. Interestingly, and counter to the behavioural theory of the time, they also found that depressive thoughts predicted higher levels of depression symptomology. This lack of ecological validity is problematic, as it restricts our ability to test out what type of impact conditioning can have upon mood, and which factors are likely to affect this impact (e.g. individual differences that make some more/less likely to be influenced by conditioning).

◉ Section summary

Behavioural approaches to depression suggest a number of explanations for how it develops and is maintained. These centre around two important types of learning – by association (classical conditioning) and by the consequences of behaviour (operant conditioning). Within these models, the symptoms of depression (e.g. anhedonia, heightened negative emotions, withdrawal and psychomotor retardation) are seen as a learnt behaviour that is shaped and maintained as a result of observable associations and outcomes.

◉ Cognitive theories of depression

Historically, cognitive theories of depression and mood disorders arose out of a belief that the behaviourists and psychoanalysts were minimising or ignoring the role that consciously experienced thoughts and feelings have upon mood and behaviour. In contrast to the behaviourists, the champions of **cognitive psychology** felt that internal mental experiences (thoughts, memory, images and so forth) were as important as environmental stimuli in understanding the human mind. In comparison with the psychoanalysts, cognitive theorists felt it was important to understand consciously experienced internal experiences, rather than focus on unconscious drives. Many of the cognitive approaches to depression emerged out of, or were influenced by, the field of **psychotherapy**. Here, the ideas of one man in particular – Aaron Beck, an American psychiatrist working with people with depression and other mental health problems – had a significant impact on our understanding of depression. There are a number of key components of Beck's cognitive approach to depression, and emotional disorders more generally:

 i Negative automatic thoughts and errors in thinking
 ii Negative, depressogenic schemas
 iii The cognitive triad

We will explore each of these in a more detail below.

Negative automatic thoughts and distorted thinking

Beck noticed in his work, initially as a psychoanalyst, that his patients had a stream of automatic, involuntary thoughts and images in their minds that they were usually unaware of but which under situations of threat or distress could 'pop up' into conscious awareness. As he spent time with his patients, helping them to pay attention to the different types of thoughts they had when depressed, he noticed a number of things. First, in depression, thoughts tended to be very negative in focus, and Beck referred to these as negative automatic thoughts (NATs). Second, that NATs were associated with negative emotion and mood. Third, when identified and verbalised during therapy, NATs tended to reflect a type of distorted or error-based thinking, in which thinking was skewed or biased, and which had a 'distorting' impact upon information processing. Finally, Beck noticed that there were characteristic styles of negative, distorted thinking in depression. Some of these are displayed in Box 4.3.

Negative schema

In 1976, Beck published work on *schemas theory* for depression in which he suggested that schemas represent ways in which information is

---

Box 4.3 Negative automatic thoughts in depression

As the name implies, automatic thoughts are those that pop into our heads without effort or thinking. In depression, these are often focused on negative self-evaluations, unresolved problems or issues from the past, or the future. Some common negative automatic thoughts in depression are:

Catastrophising – Expecting or anticipating the worst possible outcome or event to occur. For example, believing that you will fail your exams before even sitting them.

Overgeneralising – Based on one negative or distressing experience or occurrence, expecting the same thing to happen at all times. For example, 'My date was terrible tonight – I'll never find anyone' or 'These things always happen like this to me'.

Black and White Thinking – Here, thoughts are dichotomous, so that something is either all good or (more typically) all bad. For example, 'If I don't get an A, I'll be a complete failure'.

Filtering – This involves the minimisation of positives (e.g. 'I only passed the test because I got lucky') and the exaggeration of negatives (e.g. 'Now that I've passed the test, I have to do more work to pass the next one').

processed, organised and evaluated. He suggested that schemas develop over many years, and are influenced by our experiences in the world and with other people. Beck suggested that whilst we can have both positive and negative schemas, in depression we typically have access to negative schemas, and that these could be triggered by stress.

Beck suggested that when people are depressed, their schemas involve a number of core themes, which include issues of loss, failure, worthlessness and rejection. His daughter, Judith Beck (2005) suggested that negative schemas (also referred to as Core Beliefs) could fall into three broad categories: unloveability, worthlessness and helplessness. Whilst these themes themselves are not new to cognitive approaches – in fact, many psychoanalytic theorists had suggested the same decades earlier – it was how these impacted upon depression that cognitive approaches had something new to contribute. For example, Beck suggested that when depressed, an individual with a schemas of 'failure' would be more sensitive to information in the environment relating to performance, achievement and, more generally, setbacks and failure. Moreover, he suggested that this type of schemas, when activated, would alter thinking, skewing it in a negative, biased way, fuelling low mood and negative emotion, and potentially, depression.

However, Beck felt that, rather than merely operating during a depressed episode, schemas form stable vulnerability traits which guide the way an individual processes and filters information (i.e. in schemas-congruent ways) which might, in turn, make one more likely to become depressed. He suggested that the existence of certain types of schemas make some people more vulnerable to a depressed episode because of the way they bias attention towards information themed around rejection, loss and worthlessness.

Cognitive triad in depression

Beck (1976) suggested that in depressed individuals, a characteristic pattern of thinking styles tends to emerge, which is known as the 'cognitive triad'. This triad is depicted in Figure 4.2, but involves:

1 Negative evaluation of oneself, in which the person would often voice critical thoughts about themselves, such as: 'I'm useless' or 'I always fail at things'.
2 Negative views about the world, in which there is a sense of unfairness of events in life, for example 'only bad things happen to

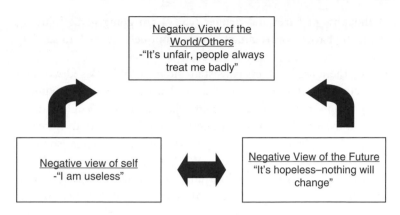

Figure 4.2 Negative cognitive triad

me', or about other people, for example, 'other people think that I'm a failure'.

3 Negative views about the future, in which there is an overwhelming sense of hopelessness and powerlessness about how life will be in days, weeks, months or years to come. For example: 'There's no point, it will always be like this' or 'I'll never find someone who will like me' or 'I'll always be a failure'.

The cognitive triad in depression is depicted visually in Figure 4.2, and shown as mutually influencing of each other.

So, is there any evidence of these types of cognitive processes in depression? Well, one of Beck's strengths was that he was keen on trying to empirically validate his ideas and encouraging others to do so as well. This has led to a lot of research looking at his theory in depression, some of which are broadly supportive of his ideas, particularly in relation to thinking styles during depression. In a good review of the evidence, Haaga, Dyck and Ernst (1991) found that when depressed, people typically describe more depressogenic cognitions in comparison with people who are not depressed. Beck and colleagues found that one could differentiate between the types of thoughts depressed individuals have from those of anxious individuals. Known as the 'cognitive content-specificity hypothesis (CCSH), Beck (Beck et al., 1987; Clark, Beck and Brown, 1989) found that depressive cognitions around failure and loss (e.g. 'I'm worthless', 'I'll never be as good as other people' and 'I'm a social failure') were uniquely associated with depression, whilst anxious cognitions around thoughts of harm and danger (e.g. 'I am going to be injured', 'I'm going to have a heart attack') were uniquely related to anxiety disorders.

However, there has been less consistent support for Beck's ideas about latent or underlying dysfunctional schemas that lead people to be vulnerable to depression. For example, although when depressed people endorse high levels of dysfunctional beliefs, there are no differences in the levels of these beliefs in people who have never been depressed, in comparison with people who have previously been depressed but who are now in remission (e.g. Miranda et al., 1990; Hamilton and Abramson, 1983). Moreover, counter to Beck's ideas, longitudinal studies have found that those people who went on to develop depression did not previously have higher levels of dysfunctional beliefs compared to those who did not go on to develop depression (e.g. Lewinsohn et al., 1981). There have been a variety of ideas and debates about these findings, and new emerging theories and evidence about how to better account for cognitive vulnerability to depression (e.g. mood-dependent hypothesis, Miranda and Gross, 1997; and diathesis-stress models of cognitive vulnerability, e.g. Scher et al., 2005).

⊙ Other cognitive components in depression

Within a cognitive approach to understanding depression, there are a number of key forms of thinking that have been highlighted as important.

Self-criticism

Somewhat similar to negative automatic thoughts, self-criticism involves a particular type of negatively focused self-talk, in which we judge and put ourselves down. Evidence has found that persistent self-criticism can reflect trait-like aspects of individuals' personality, which can increase vulnerability to suffering from depression and elevate risk for **relapse** (Blatt and Zuroff, 1992; Murphy, Nierenberg, Monson, Laird, Sobol and Leighton, 2002; Zuroff, Santor and Mongrain, 2005). Interestingly, in recent years, researchers have suggested that it is not just the cognitive content of the self-criticism (e.g. 'I'm a bad person' or 'I'm no good at my job') that is important. Rather, it appears to be that the emotions that accompany the content of the self-criticism are most powerfully related to negative emotion and depression symptomology. In particular self-criticism imbued with emotions of disgust, anger and hatred for the self is particularly associated with depression symptomology (Whelton and Greenberg, 2005; Gilbert, Clarke, Hempel, Miles and Irons, 2004). Self-criticism can, in turn, leave people feeling more beaten down and submissive to their own self-criticism (as if exposed to an 'internal bully').

Rumination

Rumination refers to the process of mentally going over events (their causes and associated feelings) in a repeated and circular fashion. Rumination is sometimes described as 'chewing over problems only makes them worse', which refers to the biological process of digestion in some mammals, in which the food is repeatedly chewed upon again and again to soften it so that it can be properly digested. Rumination is different to negative automatic thoughts (see above), in that the process of returning again and again to a particular topic is key, rather than just the content of one's thoughts. In terms of researching the effects of rumination, Professor Susan Nolan-Hoeksema, an American psychologist, and colleagues, found that high levels of rumination were related to higher levels of depression symptomology (Nolen-Hoeksema, 2000), predicted future episodes of depression and poorer regulation of negative emotion (Morrow and Nolen-Hoeksema, 1990), and were associated with negative biases in information processing.

Lack of compassion

In recent years, there has been a substantial increase in research exploring the role of compassion in well-being. One area of interest here has been whether compassion – and in particular, a lack of self-compassion – may be linked to a variety of mental health problems including depression. Compassion has been defined in a variety of ways, but a common definition is 'a sensitivity to the suffering of self and others, with a desire to alleviate the suffering'. This definition suggests that compassion is not just a way of thinking about ourselves, but also involves a particular type of feeling (e.g. warmth, kindness) and motivation (i.e. to try and alleviate suffering). Evidence suggests that in depression, people struggle to have compassion for themselves (Raes, 2010; MacBeth and Gumley, 2012), and report lower levels of compassion than those who have never been depressed (e.g. Kriger et al., 2013).

👁 Evaluation of cognitive theories

Cognitive theories of depression, particularly those influenced by Beck's work, have had a significant impact upon our understanding of depression. Although in many ways these ideas were not 'new', borrowing from **psychoanalysis** and going further back the Greek philosophers, they helped to focus our attention upon the powerful role of our thinking in affecting emotion and mood. They also helped to bridge a gap, in that whilst behavioural theories appeared to be helpful in showing how learning theory could partially account for depression in humans, people exposed to similar environmental stressors and learning contexts did not all go on to develop negative emotion or depression. The cognitive approach offered an understandable and useful explanation for this – that thinking acted as a mediator, or bridge, between a stimulus (e.g. a stressful event) and a response (e.g. depression). From a cognitive perspective, it was the way we thought about the event – either in a helpful or positive way (e.g. 'this wasn't my fault, but I'll be ok') or unhelpful or negative way ('It's all my fault, I'm an idiot – I've ruined everything now') – that directed how we responded emotionally and behaviourally.

However, there are a number of criticisms of cognitive approaches to depression. One of the main critiques of this theory is that it places conscious thinking in too prominent a role in affecting emotion, mood and behaviour. Many see this as an overly simplified way of understanding complex interactions between stimulus, attention, thinking, emotions and behaviour. Others suggest that rather than our thinking having a top-down impact upon our mood, it is our emotions and moods that can impact upon our thinking, biasing and influencing it in a variety of ways. Linked to these criticisms are concerns that whilst the focus on our conscious awareness of mind is important (i.e. the thoughts, evaluations and beliefs that we can notice consciously), this ignores important non-conscious aspects of our minds that may also play an important role in understanding depression. Finally, as we explored above, there are concerns that Beck's theory may not account well for vulnerability to depression. Whilst all of these criticisms have some validity, cognitive theories have continued to evolve and adapt to help better account for the complexity of these processes in depression.

⊙ Section summary

This section has explored cognitive explanations of depression. This perspective emerged from a dissatisfaction of existing dynamic and behavioural ideas of depression, but more broadly, how the mind 'works'. Cognitive explanations place cognition – our thoughts and beliefs – at the forefront of causing and maintaining depression. In particular, they suggest that certain types of thinking – both in terms of content (e.g. negatively biased, laden with self-criticism) and process (becoming overly fixed or ruminatory on a particular theme, or laden in negative emotional undertones) – is associated with increased vulnerability to depression.

⊙ Chapter summary

This chapter has explored three major psychological explanations of depression – psychodynamic, behavioural and cognitive – each bringing in a different slant on the disorder. We saw how historically behaviourism emerged as a contrast to the prevalent psychodynamic orthodoxy of the time, and that later, cognitive approaches emerged out of dissatisfaction with both dynamic and behavioural approaches. Each approach focuses on different elements (e.g. the unconscious, behaviour and its conse-quences, and attributions, thoughts and beliefs) in offering understand-ings to the causes and maintaining factors of depression.

Whilst offering different perspectives on depression, rather than being at odds with each other, it is likely that all three contribute to our understanding of the complexity of depression. In the next chapter, we will explore how certain types of experiences and environments may be linked to the development and maintenance of depression.

Chapter 5

Social and Environmental Explanations

Whilst the previous two chapters have focused on the *internal* mechanisms (biological and psychological) related to depression, this chapter will look at how external factors – difficult life events, or certain experiences or environments – may be related to depression. Much of this chapter will focus on experiences and environments that are stress-inducing in such a way that they may increase the likelihood of depression. For many researchers, healthcare professionals and psychologists, depression is intimately intertwined with stress, and in particular, stressful events and environments. In fact for some, depression *is* an illness of stress. Of course, biological and psychological aspects of stress can ameliorate or exacerbate the impact of stressful environments and experiences. However, our focus in this chapter will be on how certain experiences and environments may be more *depressogenic* than others.

👁 Stressful life events (SLE)

One major area of investigation of the potential role of stress in depression has been the study of stressful life events. Stressful life events have been described in a number of different ways. Some suggest that a SLE can be any event that leads to severe or prolonged strain or stress, whereas others suggest that the term involves events that lead to an individual having to change their usual behaviour or activity in some way. An initial attempt to measure stressful events was undertaken in the 1960s by two psychiatrists – Thomas Holmes and Richard Rahe – who looked into potential life events associated with illness. They developed a 43-item scale (the Social Readjustment Rating Scale – SRRS; Homes and Rahe, 1967), in which 43 different stressful situations (e.g. death of a spouse, losing your job, moving house) are ranked and given a score out of 100 (death of a spouse rated as the highest stressful life event at 100). Participants make a note of how many of the 43 stressful life events have occurred to them over the past year, and the scores given to each item are added together. The idea here is that higher total scores are associated with greater risk of physical illness. If you are interested in looking at this scale, a version can be found at: http://www.mindtools.com/pages/article/newTCS_82.htm.

Holmes and Rahe (1967) found that higher scores on the SRRS were related to higher levels of illness (although this was quite a small statistical relationship), and subsequently, to depression (Costantini et al., 1973; Rahe, 1979). From Holmes and Rahe's (1967) work, it was clear that whilst overall stress was important, certain types of stress were seen to be more significant or 'stressful'. Holmes and Rahe rated the top three most stressful events as: (i) death of a spouse, (ii) divorce and (iii) marital separation. Whilst there may be a number of elements common to these events, one issue in particular seems to be important: *loss*. In fact, the research literature over the past three decades has supported this finding, and has highlighted that interpersonal loss – be it through death, the ending of a relationship or the perception that a relationship might be permanently ending – appears to be a powerful source of stress and closely associated with depression. As a concept, loss featured as a central part of psychodynamic theories, and to a lesser extent, cognitive theories of depression explored in the previous chapter. More recently, other important life stress themes have emerged as being associated with depression, include those involving social defeat, failure, entrapment (Brown et al., 2011; Gilbert et al., 2004), rejection and/or social exclusion (Slavich et al., 2009).

Life events and depression

There is now a good deal of evidence that major life stress and events often precede the beginning of a depressive episode. For example, Mazure (1998) found that in community samples, approximately 80% of major depression episodes were preceded by significant life stress. Brown and Harris (1978, 1989) have done a lot of work looking at the role of life stress in depression. They also developed a specific interview – the Life

Events and Difficulties Schedule – that assesses the impact of stress and can be used to look at the relationship between life stress and depression. Their findings – along with those of others in the field – have highlighted that, in comparison with non-depressed controls, people with depression experience greater life stress. In fact, it was estimated that depressed individuals are 2.5 times more likely to have experienced a stressful life event, in comparison with non-depressed individuals (Brown and Harris, 1989; Mazure, 1998). These findings suggest that the experience of stressful life events may be important in depression.

Whilst the above research suggests that certain types of severe stress are associated with depression, do we have any data on whether less severe forms of stress predict depression in the same way as more severe stress does? Well, the answer is 'probably no', but that it is still likely to have an impact on depression. Studies looking at the role of less severe forms of stress suggest that whilst this can precede the onset of a depression, its effect is likely to be far less than that of severe life event stress (Brown and Harris, 1989).

Whilst there has been a greater focus in the research literature on acute and severe stressful life events, it may also be important to consider how long the stress lasts for. This is referred to as how persistent or chronic stress is, and is usually defined as stress that lasts for more than 12 months (Hammen, 2005). Whilst there has been less research looking at chronic stress in comparison with acute, severe life events, there is some evidence that chronic stress may also play a significant role in the onset of depression. For example, Rojo–Moreno et al. (2002) looked at the role of stress in the onset of depression in Spain. They found that both acute and chronic stress equally predicted depression onset. It remains unclear at this time though whether acute and chronic stress impact upon risk for depression via similar routes (e.g. changes to neurobiological systems; see Chapter 3), whether they are related to similar or different patterns of depression symptoms and severity, or whether they impact on the likelihood of relapse. As Hammen (2005) and Monroe et al. (2010) point out, methodological problems in the research literature and seemingly contradictory results make it difficult to be clear about such questions currently.

However, there are caveats to this. For at least some depressions, there appears to be an absence of an obvious stressful trigger. In the past, this type of depression was referred to as *endogenous depression*, and reflected the idea that the depression was largely biologically generated, with little or no external trigger (e.g. stressful life events). More recently, a number of researchers have referred to as the *kindling hypothesis of depression* in the literature. The term was first used by Post (1992) to denote how first episodes of depression often followed more severe life events and stress, than subsequent episodes did. So, in effect, recurrent depressions needed less severe stress to trigger them, with each further episode requiring less stress than the episode preceding it. There have been a number of studies looking at whether the evidence supports Post's ideas. Monroe and Harkness (2005) found support for the kindling model but suggest that there may be two theoretical interpretations of this. The first, which they refer to *stress sensitisation model*, suggests that with increasing numbers of episodes of depression, less severe stress is needed to trigger the episode. The second, *stress autonomy model*, suggests that whilst early episodes of depression require stress, future episodes may occur autonomously from stress, in effect occurring spontaneously in the absence of stress. They suggest that, further, high-quality research is needed to clarify which of these theories is able to best explain the kindling effect.

Box 5.1 Difficulties measuring stressful life events

Whilst research on life events has been an important first step towards understanding the role of stressful events in depression, it has been subject to a number of flaws related to use of self-report, checklist measures.

There have been a number of other concerns about this type of measurement. Relying on people to accurately report what is and isn't stressful is tricky, as we know that a variety of factors, such as poor memory and a desire to minimise perceived weakness, might influence how accurately an individual is able to recall experiences prior to the onset of a depression. Moreover, what one person finds stressful, another might take in their stride. For example, for one person the death of their mother would be highly distressing and stressful, whereas for another person (who might not have got on with or known their mother well) the death would be experienced in quite a different way. This then makes it difficult to know whether it is preferable to rate stress on some sort of aggregated hierarchy (a stress checklist) based on what people find stressful *on average*, versus relying on people's self-reports of their experience as stressful and to what extent.

In the face of these problems, Brown and Harris (1978) set out to develop a more thorough, comprehensive measurement of stressful

life events in the form of an interview called the Life Events and Difficulties Schedule (LEDS). The LEDS was developed to assess in far
greater detail the type, duration and severity of events (acute,
chronic), and their role in mental health problems. Overall, it appears
that the LEDS is a preferable, more accurate method of measuring
life events than the checklist counterpart, and has greater likelihood
of predicting depression (McQuaid, Monroe, Roberts, Kupfer and
Frank, 2000).

In the coming sections we will explore some of the different types of
stress, life events and environment that appear to be related to depression.
This will include:

- Experiences linked to the types of relationships, or relationship
  experiences, we can have.
- Types of societal view and perceptions of people.
- Social issues linked with poverty, employment and housing.

◉ Relationship experiences

As we explored in the previous chapter, a number of psychological explanations of depression highlight the importance of relational experiences –
such as loss and rejection – in shaping psychological vulnerabilities in
depression. Social theories of depression are interested in what type of
relational experiences might be related to increased levels of depression.

Early life experiences

There is a large evidence base highlighting the significant relationship
between certain types of early life experience, and increased likelihood of
depression later in life. In a large, longitudinal study of a thousand families in the Newcastle area, UK (known as the 'Newcastle Thousand
Family Study'), Sadowski, Ugarte, Kolvin, Kaplan and Barnes (1999)
looked at the relationship between a variety of early family life difficulties
(e.g. family or marital instability, poor parenting, poor physical care,

poverty, overcrowding) during individuals' first five years of life and incidence of major depression in adulthood. They found that only 7.2% of a group of 33-year-olds who had experienced no or some disadvantages prior to the age of five experienced a major depression in the previous year. In comparison, 28.2% of the same group, who had experienced multiple disadvantages in early life, had experienced a major depression in the previous year.

The National Society for the Prevention of Cruelty to Children (NSPCC) suggests that child abuse includes any type of emotional, physical or sexual treatment that leads to injury or some form of harm. They also suggest that a lack of care can also form an abuse in some situations. A number of large-scale meta-analyses have shown that child abuse is significantly related with increased likelihood of depression (and other mental health problems) later in life. Nanni, Uher and Danese (2012) conducted a meta-analysis on 16 epidemiological studies (with over 23,000 people) looking at the relationship between childhood maltreatment (physical abuse, sexual abuse, neglect, or family conflict or violence) and depression onset later in life. They found that children who had experienced childhood maltreatment were significantly more vulnerable to recurrent and persistent depression, in comparison with those who had not experienced childhood maltreatment. They calculated that there was a 2.27 odds ratio of recurrent or persistent depression in individuals who experienced childhood maltreatment. In other words, people who were maltreated as children were over two times more likely to develop recurrent or persistent depression than those who had not experienced childhood maltreatment.

Although often not described as abuse, there are a variety of ways that parents can interact with their children – such as with no (or low) care and warmth, or high levels of criticism, overprotection and rejection – which also appear to be related to depression later in life. A number of studies have asked participants to recall how their parents behaved towards them when they were younger, and then examined whether these ratings were associated with higher levels of depression symptomology. For the most part, research has found that higher levels of recalled lack of parental care, overprotection and rejection are associated with higher levels of depression symptomology in adulthood. For example, Rosenfarb, Becker and Khan (1994) found that, in comparison with non-psychiatric controls, moderately and severely depressed individuals recalled their childhood as having less love and affection. There have been a variety of studies demonstrating that when asked about their memories of growing up, depressed adults are more likely to describe their parents as being low in emotional warmth, overly controlling and more rejecting (Perris, Arrindell, Perris, Eiseman, van der Ende and von knorring, 1986; Gerlsma et al., 1990).

There have been a number of criticisms of the parent-rearing litera-ture. In particular, a number of concerns have been raised regarding the reliability of recall of past experiences, including upbringing, as this might be influenced by current levels of low mood or depression (McFarland and Buehler, 1998; Calev, 1996; Lewinsohn and Rosenbaum, 1987). However, a number of studies have suggested that recall of early parental experiences is at least moderately reliable (Cournoyer and Rohner, 1996) and is independent of changes in depressed mood (Gerlsma, 1994; Gerlsma, Das and Emmelkamp, 1993; Brewin, Andrews and Gotlib, 1993). With specific regard to clinical samples, it seems that there may not be a 'depressed' skew on recall, as studies have shown that individuals' ratings of parenting whilst depressed and whilst in remission are not significantly different (Parker, 1981). Overall, it seems that recall of parental behaviour remains relatively stable in clinical and non-clinical populations (Wilhelm and Parker, 1990).

Box 5.2 How common is childhood adversity?

A number of researchers have tried to ascertain how common expe-riences of adversity are in childhood. It is actually quite difficult to get an accurate measure of this, partly because different people use different definitions of what stands for childhood adversity. In a recent review of the association between childhood adversity and mental health, Kessler and colleagues (Kessler et al., 2010) suggest 12 types of childhood adversity:

(1) Interpersonal Loss
(2) Parental Maladjustment
       (i) parental death; (i) mental illness
       (ii) parental divorce; (ii) substance misuse
       (iii) other separation from parents; (iii) criminality
       (iv) violence

(3) Maltreatment
(4) Other Adversity
   (i) physical abuse; (i) life-threatening physical illness
   (ii) sexual abuse; (ii) family economic adversity
   (iii) neglect

Kessler et al. (2010) analysed data from over 50,000 adults from 21 different countries as part of a broader World Health Organization (WHO) World Mental Health (WMH) survey. Participants were asked to give information about early life adversity (before the age of 18). In total, 38.8% of people surveyed had experienced one childhood adversity, of which parental death was most common (12.5%), followed by physical abuse (8%), parental divorce (6.6.%) and family violence (6.5%). The lowest recorded adversities were sexual abuse (1.6%) and parental criminal behaviour (2.9%).

Expressed emotion (EE)

Expressed emotion is a description of a family environment that has been found to be associated with the development, maintenance and relapse of mental health problems, particularly schizophrenia but also mood disorders like depression. EE refers to the way that family members/relatives talk or treat a member of the family with depression, and using a measure called the Camberwell Family Interview (CFI; Leff and Vaughn, 1985), three facets of expressed emotion are coded:

- Hostility – a negative attitude expressed to the person suffering from depression, in which family members feel that depression is the person's fault, and could be alleviated if the person chooses to. Hostility can also refer to blaming the depressed individual for other family problems.
- Emotional Over-involvement – family members high in emotional over-involvement can often be intrusive.
- Critical Comments – here, there is less blaming of the patient for their depression, and family members may be more open to other explanations for its cause. However, there are still critical comments directed towards the depressed individual.

A variety of studies have found that families high in EE are associated with the development and maintenance of depression. In a small study,

Hooley, Orley and Teasdale (1986) found that over a nine-month period, 59% of people with depression who had spouses with high EE experienced a relapse. In comparison, none of those people with depression who lived with low-EE spouses became depressed. In a meta-analysis, Butzlaff and Hooley (1998) found that the experience of EE predicted stronger effects in depression than in schizophrenia, and calculated a significantly higher depression relapse rate (69.5%) for those patients with high-EE relatives than those patients with low-EE relatives (30.5%). However, in a 10-year longitudinal study, spousal high EE was not a significant predicting variable in depression outcome. This led the researchers to caution against a clear, causal role between high EE and depression in adults (Kronmuller et al., 2008), although they do note some limitations with their study, such as not using the CFI to measure EE, and only measuring levels of EE at the start of the study (i.e. EE could have changed in spouses over the course of 10-year study). It is likely that further and more methodologically tight research will help us understand the relationship between EE and depression.

Bullying

Whilst many of us might look back at our childhood as halcyon days of fun and freedom, many others remember – or may prefer to try not to remember – that growing up involved a lot of pain and suffering. One common source of childhood difficulty is being bullied. Estimates of how common bullying is vary hugely, but in a large study of 7000 11- to 16-year-olds in the United States, Wang and colleagues (2009) found that, in the previous two months, 12.8% of respondents had experienced physical bullying, 36.5% some form of verbal bullying, 41% relational bullying and 9.8% 'cyber' (online bullying).

Research has been particularly interested in the *consequences* of being bullied, and studies have consistently found that being the recipient of bullying is associated with a variety of deleterious health outcomes, including depression. For example, Klomek et al. (2007) asked over 2000 students, aged between 13 and19 years old, whether they had experienced bullying, and the frequency to which this had occurred if they had. They found that adolescents with frequent experiences of being bullied were more likely to be depressed in comparison with those adolescents who had never been bullied. Whilst much of the literature on bullying has focused on the consequences of being a victim of bullying, a number of studies, including Klomek et al. (2007), have also shown that being a bully, or being a bully as well as a victim of bullying, are also associated with increased levels of depression.

With recent technological advances and the development of social media, the phenomenon of cyber bullying has also become a feature of the bullying landscape. Social networking sites, such as Facebook, Twitter and Bebo, along with other forms of communication such as BBM and WhatsApp, are commonly used by bullies to target victims, providing a new, indirect and extended route for bullying to continue even outside of the normal confines of the school or workplace. Although we have no data yet, it is interesting to consider the potential impact of bullying 'following you' (through the use of social media), rather than it just being confined to a particular place (e.g. school).

There is also some intriguing evidence that other social factors might interact with bullying to convey greater risk of depression. For example, Due et al. (2009) found that Danish children from poor households who were bullied were more likely to be depressed as adults, than children who were bullied but were from affluent households. We will explore the potential role of poverty and depression below, but these findings suggest that multiple stressful experiences/environments may interact in a cumulative way to make us more vulnerable to depression.

Bullying is not just confined to childhood and adolescence. Most adults spend a significant amount of their life in the workplace, where bullying from colleagues or managers can also be common. In two large meta-analyses, Nielsen and Einarsen (2012) looked at the cross-sectional and longitudinal impact of bullying at work and a variety of deleterious outcomes, including depression. They found that individuals with current experiences of workplace bullying reported significantly more depression symptoms than people who did not experience workplace bullying.

Social support

Having social support – colleagues, friends or family who we feel are there for us when needed – has long been seen as important for psychological well-being and as a buffer against the potential depressogenic impact of stress (e.g. Cohen and Wills, 1985). It is not surprising that a lack of social support has been found to be related to depression. In a group of depressed patients being treated as inpatients, George et al. (1989) found that size of social network and, in particular, perception of social support, were significantly associated with depression symptomology between 6 and 32 months later.

Why might the lack of social support be related to greater vulnerability to depression? Well, one explanation is that a common consequence of lacking social support is loneliness. Loneliness has been defined as the distress that results from discrepancies between ideal and perceived social relationships, and can reflect actual lack of contact with people/ social support, or the perception of this, even if there are people close by. In a great book discussing the power of loneliness, John Cacioppo and William Patrick (2008) discuss how humans have an innate need for social connection due to our evolutionary history, and that loneliness is tied to a sense of being socially disconnected.

Studies have found that higher levels of reported loneliness are related to higher levels of reported depression symptoms. In 2006, John Cacioppo and colleagues published a study looking at the relationship between loneliness and depression. They found that higher loneliness ratings in middle-aged adults (over 54 years old) were associated with higher severity of depression symptoms, even when other factors related to depression (such as, income, marital status, social support and perceived stress) were controlled. They also found that in a sample of 50- to 67-year-olds, higher levels of loneliness at Year 1 were associated with increased depression symptomology three years later, and that this relationship was again independent of the impact of other important factors like social support and perceived stress. Using a complex type of statistical analysis, Cacioppo and colleagues showed that, over time, loneliness and depression had a reciprocal relationship in that levels of depression in Year 1 went on to predict levels of loneliness in Year 3. From these findings, it appears that an interacting vicious cycle may be at play between depression and the (real or perceived) lack of social support.

◉ Societal views and expectations

Whilst our experiences with other people seem to have an important impact upon our risk to depression, it may be that at broader level, certain group, cultural or societal factors could also play a role in depression vulnerability.

Gender

Although we explored whether there might be certain biological gender differences that could account for women being far more likely to suffer from depression in their lifetime (e.g. hormonal), it is likely that certain social factors in gender roles may predispose women to greater vulnerability for depression. These include:

- Help-seeking: One of the most consistent findings in the research literature is the difference between male and female help-seeking behaviour when depressed (also evident for a variety of other health and mental health problems). Studies have found that men are significantly less likely to attempt to access help from healthcare professionals for depression. It is likely that a substantial block to men's help-seeking are cultural ideas that men should be strong and not show feelings, and that having mental health problems is somehow indicative of weakness. So if this is true, it is possible that the higher incidence of depression amongst women reflects gender differences in social behaviours (i.e. help- seeking, with women more likely to seek help), rather than actual differences in experiencing the illness.
- Professional Bias: In a study looking at clinician rating of depression, Potts et al. (1991) found that women are more likely to be diagnosed with depression than men, even when they both met objective criteria for depression based on structured assessment interviews. It may be that our stereotypes of women and men – that women are more emotional and prone to distress, whereas men are 'stronger' and less in touch with their feelings – may influence diagnosis even when the symptoms are identical.
- Media and Body Image: Aspects of the media, female social roles and emphasis on female body image have also been suggested as potential sources of threat, increasing women's vulnerability to depression. Interestingly, recently there have also been accounts of how media images of the 'ideal' male body has also led to an increase in body-related issues in men (a subtype of these being labelled as 'bigorexia', reflecting a preoccupation with negative feelings about one's body and desire to work out and become muscular).
- Role in Life: There appear to be important aspects of gender role that may also place women under increased stress. These include the idea

of 'supermum' – working mothers holding down fulltime jobs whilst also having to juggle child rearing, household chores and a variety of other tasks. Other ideas point towards the experience of sexism in work, particularly in terms of iniquitous pay and the 'glass ceiling', where promotions essential stop at a particular level of seniority.

Stigma

Stigma is often defined as a strong disapproval of someone due to a particular characteristic they have, and commonly operates on a group, cultural or societal level. It can relate to direct or indirect experiences of being stigmatised, or to a perception that 'people' in general think negatively about us. For many people, experiencing stigma for a particular aspect of themselves or their identity – such as their ethnicity, sexuality or a particular type of illness or condition (e.g. depression, vitiligo or HIV) – can be highly stressful.

There are different ways to think about stigma, culture and depression. The first is linked to depression itself being highly stigmatising. For example, studies have found that those people who feel stigmatised for having depression find it harder to seek help and access treatment for their depression (Barney et al., 2006) and are more likely to discontinue treatment (Sirey et al., 2001). In a study published in 2008, Griffiths et al. (2008) investigated factors that were associated with increased stigma in Australians with depression. They found that stigma for having depression was higher in men rather than women, non-native Australians and those with less education. Interestingly, they also found stigma levels were also higher in those people with less contact with depression (i.e. not having had depression or not having a close family member who had depression) and lower knowledge of depression (i.e. reduced ability to recognise the symptoms of depression). In a very honest and insightful article, Lewis Wolport, a biologist and author, describes his experience of depression and the stigma surrounding it (Wolport, 2001). He describes how on one occasion, on being discharged following an inpatient admission, he found that his wife had not told anyone why he had been in hospital because she was ashamed of what they might think. Instead she told people that he had a minor heart problem (you can read Lewis' account here: http://bmb.oxfordjournals.org/content/57/1/221.full).

The second way of understanding the relationship between stigma and depression involves the experience of depression as a result of stigma surrounding a different condition or situation. For example, there are a number of studies that show that higher levels of perceived stigma about certain illnesses are associated with higher levels of depression symptomology. For example, higher perceived stigma for having HIV was associated with higher levels of depression symptomology (e.g. Tanney et al., 2012).

⊚ Social issues – poverty, unemployment, housing problems and violence

A key concern for many people in healthcare is the damaging impact that a variety of social issues can have upon physical health and illness. Interestingly, it is not just our physical health that seems to be associated with economic problems – our mental health is also negatively affected as well.

Social status and poverty

As discussed in Chapter 2, there is good evidence that a person's socioeconomic background – and in particular, lower socioeconomic background – increases the likelihood of depression. There are numerous explanations for why this might be. In their far reaching and powerful book *The Spirit Level*, Richard Wilkinson and Kate Pickett (2010) provide a wide range of evidence for how depression – and mental health problems, in general – is related not to how wealthy a country is, but to how unequally wealth is distributed in that country. They highlight that depression is more prevalent in societies in which there is a greater stratification of wealth, in other words, where there is a big gap between people with the most amount of money and those with the least. Moreover, research by Wilkinson and colleagues (e.g. Singh-Manoux et al., 2003; Marmot et al., 1991) found that in specific groups (such as staff in an organisation), those at the 'bottom of the pile', who occupy the lower occupational grading and/or rate themselves as having lowest social status and power, and more likely to suffer with a variety of health problems (e.g. heart disease, cancer and back pain), including depression.

Many other researchers have also investigated the relationship between poverty and mental health, including depression. Sandro Galea and colleagues (Galea et al., 2007) found that, in a longitudinal sample of over 1000 adults living in New York City, the incidence of depression was

19.4% in people living in low-socioeconomic neighbourhoods, in comparison with just 10.5% amongst those living in high SES neighbourhoods. When controlling for a variety of individual factors (such as age, gender, individual SES, stress and social support), they found that people living in low SES neighbourhoods were 2.19 times more likely to be depressed than those in high SES neighbourhoods.

Box 5.3 Disparity of wealth and depression

The research presented above does not suggest that rich people don't get depressed, or that in countries where there is less wealth inequality, people will not suffer from depression. Rather, it highlights that there is increased vulnerability for depression in environments where wealth is unequally distributed. So, how might greater disparity of wealth make people more likely to be depressed? In my job as a Clinical Psychologist working in the National Health Service (NHS), I have had some examples of working with patients that has helped me to understand this better. One patient I used to work with ('David') lived in an area of East London (called the Isle of Dogs), which happens to be one of the poorest areas in the UK, with high levels of poverty, unemployment and hardship. David described to me what it was like growing up in a high-rise estate in the Isle of Dogs. He told me about how his mother would work two jobs to pay the bills and keep him and his siblings fed and clothed, and how he would regularly feel cold in the winter and have to wear many layers of clothes, because his family didn't have enough money to keep the heating on.

He went on to tell me that in many ways, he felt ok with people on his estate, because everyone was the same – 'everyone was in the same boat' – struggling to get by, working hard to make ends meet and take care of the basics for survival. However, what he found most difficult was looking out of his bedroom window and seeing an *alternative world*. David was referring to probably one of the most affluent areas in the world, Canary Wharf, a major banking and financial district set in the middle of the Isle of Dogs. He went on to describe to me how, as a child, he observed the people who worked there, dressed in smart suits and dresses, expensive mobile phones and driving BMWs and Mercedez Benz cars. For David, this was a world in which he did not belong, could not get to, but wanted to be a part of. He described his desire to have what these people in Canary Wharf had – money, nice clothes, expensive cars and so forth. However, as he struggled through school and then became unemployed at the age of 16, he described how he felt that there must be something wrong with him, something inferior or bad that would explain why he was on his side of his window, inside a cold dark flat, and different to those 'successful and happy people' across the road.

There are two main theories to explain why the relationship between socioeconomic status and depression may exist; the *social causation hypothesis*, which states that low socioeconomic status and poverty cause depression, and the *social selection hypothesis* (also known as the *social drift hypothesis*), which suggest that being depressed leads to lower socio-economic status (through, for example, problems with motivation and concentration making it difficult to maintain paid employment). So, what is the verdict? Does one of these theories best reflect the data, or is there a reciprocal and interacting relationship between them? It seems that more research is needed to clarify these processes, but at the moment, there may be more evidence for low socioeconomic status causing depression, rather than depression leading to lower socioeconomic status (e.g. Ritsher, Warner, Johnson and Dohrenwend, 2001; Warren, 2009).

Unemployment

It is perhaps unsurprising that researchers have been keen to investigate whether there is a relationship between unemployment and depression. This, of course, has a particular prominence currently given the impact of the financial crisis in 2008 and the subsequent increase in unemployment across much of the globe. In a large meta-analysis of the findings of previous studies, Paul and Moser (2009) found that unemployment was associated with significantly higher levels of depression symptomology. In the UK, the case for the link between unemployment and depression was made by economist Lord Richard Layard. Layard posited the idea that unemployment cost the economy a huge amount of money and that part of this cost was due to poorer health outcomes (including depression) associated with unemployment. Based on Layard's work, the government invested in the Improving Access to Psychological Therapies (IAPT) service, with the suggested aim of providing effective psychological therapies to unemployed people with depression, to enable them to get back into the workforce.

Housing and local environment

Most of us will have experienced times when, being in a beautiful scenic location, or surrounded by attractive surroundings, we feel good – excited, uplifted, relaxed and soothed. It also appears that the opposite is true; that is, being in physically unattractive environments, or environments in which there are signs of disrepair, can lead to an increase in negative feelings, including depression. In a study of residents living in New York, USA, Galea and colleagues (Galea et al., 2005) were interested to see whether the characteristics of the inside of people's accommodation (e.g. percentage of homes with problems with toilets, lack of heating, or peeling wall plaster or paint) and the outside features (e.g. percentage of buildings with a dilapidated appearance or percentage of unclean streets) were related to propensity to depression. They found that people living in areas rated as having poorer built features were between 29% and 58% more likely to have experienced depression in the previous six-month period, in comparison with people living in neighbourhoods which had a higher quality of 'built environment'. This finding was maintained when controlling for the impact of a variety of other factors, such as age, gender, ethnicity and household income.

Mair et al. (2008) conducted a review of studies published that had looked at the relationship between depression symptoms and neighbourhood characteristics. Of a total of 45 studies identified, 37 of these found at least one neighbourhood characteristic that was associated with increased depression symptomology, after controlling for a variety of individual differences, such as age, gender, ethnicity, education level and income. The likelihood of finding a relationship between neighbourhood characteristics and depression were broadly similar for cross-sectional and longitudinal studies. When looking at structural features of the environment, Mair et al. found that there was a more consistent relationship between quality of built environment and depression, than socioeconomic deprivation, residential stability or ethnic composition and depression.

Mair et al. (2008) suggest caution when interpreting studies looking at the relationship between depression and neighbourhood characteristics, as there are numerous methodological issues with existing studies. They suggest future studies would benefit from having greater clarity on the processes through which neighbourhood features may influence depression, as well as improving measures used to test neighbourhood factors.

One particularly stressful experience linked to housing is when we lose our home. There have been a variety of studies that have looked at the relationship between homelessness and depression. Over 20 years ago, Ritchey et al. (1990) found that homeless people were four times more likely to meet 'caseness' ratings (achieving a certain score which research suggests would be a 'cut off' indicating likely depression diagnosis) on a depression symptomology measure than the general population. In fact, almost three-quarters of those homeless sampled scored above the cut-off for caseness. In a study looking at mothers of homeless families, Weinreb et al. (2006) found that a massive 52.4% met criteria for diagnosis of a major depressive episode, and moreover, 85% had experienced a major depression in the past. These figures are far higher than those in the general population. It is difficult to clearly identify whether being homeless causes depression, whether existing depression makes homelessness more likely, or whether causality flows both ways. Whilst all of these appear possible, Rohde et al. (2001) found that in a group of homeless adolescents, depression tended to precede homelessness.

Societal violence

There have been a number of studies looking at the relationship between the level of violence individuals are exposed to and mental health outcomes. Some of these studies have focused on the level of neighbourhood violence – that is, how much violence people observe or experience in their local community or neighbourhood. In a group of over 300 mothers recruited from different neighbourhoods in northeastern US, Clark et al. (2007) found that exposure to neighbourhood violence (defined as hearing gunshots, kicking, punching, knife attacks, shootings) was associated with significantly greater reporting of depression and anxiety symptomology. In a large longitudinal study of over 2000 14-year-olds in Chicago, USA, Slopen et al. (2012) measured levels of home and neighbourhood violence, and then reassessed the same adolescents two years later for presence of depression. The authors found that those adolescents who had been exposed to violence at home were 1.62 times more likely to be depressed than those who hadn't been. Moreover those adolescents who had experienced neighbourhood violence were 1.47 times more likely to be depressed than those who hadn't experienced neighbourhood violence. Interestingly, experiencing violence in multiple settings increased the likelihood of depression by 2.44 times, suggesting a cumulative effect of experience of violence and depression. The researchers also found similar results for anxiety.

Given the relationship between depression incidence and exposure to violence in the local community, it is unsurprising that exposure to mass levels of violence, such as a war, has also been found to be associated with increased rates of depression. In a good article on the impact of war on mental health, Murthy and Lakshminarayana (2006) review studies highlighting the link between war and increased rates of depression in a variety of countries and conflicts, including Iraq, Afghanistan and Cambodia. Karam and colleagues (Karam et al., 1998) explored the prevalence of depression diagnosis following the Lebanese wars of 1975–1990 where the country was torn apart by civil war but which also included invasion from Israel on two occasions. They found that exposure to war increased the likelihood of depression in four different areas in Lebanon. The researchers found lifetime prevalence of major depression (using DSM-III-R criteria) between 16.3% and 41.9%. Crucially, they found that the lower prevalence rates were found in communities that were less affected by the war, whereas greater prevalence of depression occurred in those areas of the country that experienced greater exposure to the war itself.

◉ Chapter summary

This section has looked at a variety of social factors that can play a role in causing or contributing to the development and maintenance of depression. It is clear that, for some depressions in particular, significant life stress and events are an important precipitant. However, it also appears likely that certain early life experiences – often far removed from the actual onset of depression – can make a person more vulnerable to depression later in life. Moreover, there also appear to be aspects of our culture and physical surroundings that may also play a role in increasing vulnerability to depression. It is likely there may be two important and related links between life/environmental stress and depression:

- That stress impacts upon certain biological systems and psychological mechanisms, as discussed in Chapters 3 and 4, and that through these we become more at risk of depression.

- That underlying biological or psychological vulnerability increases the potential of life and environmental stress to lead to depression.

Further reading

Wilkinson, R. and Pickett, K. (2010) *The Spirit Level: Why Equality is Better for Everyone*. Penguin: London.

Chapter 6

Evolutionary Approaches

Evolutionary psychology is concerned with understanding moods, emotions and other mental experiences in terms of their evolved function and natural triggers. For example, the evolved function of anxiety is to detect threat and take defensive actions, whereas love binds us to each other and facilitates caring behaviour. As David Buss (2012), a prominent evolutionary psychologist, points out, an important area of enquiry for evolutionary psychologists is to understand why and how the human mind was shaped through evolutionary processes. Given that depression is a highly aversive experience, impacting in negative ways on peoples' physical health, relationships, motivation and ability to experience pleasure, evolutionary explanations focus upon what (adaptive) functions depression may have in our lives. In other words, why does such a debilitating, unpleasant experience like depression occur, particularly given that many of its symptoms seem to inhibit key evolutionary drives for survival and reproduction?

As we have discussed, although depression is a highly heterogeneous disorder, at its core is a reduction in positive affect and an increase in negative affect. An evolutionary functional analysis (EFA) of depression therefore considers under what conditions might it have been useful for animals to experience a loss of positive affect, drive and activity, and instead, experience an increased level of a variety of negative feelings. If these can be identified then we might be able to understand depression not so much as a pathology in itself but as the triggering of evolved patterns of defence. This chapter will explore some of these possible triggers and functions of depression:

- Learned helplessness – depression as a response to uncontrollable stressors

- Disengagement theory – depression as a response to blocked or thwarted motivations and goals
- Attachment theory – depression as a response to disruption or problems in attachment and social bonds
- Social competition/rank theory – depression as a response to social conflict, defeat and entrapment
- Emotion regulation systems – how depression emerges from a particular patterning of emotion regulation systems designed to respond to different contexts, for example, threat, achievement or caring.
- Dysregulation of evolved emotion–motivation systems – depression as a response to 'loops' in the mind between more recently evolved cognitive systems and ancient emotional motivational systems

◉ Learned helplessness

A number of theories have suggested that aversive, uncontrollable events can cause depression-like symptoms. One of the most well-researched theories is learned helplessness. In the mid- to late 1960s, psychologist Martin Seligman and colleagues were investigating principles of behavioural conditioning in dogs. In these initial experiments (Seligman and Maier, 1967; Overmier and Seligman, 1967), three groups of dogs were placed into harnesses. In the first group, the dogs were placed in a harness for a set amount of time, and then released. Dogs in the second group were also harnessed, but were given a painful electric shock, which they were trained to learn how to stop by pressing a lever. The third group of harnessed dogs was also given an electric shock (of the same intensity and duration as the second group); however, here pressing the lever did not stop the electric shocks. Thus, these dogs did not have a way of preventing or escaping the pain of the electric shock. Following these initial experiments, Seligman placed all the dogs in a container and gave them an electric shock from which they could escape by jumping over a small barrier. The dogs from groups one and two of the initial experiment quickly learnt to avoid the electric shock by jumping over the barrier. However, the dogs from the third group did not do this. Instead, on experiencing the electric shock these dogs tended to lie down and make whining noises. Seligman concluded that these dogs had learnt from the previous experience of not being able to prevent the electric shock that there was no way to stop the aversive experience and therefore, in the second condition, did not try to engage in any behaviours that would help them escape from it. In arriving at an explanation for this behaviour, Seligman suggested that controllability was key – in other words, dogs exposed to the inescapable electric shocks had learnt that this aversive experience was uncontrollable. Seligman and colleagues referred to this phenomenon as learned helplessness, and suggested that the profile of helplessness in animals was analogous to depression in humans.

Box 6.1 Why do we use animals to study human depression?

There are a variety of reasons why scientists use animals to study depression. As with other health problems that humans suffer from, animals also appear to experience depression, and this has been observed in a variety of animals, including our closest relatives, non-human primates, but also in dogs and rats. Therefore, one of the main reasons for studying depression in animals is their similarity to humans. Mammals have similar emotional, behavioural and motivational repertoires as humans. For example, many mammals share similar types of behaviours and 'mentalities', such as nurturance, bonding and competitiveness, and in basic forms, emotions such as anger, anxiety and sadness. Because we have evolved from other animals, the parts of our brains that are involved in our emotions and behaviours are structurally very similar to those of animals. Moreover, sequencing of human and non-human DNA has shown a high level of overlap. For example, we share approximately 98% of our genes with chimpanzees and 36% with fruit flies!

One of the main reasons for studying depression in animals is that in some respects, they are easier to study than humans. Generally, in comparison with humans it is easier to identify specific genes and measure brain responses/changes in animals. It is also easier to control the environment animals live in (e.g. the amount of stress present in the environment). All this means that scientists can set up experimental conditions which can help us to understand how depression might arise out of a complex interaction between genes, biological responses and environmental experiences, and test out treatments (e.g. antidepressants). There are increasingly sophisticated models of animal depression being studied (Cryan and Slattery, 2007), and the results of these are providing important insights to the understanding and treatment of human depression.

There are of course a number of criticisms about using animals to study depression (and other health problems). One obvious yet important point relates to ethical concerns, particularly if experiments cause the animals pain or discomfort. Some people are critical of attempts to understand complex human behaviour from non-humans, even from species closely related to us (e.g. chimpanzees). For example, a number of traits that appear to be central in the experience of depression (such as capacity for self-reflection and self-consciousness) are seen as uniquely specific to humans. One can therefore argue that the outcomes from animal studies have limited generalisability to human experience.

One of the key concepts of learned helplessness involves the initial increase of effort (attempts to escape) upon experience of a stressor (electric shock). If this increased mobilisation of energy and attempt to avoid the stressor is unsuccessful (i.e. the stressor is uncontrollable or unavoidable), then there will be a change in response with a down mobilisation of energy/effort and a depressed-like response. Psychologists saw these changes as similar to those that occur when humans become depressed. This led to attempts at translating learned helplessness theory to humans, and this was initially met with partial success. However, it soon became evident that humans did not consistently respond with helplessness in similar types of (uncontrollable) scenarios as other animals did. Seligman and colleagues eventually 'reformulated' (adapted) learned helplessness theory with some important changes (Abramson, Seligman and Teasdale, 1978) stressing the importance of the way humans thought about events in determining their response to them. In particular, they integrated learned helplessness theory with concepts from attribution theory, which is interested in how people make sense of events (e.g. with regard to their causality). Seligman and colleagues suggested that in humans, rather than events directly predicting the development of learned helplessness (as in animals), learned helplessness is the result of certain types of events, in combination with the attributions regarding the causality of those events. In other words, individuals' explanations about 'why an event happened' were key in contributing to learned helplessness. With regard to depression and feelings of helplessness, it was suggested that the following types of attributions were common:

- The cause of the event was viewed as relating to internal causes ('it's my fault') rather than external ones ('it's someone else's fault')
- Global ('this will happen in all situations') rather than specific ('it was just a one off')
- Stable ('it will always be like this') rather than unstable ('it may change')

So, is there any evidence that internal, global and stable attributions following an aversive event are linked with depression, more than external, specific and unstable attributions? Well, on the whole, yes, there is. In a large meta-analytic study that pooled data from over 100 studies (involving over 14,000 participants) looking at attribution theory in relation to depression, Sweeney et al. (1986) found that for negative events, internal, global and stable attributions were significantly associated with depression.

◉ Disengagement theory

Other theories about the evolved function of depression have tied this to disengaging from the pursuit of goals. Klinger (1975) suggested that the reduction of positive affect in depression was adaptive when someone was pursing an investment (achievements, goals) that they were then blocked from. He called this the incentive-disengagement theory of depression. In other words, low mood and the lowering of positive affect help a person to disengage from the obstacle blocking a goal, rather than getting 'caught in the cycle' and wasting energy in something that could not be attained. Klinger suggested that if the person could not disengage from the obstacle, then depression would increase.

In a similar approach, evolutionary psychologist Randolf Nesse (2000) suggested that depression might be an adaptive response in helping to regulate how much we invest in something based upon the likely payoffs that it will bring. Thus, in favourable situations, there may be an increase in positive mood and effort to take advantage of the potential positive tradeoffs. However, in unfavourable situations, he suggested there would be a reduction of motivation and positive emotion, as likely tradeoffs would not be worth the input expended. The reduction of positive feelings and effort here help to disengage someone from continued pursuit of something that was unlikely to be successful. You see versions of this when watching natural world programmes on TV. For example, a hungry lion will chase after a zebra for a period of time but at some stage will stop chasing and refocus its attention to something else. From an evolutionary point of view, this makes sense, as whilst the lion needs to catch the zebra to survive, there is a tipping point at which, if it keeps on chasing, the pursuit of this goal (to catch the zebra to eat) becomes harmful in that it expends precious energy. Thus, the lowering of positive affect and effort in humans could function on a similar idea, reducing our motivation to pursue and achieve things, therefore preventing us from a dangerous overinvestment in something that may be unobtainable.

⦿ Arrested defences model

Another evolutionary model, with some similarities to Learned Helplessness, suggests that depression may be related to arrested defences in the face of stress (Gilbert, 1992, 2001). In this context, defences are defined as evolved responses to being threatened – for example, feeling anxious with the motivation to move away or escape (flight) or to respond with anger and aggression (fight). These responses to stress are associated with short-term increases in the physiological stress response and mobilisation of energy that can be helpful in dealing with a threat, following which the animal can return to a non-threatened state. Gilbert (1992, 2001) suggested that when these evolved defensive capacities to escape or fight are blocked or arrested in some way, this can lead to chronic activation of stress response. Under these circumstances, the chronic activation of these responses (and therefore stress) 'tone down' the capacity to experience positive emotion and exacerbate negative emotion. Similar to the reformulated learned helplessness model (i.e. attribution theory), conscious perceptions of control in these circumstances also play a role in the arrested defence theory, but as Gilbert (2005) points out, the salient factor here is the blocked nature of evolved defences.

A number of researchers have found that blocked desires to escape – also known as feeling trapped or entrapment – are associated with elevated levels of depression in both clinical and non-clinical samples

(Brown et al., 1995; Gilbert and Allan, 1998; Gilbert et al., 2004). In fact, the association between feelings of entrapment and depression was found to be of moderate to large magnitude. In my work as a clinical psychologist, many depressed people that I work with describe feeling trapped in some way. This is sometimes linked to a particular relationship. For example, a woman wanting to get away from an abusive marriage, but having young children and no income, felt she could not survive on her own with the children, and therefore, was unable to end the relationship and subsequently, in the face of ongoing abuse, became very depressed and suicidal. A number of men and women I work with feel trapped in stressful jobs, working very long hours and with few holiday or weekends off, but feel unable to leave as the job pays well and they have a large mortgage to pay each month. Other people can feel trapped with aspects of themselves, for example, having a long-term medical condition (e.g. diabetes or HIV) or mental health problem (recurrent depression, schizophrenia). It appears that feeling trapped can also be linked to suicidal feelings (e.g. Taylor et al., 2011). One of the ideas here is that suicide represents the ultimate escape behaviour from feeling trapped.

Other researchers have found that blocked anger – known as arrested fight – is associated with depression. In a study with Paul Gilbert (Gilbert, Gilbert and Irons, 2004), we looked at the experience of life events and difficulties in people who were depressed. 82% of the sample felt they had suppressed their anger, and of these, 56% felt this problem predated their depression. Participants gave a number of reasons for this, including self-blame but also a sense of blaming other people for their current difficult circumstances. Other researchers found that in comparison with a group of people who have never been depressed, recovered depressed people reported greater suppression of anger, feeling afraid of expressing anger and believing that feelings should be withheld to maintain relationships (Brody et al, 1999).

These ideas on arrested anger have overlaps with psychoanalytic ideas of depression (see Chapter 5 for further discussion). In my clinical work, people who are depressed sometimes describe being fearful that becoming angry will upset other people, making them less likely to be supportive, caring or available when needed. Others are concerned that if they become angry, they may provoke an angry (sometimes violent) attack from others in response. For some, the concern is that if they get angry, they might become aggressive and violent and hurt people that they love or care for, or face negative consequences because of their violence (e.g. incarceration).

Whilst appreciating the potential link between depression and lack of control over stressors or positive events/goals, Gilbert (2005) drew attention to how these theories typically explain depression in terms of non-social threats. Humans, however, are a particularly affiliative species, and consequentially, many of our threats are socially based. Gilbert suggests that there are two important socially based evolutionary theories: those that look at disruption to affiliative bonds (attachment theory) and those that relate to disruption of social competition and rank (social competition/social rank theory).

◁⊙▷ Attachment theory

The most well-known social evolutionary theory is **attachment theory**, which was developed by John Bowlby (Bowlby, 1968, 1973). Bowlby was interested in child development, and in particular, how loss and separation impacted upon children's well-being. Attachment theory suggests that human infants (like other mammals) are born with innate motivational, behavioural and emotional repertoires that aid survival by predisposing them to seek closeness to their caregiver (typically, their mother) and to signal when in need of food, reassurance and care.

Bowlby suggested that infants have different responses depending upon their proximity to the parent. When a parent is close by, the infants tend to explore their surroundings, by way of using the attachment figure as a safe haven or secure base. However, if there is a separation between infant and parent, then the infant becomes alarmed and distressed, and engages in specific behaviour – distress calling and seeking – to reinstate the return of the parent, and therefore, safety. Bowlby suggested that in the initial phase of the threat response to being left (separated), the infant would respond with increased arousal, distress, crying, anxiety/anger and searching behaviour. He called this stage 'protest', and from an evolutionary perspective, it is designed to signal to one's parents to return. However, whilst this strategy makes sense to begin with, an infant who continued in this state would risk becoming lost, dehydrated or attracting the attention of predators. Consequentially, if protest behaviours fail (i.e. the mother does not return), the safest thing to do in order to avoid negative consequences would be to reduce activity and arousal, instead 'staying put' to wait for reunion with mother. This state was termed 'despair'. Bowlby suggested that these basic templates, with the defensive strategies for protest and despair, have been phylogenetically conserved and are active in human infants today. In terms of depression, you might be able to see overlaps with ideas of protest-despair. For example, some depressions have aspects of protest behaviour, with the wish and yearning for closeness to others or the return of someone who has been lost (e.g. through a relationship break-up or death), but on the other hand, as time progresses people may increasingly feel shut down, demotivated and lacking in energy, which are all similar to the behaviours observed in despair states.

Box 6.2 Harlow's monkeys

Bowlby's work influenced, and was then influenced by, the work of an American psychologist, Harry Harlow. Harlow was interested in understanding the bond between infant and mother. Some of the leading theories at the time suggested this bond was based upon a behavioural model of conditioning (see below for discussion of behavioural theories), in that infants sought their mother because they provided food. In a series of experiments, Harlow (1958) separated baby rhesus macaque monkeys from their mothers and reared them in nurseries. In his most famous study (known as the 'Surrogate Mother' experiment), Harlow built approximations of a 'mother monkey' out of wire. Harlow had one of the surrogates covered in a soft cloth material, with a light shining behind it which created a tactile sense of warmth, while he left the other uncovered, so only the wire mesh was showing. He then carried out two experiments. In the first, Harlow placed the two surrogate mothers together, but only gave the wire mother a feeding bottle. In the second, the feeding bottle was only given to the cloth mother. When given the choice, Harlow found that the infant rhesus monkeys consistently selected the cloth mother to spend time with. Even when the wire mother had the feeding bottle, infant monkeys still spent the majority of time with the cloth mother, only leaving her to feed briefly, before returning again. For Harlow and Bowlby, it was evident that the attachment to the 'mother' was not only to receive nourishment, but rather, qualities such as warmth and 'contact comfort' were key.

In an attempt to develop an understanding of depression in monkeys, Harlow's most controversial experiment involved exposing infant monkeys to extended periods of social depreciation. He found that if you separated an infant monkey for a prolonged time (up to 24 months) from its mother and other monkeys, this left is severely disturbed. These monkeys would emerge as psychologically scared, showing significant difficulty interacting with other monkeys, but also showing specific signs of physiological distress, including prolonged rocking, staring 'blankly' and self-mutilation, and restricted (or no) appetite. Some of these responses are similar to symptoms of depression in humans, and pointed towards separation as a potential trigger for depression.

Harlow's experiments can be criticised on many grounds, not least for the unethical treatment of the rhesus monkeys he bred. Moreover, there are also concerns about the comparative aspects of his work, given the differences in behaviour between rhesus monkeys and humans (e.g. 'clinging' behaviours being prevalent in monkeys but absent in humans) and the degree to which one can extrapolate human psychology from non-human species. However, these studies are important as they help us to understand the role of care, affection and physical contact on regulating distress and helping to manage threat, processes implicated in depression.

You can watch videos of Harlow's experiments and findings on YouTube, by typing in 'Harlow studies on dependency in monkeys'.

In terms of depression, Bowlby (1980) felt this was the result of the disruption in the attachment bond. In infants and children, he suggested that this disruption may be through the loss (e.g. death), separation (e.g. hospitalisation of the infant so they are no longer with their mother) or emotional unresponsiveness/inaccessibility of the attachment figure. Bifulco, Harris and Brown (1992) suggested it was the quality of care pre- and post-separation/loss that increased an individual's vulnerability to depression, rather than the experience of loss as such.

Although attachment theory began with a focus on infants and children, much of the subsequent work has focused on how attachment patterns developed in childhood may persist into adulthood in the form of 'attachment styles' (see Box 6.3 for further description), and how these attachment styles may be related to depression and other mental health problems. In terms of research evidence looking at attachment styles and depression, there exists a large and consistent series of studies that have found an association between insecure attachment and depression (e.g. Murphy and Bates, 1997; Mickelson, Kessler and Shaver, 1997). In a sample of at risk women, Bifulco et al. (2002) found that more severe levels of insecure attachment were associated with depression. These studies have shown that people with insecure attachment styles are more likely to be depressed, and to report higher levels of depression symptomology, than those rated as having secure attachment styles. Blatt and Homman (1992) suggested that the type of depression experienced may be different for people with insecure-ambivalent and insecure-avoidant attachment styles. The authors postulated that in individuals with ambivalent attachment styles, depression is commonly related to issues of loss, abandonment and dependency, whilst amongst people with avoidant attachment styles, issues of self-worth and self-criticism are implicated.

Box 6.3 Attachment styles

Mary Ainsworth, a colleague of Bowlby developed a novel procedure – called the 'Strange Situation' – to investigate differences in children's attachment behaviour (Ainsworth, Blehar, Waters & Wall, 1978). This procedure involves young infants (aged under 18 months old) being placed in increasingly stressful scenarios designed to assess how they behave during systematic interaction, separation and reunion with their mother and a stranger. The experimenters were particularly interested in the quantity and quality of the infant's explorative behaviour when separated from mother, their reaction to mother leaving (e.g. distress, searching for mother), their reaction to the presence of the stranger in the absence of mother (i.e. acceptance of stranger's presence, whether infant is calmed by stranger's presence), and their response when mother returned. You can watch the different stages of this experiment – and the infants' reactions – on YouTube by typing in 'strange situation experiment'.

Using a systematic measurement tool of infant responses to this procedure, Ainsworth et al. (1978) found that infants appeared to react in three distinctive patterns during this experiment. They described these patterns as attachment styles, and more specifically, named them Insecure-avoidant (Type A), Secure attachment (Type B) and Insecure-ambivalent (Type C) attachment. The characteristics of these styles are described below:

Insecure-avoidant (Type A): The infant shows little interest in interacting with the attachment figure (mother), and on separation shows little or no sign of missing her. During the first stage of the experiment, the infant actively avoids proximity and interaction with the stranger. On mother's return, the insecure-avoidant infant tends not to seek closeness or initiate contact, and may even avoid the attachment figure altogether. The infant does not seem to differentiate between an unknown person and the attachment figure, or may even show preference for the stranger.

Secure attachment (Type B): Secure infants are able to use their attachment figure as a secure base from which to explore the environment. When left alone, the infant may show some distress, which appears to be related to the absence of the mother, rather than being left alone. There is clear differentiation between the attachment figure and the stranger, with greater preference shown to the attachment figure, although the infant may be somewhat comforted by the presence of the stranger. On reunion with the mother the securely attached infant seeks proximity and maintenance of contact, and displays low resistance and avoidance behaviour. He/she is easily comforted and soon feels safe again to play and explore the environment.

Insecure-ambivalent (Type C): These infants seem anxious even in the presence of the attachment figure, and tend to become rather distressed on separation from the mother, but are neither easily comforted by the stranger nor, crucially, reassured upon the mother's return. While they attempt to seek and maintain proximity with the mother, once in contact, they appear to respond with anger or passivity, and do not re-engage in play activities.

Using the Strange Situation procedure, Ainsworth et al. (1978) found that 65% of infants had a secure attachment style, whilst 22% were insecure-avoidant and 13% were insecure-ambivalent. Broadly, these distributions have also been found in other studies (e.g. van Ijzendoorn, Sagi and Lambermon, 1992). In subsequent studies using the Strange Situation, a fourth attachment style – Insecure-disorganised – was found (Main and Weston, 1981; Main and Cassidy, 1988; Main and Solomon, 1990; Bartholomew and Horowitz, 1991). This attachment style is characterised by a tendency for the infant to cry during the separation stage of the Strange Situation and, on reunion, approach the mother with averted eyes, or by quickly 'freezing up', or holding on to the mother whilst leaning away at the same time. These infants do not seem to cope with the anxiety of separation, and display a mixture of approach and avoidant behaviour. Roughly 15–20% of infants have been subsequently classified as disorganised (Main and Weston, 1981; Main and Solomon, 1990).

If you are interested in thinking about your own attachment style, you can complete an online questionnaire found at http://personality-testing.info/tests/ECR.php. This questionnaire is based on the commonly used self-report attachment measured called the Experiences of Close Relationships Scale (ECR; Brennan et al., 1998).

◉ Social competition and social rank

Whilst attachment theory focuses upon how the relationship with one's caregivers shapes behavioural and emotional regulation, a second social, evolutionary-derived theory has also been posited as important in depression. This theory was developed by Psychiatrist John Price who like Bowlby, was also interested in the application of evolutionary and ethological theory to understand mental health problems. However, rather than focusing on children, his focus was on adults, and in particular, his patients who were suffering from depression. In his clinical work, he began to observe that some of his depressed patients described feeling defeated in the face of social conflicts. He suggested that depression may be an understandable defensive strategy in the face of conflict with powerful others. He compared the symptom profile of a depressed person – often characterised by demobilisation, reduced eye contact and emotional reactivity – with that of an animal that has been defeated in a conflict. Price suggested that depressive symptoms signal to a powerful other to terminate conflict and thus reduce the likelihood of continued conflict and potential injury, or even death. There are two functional aspects to these signals. First, the external expression of a defeat state indicates to potential competitors that 'the loser is out of action' and is no longer a competitor. Second, as part of the subordinate or defeated response, the animal experiences reduced motivation and increase in fear, thus making it less likely that they engage in further competition (thus, ultimately reducing the likelihood of further defeat, injury or death). Both of these are believed to serve the purpose of yielding (Price et al., 1994) through disengaging the individual from a fruitless and pointless struggle. Price and colleagues (Price, 1976; Price et al., 1994) labelled this theory the Social Competition Theory of depression.

Research has provided good support of the social competition hypothesis in animals. For example, in comparison with dominant monkeys, subordinates have been found to have higher stress levels (e.g. cortisol; Sapolsky, 1989). Chronic and acute exposure to social defeat was associated with a variety of physiological stress responses in mice (Keeney et al., 2006). Experiments looking at social competition and stress have consistently found an association between social defeat/stress and increased anxious and depressed-like responses in a variety of animals, including monkeys, pigs and rats (e.g. Bjorkqvist, 2001).

In humans, threats, harassment and the experience of being in a (unwanted) subordinate position can occur within a myriad of relationships or groups, including parent-child, sibling, peer, romantic, occupational, cultural, religious, racial and socioeconomic group (Gilbert, 2005). We explored some of the evidence looking at the frequency of depression in different relational and social contexts in Chapter 4. However, it is important to emphasise that it is not just the experience of threat per se that is associated with depression – rather, it is the subjective experience of threat that is important in whether an individual develops depression. For example, in a study looking at the interrelationship between stress, defeat, entrapment and depression in stressed mothers, Willner and Goldstein (2001) found that the subjective sense of defeat and entrapment mediated the link between stress and depression levels. In other words, it wasn't just feeling stressed that made these mothers likely to experience depression, but rather, it was when their stress made them feel trapped and defeated that they were likely to become depressed.

In the late 1980s and early 1990s, psychologist Paul Gilbert adapted Price's theory (Gilbert, 1992; Gilbert, Price and Allan, 1995). Gilbert argued that, for modern humans, competition is more frequently focussed on social status, attraction and belonging (i.e. being chosen or liked by others, e.g. friends, colleagues, lovers), rather than on physical survival, such as food, territory and sexual partners (although of course, these types of competition can still be common for humans). Gilbert suggested that it was the subjective experience of feeling inferior or losing rank in the social domain that can activate a sense of defeat, inferiority and low self-esteem, as well as increase submissiveness and, ultimately, depression. He called this competitive concern 'Social Rank Theory' (Gilbert, 1992, 2004). Within this theory, it has been hypothesised that humans have a variety of endowments (thinking styles, behaviours, emotions) that help them judge and respond to these forms of competition. Three important psychological processes relating to social rank are:

(i) Cognitive – the degree to which people compare themselves negatively to others (Social Comparison)
(ii) Behaviour – the degree to which people feel they have to behave in non-assertive or submissive ways (Submissive Behaviour)
(iii) Emotional – the degree to which individuals feel ashamed about themselves or feel that others look down on them (Shame)

There have been a variety of studies looking at the association between these aspects of social rank theory and depression in humans.

Social comparison and depression

In an attempt to measure social comparison more directly with self-report scales, Gilbert and Allan (1994; Allan and Gilbert, 1995) developed the Social Comparison Scale. This questionnaire asks people to rate themselves on a range of dimensions, including attractiveness, rank and sense of belonging in comparison with other people. In a series of studies, Gilbert and colleagues found that those people who rated themselves as inferior in comparison with others had higher levels of depression symptomology, and that depressed people rated themselves as more inferior than non-depressed people (Allan and Gilbert, 1995; Cheung, Gilbert and Irons, 2004; Gilbert and Allan, 1994; Gilbert et al., 2002; O'Conner, Berry, Weiss and Gilbert, 2002).

Submissive behaviour and depression

There has been a range of studies looking at the relationship between submissiveness and depression. In fact, Gilbert and Allan (1994) developed a submissive behaviour scale asking participants to rate themselves on items such as 'I agree that I am wrong even though I know I'm not' or 'I pretend I am ill when declining an invitation'. Studies have shown that higher levels of submissive behaviour are associated with higher levels of depression symptomology, and that people with depression have on average higher levels of submissive behaviour than people who aren't depressed (Allan and Gilbert, 1995; Cheung, Gilbert and Irons, 2004; O'Conner, Berry, Weiss and Gilbert, 2002).

Shame and depression

Shame has been described as the 'affect of inferiority' (Kaufman, 1989), and has been discussed as an important emotion linked to the social rank system (e.g. Gilbert, 2000). A range of research studies have found that shame-proneness and the experience of shame are closely associated with depression. In a sample of individuals who had been abused, Andrews (1995) found that bodily shame was a strong predictor of chronic depression. In a sample of 35 depressed patients, Andrews and Hunter (1997) found that three types of shame – character, behavioural and bodily – were related to the course of depression (its chronicity and recurrence). Gilbert (2000) found that higher levels of self-reported shame were related to higher depression symptoms.

Interaction between social evolutionary systems

Although there has not been much work looking at the interaction between the attachment/affiliation and social rank evolutionary models of depression, these are complementary models (Sloman et al., 2003) and are likely to interact. For example, Paul Gilbert and myself (Irons and Gilbert, 2005) looked at how attachment styles (secure, ambivalent and avoidant) and social rank perceptions (sense of inferiority and submissiveness) were associated with depression symptoms in adolescents. We found that insecure attachment was associated with perceptions of lower social rank (i.e. greater sense of inferiority and submissiveness). Moreover, insecure attachment styles were related to higher depression symptoms through their association with low social rank (inferiority and submissiveness). One interpretation of these findings is that adolescents who have insecure attachment relationships may need to be more orientated to social competition, rank (e.g. sense of inferiority in comparison with others) and behaviours to manage this (e.g. higher levels of submissiveness) than adolescents who had secure attachment styles. In fact, we found that secure attachment was directly associated with lower levels of depression symptoms, and seemingly, these individuals did not have to engage in unhelpful social rank related thinking or behaviour.

These studies suggest different socially based, evolutionary-derived pathways that may contribute towards depression; these pathways, although evolved to deal with different survival pressures, may interact in important ways in dealing with social threats. It may also be that different types of depression symptomology are associated with different social evolutionary threats. For example, in a study looking at different symptom profiles of depression based on different types of stressor, Keller and Nesse (2005) found that crying and sadness tended to follow stressors involving social loss, whereas pessimism, rumination and fatigue was associated with thwarted goals/failures.

⊙ Emotion regulation systems in depression

The theories that we have discussed so far in this chapter help us to understand depression in the context of some of the different social and non-social challenges that we have to traverse in life. They have highlighted how in depression, common changes in our emotions and motivation may serve important, adaptive purposes in the context of particular contexts or environments. The relationship between emotions and motivation is complex, but commonly emotions track motives. For example, we get bursts of positive emotion when we're successful in our motivations and goals, such as getting a good mark in an essay. In contrast, we may experience negative emotions when we are thwarted, struggling or unsuccessful in our efforts, such as getting a poor mark or failing an essay.

As we have seen already, in depression the texture of our emotions and motivation are quite different to when we're not feeling depressed. Although there are a variety of ways to explore the relationship between our evolved emotions and motives, one simplified but helpful approach was developed by psychologist Paul Gilbert (Gilbert, 2005, 2014), in which he suggests we have three key, emotion regulation systems:

1 Those that detect threat and promote the seeking of self-protection and safety
2 Those that focus on doing and achieving things
3 Those that focus on contentment and feeling safe

These are described in more detail below, but also depicted visually in Figure 6.1

Figure 6.1 Emotion regulation systems – Three circle model
From P. Gilbert, *The Compassionate Mind* (2009), reprinted with permission from
Constable & Robinson Ltd.

The threat and self-protection system

This system evolved to detect and respond to threats to ourselves and
people we care about. It is linked to certain biological and neurophysiological systems that we discussed in Chapter 3, such as the hypothalamic–
pituitary–adrenal (HPA) axis, the amygdala, the neurotransmitter
serotonin and the hormone cortisol, which all play a role in threat detection and how the body begins to mobilise a response to threat. To help
with this, the threat system has a variety of threat-based emotions, such as
anger, anxiety and disgust, and can trigger a number of defensive behaviours, such as freeze, flight, fight and submission. On a psychological
level, this system commonly works on a better safe than sorry principle
(Gilbert, 1998). The threat system evolved to keep us safe, so is therefore
often easy to activate. It is also a 'learning' system, which means that if we
experience stressful events in life (e.g. abusive relationships, bullying,
poverty) it can become more sensitive, and it is highly conditionable
through the process of classical and operant conditioning.

The drive-seeking system

This system evolved to detect, seek out and acquire resources that are advantageous or helpful to us in some way. It gives us bursts of positive emotion and feelings that energise and motivate us towards the acquisition of resources, and then leaves us feeling good when we achieve them. Whilst the drive system can be associated with things like food, shelter or sexual opportunities (things that were fundamental to our survival), for humans it can be linked to any number of rewards and reinforcers – especially social ones like status, approval and affection. It is therefore associated with aspects of both the social rank and attachment systems described above.

The soothing–affiliative system

When mammals are not managing threats, and are not driven to achieve something, they can move into a state of recuperation and calmness. This system is associated with the parasympathetic nervous system, which helps to slow down the body and is sometimes called a 'rest and digest' system. The emotional tone is one of soothing, calming and peaceful well-being. We think this system developed during the evolution of the attachment system, and consequentially, this means that affiliative relationships can stimulate this system, giving a sense of calming and soothing. Although complex, these emotional qualities are linked neurophysiologically to **hormones** such as oxytocin and the neurotransmitter endorphin. Oxytocin has been described in various places as the 'hormone of love' or the 'cuddle hormone' as it is associated with child birth, breast feeding, close contact with loved ones and bonding and trust. Evidence suggests that it may be a natural regulator of threat.

It can be helpful to consider how the three emotion systems are affected or balanced in depression, with a particular focus upon the different biological, psychological and social aspects.

Depression and the threat system

Depression often emerges from a background of chronic stress, and as we learnt in Chapter 5, there appear to be certain types of social and environmental threats and stresses that are associated with increased levels of depression. These include stressful relationships, such as abuse in early life, bullying or racism. However, we have also seen that certain environmental contexts, such as deprivation, a wide gap between rich and poor, and dilapidated housing, are also associated with increased levels of depression.

These types of stressful environments impact upon the biological and physiological systems underpinning the threat system, such as the sympathetic nervous system, HPA axis (cortisol), altered levels and functioning of neurotransmitters (e.g. serotonin), and our immune systems. Those of you who are eagle eyed will remember that these also happen to be systems that were highlighted as important in depression in Chapter 3. Key here is that depression seems to involve increased and prolonged activity in the biological and physiological components of the threat system.

The threat system is also associated with certain types of emotion (anger and anxiety), and as we have seen in Chapter 4, there are a number of psychological theories that have highlighted the important role of these threat emotions in depression (see in particular, the role of anger in depression as highlighted by the psychodynamic approach). The threat system is also associated with certain types of protective behaviours (flight, freeze, shut down, submissiveness) and these behaviours can be more or less common in different variants of depression. The threat system is also a 'learning system' and highly prone to conditioning, and it is thus sensitive to the behavioural learning principles of operant and classical conditioning that we learnt about in Chapter 4.

The threat system is also related to a particular 'better safe than sorry' thinking that naturally means that it will bias your thinking to be overly focused upon threats and negative things. For example, if you go shopping for a present for your best friend, and in nine of the shops you go to, the sales assistant is cheerful, helpful and polite, but in the tenth shop, the assistant is rude, dismissive and unhelpful, which one do you focus on and talk about when you get home? There is a well-known saying in evolutionary psychology: 'You can have lunch many many times in life, but you can only be lunch once!'. What this means is that your threat system always needs to be on alert and will actually overestimate threats in order to keep you safe. In depression, our thinking is further biased to the 'negative' by our increased negative emotions and altered motivation, and this can lead to typical thinking patterns in which we become increasingly negative, self-critical and stuck in rumination cycles when depressed. We will return to the idea of these types of thinking-emotion loops later on in this chapter, but for now it is worth remembering that some of the cognitive psychologists refer to these typical types of thinking style in depression as 'negative automatic thoughts'.

Depression and the drive system

Given the importance of anhedonia and problems with motivation in depression, it is unsurprising that the drive system, which is linked to a particular type of positive emotion associated with reward, achievement and wanting/getting is affected in depression.

There are important biopsychosocial linkages between the drive system and depression. On a biological level, the drive system is associated with dopamine, a neurotransmitter that we discussed in Chapter 3 which is thought to play an important role in difficulties in experiencing positive emotion, motivation and energy that are often common in depression. We can see here that drive system in depression may mirror the two forms of anhedonia that we explored in Chapter 3. The first involved difficulties with motivation, anticipation and 'wanting' things, in which people who are depressed struggle with the energy or **drive** to move them towards a particular goal. Here, people will often say: 'There's no point trying, as I won't enjoy it anyway' or 'It's too much effort to make it worthwhile'. The second aspect of anhedonia focuses more on struggles to enjoy or derive pleasure from something when we have got/achieved it. These differences are important when considering depression, as a number of authors highlight that in depression, it may be the anticipatory, motivational aspect of the drive system that is most frequently affected (e.g. Gilbert, 2013, Argyroploulos and Nutt, 2013). Further research is required here to help us understand aspects of drive system functioning, positive affect and anhedonia in depression.

As we explored in Chapter 4, the psychological impact of setbacks, failures and defeats may be a powerful trigger for depression, and it is clear in these situations that they involve a down-regulation of positive emotion and the ability to experience pleasure. You might be able to remember yourself a time that you failed in some way (maybe an exam or test), and how following this, it was difficult to enjoy things in the same way in the hours afterwards. Many people have this experience when their football team loses – the rest of the day/weekend just isn't the same! However, of course in depression this loss of the ability to enjoy things doesn't just last a few hours, but over a period of weeks and months. We discussed some of the evolutionary psychology explanations of depression earlier in this chapter, and saw how some of these suggested that depression (and in particular, the loss of drive and motivation) was associated with ways to disengage from situations in which, if we continued striving and pursuing a goal, we might hurt ourselves or suffer from serious defeats. The drive system is also associated with social rank difficulties. For example, chronic stress associated with being in a subordinate, lower rank position is associated with lower functioning of dopamine receptors (Shively, 1999).

For some people, drive-based feelings are actually quite scary. For example, if as a child you feel anxious and scared after being punished by your parents for celebrating passing a test, or when beating your brother or sister in a game, this can lead to a classically conditioned experience. Here, pleasure, joy and excitement may have been conditioned to shame and anxiety. Later in life it may be more difficult for you to experience positive emotion, particularly when competing or striving to achieve or win something, because negative, conditioned emotions of shame and anxiety arise instead. We know that those people who have a fear of positive emotion have significantly higher levels of depression symptomology (Gilbert et al., 2013).

There may be a variety of social and societal factors that influence the functioning of the drive system in depression. As Gilbert (2014) points out, there are worries that in many Western countries, economic systems like capitalism and consumerism lead to a societal overemphasis of the importance of drive-based goals of wanting, achieving, 'getting' and, in general, competing. A concern here is that this type of focus may lead to an unhealthy 'overheating' of the drive system, and leave some people vulnerable to types of depression linked to this system, including primary symptoms of feeling defeated, fatigued and lacking motivation.

Depression and the soothing–affiliative system

Although there is a complex biological and neurophysiological interactions here, affiliative experiences and emotions (e.g. safeness, contentment, connection) have been found to be associated with both a vulnerability to and maintenance of depression (Cacioppo and Patrick, 2008; Cozolino, 2008; Gilbert, 2013). The soothing-affiliative system is associated with certain neuropeptides, such as oxytocin and endorphin. As mentioned above, oxytocin has variably been referred to in the press as the 'hormone of love' or the 'hormone of trust'. As these descriptions allude, oxytocin appears to be associated with being in caring, supportive relationships. Given that in some depressions, we feel a sense of increased loneliness, isolation and separation, it may be that this could be linked to problems on a neurophysiological level within the soothing–affiliative system. Although evidence here is tentative, some researchers have found a relationship between oxytocin levels and depression symptoms (e.g. Scantamburlo et al., 2007; Ozsoy, Esel and Kula, 2009).

As we discovered with our exploration of attachment theory earlier in this chapter, and our discussion of some of the explanatory ideas within some of the major psychological theories of depression in Chapter 4 (e.g. psychodynamic and cognitive), a number of psychological explanations suggest that some depressions may be associated with difficulties in the soothing–affiliative system. Invariably, these approaches highlight the inconsistency or absence of soothing–affiliative relationships and experiences, particularly in early life, as potentially contributing to future risk of depression. As Gilbert (2013) points out, depressions with features of sadness, tearfulness, feeling unloved or alone, with the yearning for closeness with others and to be nurtured and cared for, may well be linked to problems with the soothing–affiliative system rooted in attachment difficulties (i.e. Bowlby's concept of the 'protest' phase of separation). In contrast, those individuals who have had stable, affiliative relationships, characterised by love, care, warmth, consistency and availability, are more likely to develop secure attachment styles, and less likely to be depressed (e.g. Roberts et al., 1996; Marganska et al., 2013).

For some of the depressed patients I work with, the soothing–affiliative system has become contaminated by previous experiences. For example, a tragic yet too common experience is of having memories of feeling safe, calm and close to someone (e.g. a parent or relative) just before being sexually abused by that person. One of the unfortunate aspects of this is that, through a process of classical conditioning, the presence of others' care and warmth, or the internal experience of the feelings associated with the soothing–affiliative system (e.g. calmness, contentment) actually trigger threat based response instead, such as anxiety, anger or shame. In fact, we now know that the fear of care and compassion is associated with higher levels of depression, anxiety and stress (Gilbert, McEwan, Matos and Rivis, 2011).

On a social level, there are also concerns that societal changes, particularly in the West, may be having a negative impact upon our soothing–affiliative system and, consequentially, create vulnerability to depression. For example, our gradual movement away from extended familial caring and the use of touch to sooth our children, and the inhibition of adults in using touch to display care and help to sooth distress (e.g. teachers prevented from doing this due to concerns of abuse), may lead to a reduction or absence of a potentially potent source of distress regulation (e.g. Gilbert, 2013).

◉ How are the emotional systems organised in depression?

So, how do the three different emotion systems function in depression in relation to each other? In depression, we often see a familiar pattern of functioning which can be described in a simple way as:

- Under activation of the drive system
- Under activation of the soothing–affiliative system
- Over activation of the threat system

Often, if I ask my depressed patients to draw out the three circles but with the types of experiences they are having at the moment written inside them, and the size of the circle determining how much of each system they experience when depressed (i.e. threat, drive and soothing), Figure 6.2 is a common depiction.

It is also helpful to understand a little about how these systems interact with each other in depression. For example, it might be that blocks to drive system (e.g. attempts to achieve that are not successful) can lead to down-regulation of this system, which, if they persist, can lead to a form of anhedonic depression. In other depressions, it might be losses associated with the soothing–affiliative system, such as the death of a parent, or being rejected by a partner, that disrupts functioning in this system to such an extent and triggers firing of the threat system, that leads someone feeling depressed. Other depressions may involve more specific activation of the threat system, which then cuts out the ability to feel positive emotions of the drive or soothing system. For example, we know that positive emotion will go offline if you are suddenly threatened (imagine you are enjoying having a picnic in a field on a warm summers day, when suddenly a large snake slides out of the grass – it's likely your positive emotion systems would shut down immediately). In depression, it might be that we lose access to the drive and affiliative positive emotions

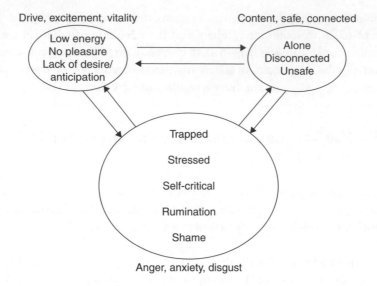

Figure 6.2   Three circle model in depression
Adapted from P. Gilbert, *The Compassionate Mind* (2009), reprinted with permission from Constable & Robinson.

through acute or chronic activation of the threat system. So it is helpful when thinking about depression to consider the different ways that the three circles can interact, affect and influence each other, and the types of triggering events that might lead to depression.

⊙ Summary: Three circle model

As we have explored in the above section, the three circle model can be quite helpful for us in considering how our emotions and motivations are affected in depression. This model also holds as an important way of bringing together key biological, psychological and social factors in depression that we have discussed in Chapters 3, 4 and 5.

As we move on now to the next section of the book, we will begin to explore some of the different interventions for depression, again structured around the three categories of biological, psychological and social. As you are reading the coming chapters, it will be helpful to keep in mind how each of these approaches to treating depression may impact upon the functioning of the typical three circle pattern in depression, as shown in Figure 6.2.

◉ Are all depressions evolutionary 'adaptive'?

It can be tempting when reviewing the above theories to consider depression as always being 'adaptive' – that is, functioning in a way that confers some sort of benefit to the individual. The problem with this is that given the heterogeneous nature of depression – the different mix of symptoms, types of symptoms or length of symptoms – it is hard to separate what is evolutionarily functional or not. Because we can identify adaptive systems underpinning a disorder, this does not mean that it is always adaptive. Gilbert (2005) suggests that not all depressions are adaptive. Rather, evolutionary accounts suggest that a depression, as is the case with all **phenotypes**, can function outside of its evolved repertoire if it is too easily or powerfully triggered, or last longer than is helpful. Moreover, Gilbert suggests that it is difficult to identify clearly which depressions are adaptive and which aren't. In thinking about this, it is helpful to consider how as a biopsychosocial interaction, depression can arise in complex ways that involve the interplay between biological, psychological and social factors that may be a reflection of very recent stressors that our ancestors did not encounter. In other words, it might be that ancient physiological systems which evolved to tone down positive emotion and increase negative emotion in certain contexts may get triggered by stimuli that they were not designed to. To elucidate this, we will focus on how interactions between biological and psychosocial factors may trigger depression in ways that may not have adaptive functions.

Old and new brain loops

One reason why depression can function in a maladaptive way may be because it is a 'quirk', or by-product, of other evolutionary processes. As MacLean (1990) argued, the human brain has gone through different (evolutionary) stages of change. This change has left the brain with different 'parts' which are linked to specific types of competencies or abilities (e.g. to control physiological homeostasis like body temperature or to facilitate emotions or thinking). Building upon this, Gilbert (Gilbert, 2005, 2009, 2013) has pointed out that we have an 'old' part of our brain which is over 100 million years old, and is involved with some of key motivations, primary emotions (anger, anxiety, sadness, disgust, joy) and behaviours (e.g. fight-flight). However, we also have a more recently evolved (within the last two million years) 'new brain' which is associated with very human abilities to imagine, ruminate, plan and self-monitor. Whilst these parts of our brains can interact well, they can get into unhelpful feedback loops or glitches. As Gilbert (2005) points out, it may well be that adaptations in new brain abilities, which were helpful in humans 'getting smart', can stimulate old brain pathways involved in depression. For example, our capacity for planning, imagining and self-reflection are wonderful endowments, but if they focus upon the difficulties of leaving, say, an abusive husband (e.g. imagining struggling with little money, nowhere to live, and having to move young children to a new school) this may block the flight defence, leading to a sense of entrapment and ultimately, depression.

As far as we know, no other animal can become depressed in this way; that is, these types of loops in the mind between new and old brain abilities seems to be a uniquely human ability, and in some instances, problem. We do know these types of loops can be a very common experience for many people, and may underpin many depressions (Gilbert and Irons, 2005). A simplified depiction of old and new brain loops common in depression is shown in Figure 6.3.

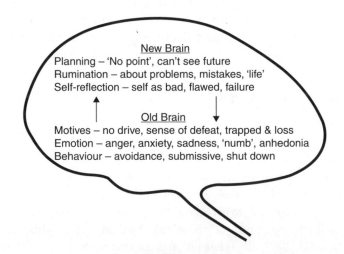

Figure 6.3 Interaction between old and new brain psychologies
Adapted from Gilbert and Choden, *Mindful Compassion* (2013), reprinted with permission from Constable & Robinson Ltd.

Stressful modern environments

Depression may also operate in a maladaptive way due to specific stresses in modern living environments that stimulate ancient biological emotion-motivation systems. As we saw in Chapter 4, certain aspects of modern day living, such as deprivation, poverty and high levels of social isolation, are associated with higher levels of depression. It is therefore important to consider what it is about these environments that may be stressful for humans. One answer is that these types of challenges are a very modern one, and one that our ancestors – and therefore our brains – did not have to cope with or adapt to. Our human minds evolved in particular environments (known as the 'environment of evolutionary adaptedness' or EEA for short). As best as we can work out, these environments were characterised by small groups of people living together. Many of these people would be relatives, and survival was built upon supporting and looking after each other. However, in comparison modern environments place our brains in very different situations. Many of us now live in large cities, surrounded by lots of people, in close proximity, who we don't know. Moreover, many of us have little contact from family members, and consequentially, low levels of social support. Given the social evolutionary theories outlined above, and consideration of our species being the most affiliative and in need of close, supporting relationships, it may be that the absence of these, linked to modern forms of living, create chronic stress in our brains, and potentially, the conditions for depression.

◉ Section summary

The above reflections are important when considering why we can develop depression. They still fit within evolutionary explanations, but what is key here is to understand how evolved, adaptive responses for the toning down of positive emotion and heightening of negative emotion may be stimulated in unintended ways for modern humans.

◉ Chapter summary

This chapter has explored a number of different evolutionary psychology explanations of depression. In particular, it has focused upon an idea that may be counter-intuitive at first, that depression may have an adaptive value to our overall survival and well-being. In particular, we have looked at this from two different perspectives – non-social causes (learned helplessness theory) and social theories (attachment and social rank models). We have seen that depression may emerge from an adaptive need to reduce positive affect in certain types of contexts, including those involving poor attachment relationships, difficulties competing for social resources, and/or difficult social environments. In other words, depression, and the toning down of positive emotion and exploratory/competitive behaviour, may arise through the activation of defensive/protective strategies in difficult social contexts (e.g. when competition is going badly) that evolved over millions of years to increase survival and inclusion within social groups.

However, whilst we have explored ideas for why some depressions arise and are beneficial to us, it may be that other depressions do not serve an adaptive function per se. Here, we explored how depression can emerge as a by-product of our ancient, inherited capacity to downregulate positive emotion being stimulated by our recently evolved new brains (e.g. our increasing cognitive capacity triggering 'old brain' emotions and motives), or stressful modern environments.

We have also explored a model of understanding our emotional changes in depression (the 'Three Circle Model') and seen how this may be a helpful way of bringing together biological, psychological and social factors that might lead to some of the changes seen in depression.

◉ Further reading

Gilbert, P. (2006) 'Evolution and depression: Issues and implications'. *Psychological Medicine*, 36, 287–297.

Gilbert, P. (2013) 'Depression: The challenges of an integrative, biopsychosocial evolutionary approach'. In M. Power (ed.), *The Wiley-Blackwell Handbook of Mood Disorders* (2nd ed., pp. 229–288), Chichester, UK: J. Wiley.

Chapter 7

Biological and Physiological Treatments

Treatments for depression that aim to impact on a biological or physiological level have existed for thousands of years. Many of these emerged from the use of plant extracts, such as *opium* (from poppys), *hashish* (from hemp plants) and *deadly nightshade* (from the plant Atropa belladonna). More recently, the advance of the scientific method brought experiments with a variety of chemicals such as barbiturates and codeine in an attempt to alleviate low mood. Although these treatments were initially met with excitement and enthusiasm about their effectiveness, their early promise did not persist, and awareness grew that, for many, there were significant issues with side-effects and addiction that only exacerbated the original suffering.

👁 Pharmaceutical treatments for depression

As scientific exploration became more sophisticated, organised and well funded, and with the discovery of the potential benefits (and profits!) of new drugs such as penicillin in the 1920s and 1930s, increasing focus turned to pharmaceutical treatments for a variety of physical and mental health difficulties. As with the discovery of penicillin, the first medications for depression – which went on to be known as antidepressants – were stumbled upon serendipitously. Whilst trialling a new drug called iproniazid for tuberculosis in the early 1950s, researchers noted that this had the unexpected result of making patients more physically active, cheerful and hopeful. Doctors working in psychiatric settings in the US and France soon learned of these findings, and initially started using this drug 'off-label' with some benefit in alleviating depression symptoms for their patients. Although these medications were later withdrawn for the use of depression following the discovery that they led to significant side-effects, research suggested that they operated through inhibiting an enzyme called monoamine oxidase (which has a role in the breakdown of monoamine neurotransmitters such as serotonin, dopamine and norepinephrine). This subsequently led to the development of a class of medications called monoamine oxidase inhibitors (MAOIs), one of the first types of antidepressants. In 1957, a separate class of drugs, known as the tricyclic antidepressants (TCAs), were developed, following initial observations of the antidepressant effects on mood of chlorpromazine on people suffering with psychotic illnesses. Using chlorpromazine as a blueprint, scientists started developing and studying derivatives, such as imipramine, the first of the TCAs. Together, these two types of medication – MAOIs and TCAs – are referred to as the first generation of antidepressants.

◉ Antidepressant medication

Although the first generation of antidepressants emerged as a treatment between the late 1950s and early 1970s, it was not until the development of the second generation of antidepressants, in particular the introduction and marketing of fluoxetine hydrochloride (commonly known as Prozac) in the early 1980s, that the prescribing of antidepressants became more common. Over the following decades, antidepressants, and Prozac in particular, became so frequently prescribed, but seemingly so effective in alleviating depression, that they entered social and cultural awareness like few medications before them. In a book called *Prozac Nation*, journalist and author Elizabeth Wurtzel highlights aspects of this phenomenon, and describes both her struggle with depression and the effect of Prozac in alleviating her symptoms almost overnight.

Antidepressants are the most common biological treatment for depression. Since the mid-1980s, there has been an explosion in the prescribing and use of antidepressants. Although it is difficult to get worldwide figures for the use of these drugs, Gusmão et al. (2013) looked at estimates of the proportion of a population receiving antidepressant treatment in 29 different European countries. In total, the researchers found a year-on-year increase of almost 20%. In the UK alone over a

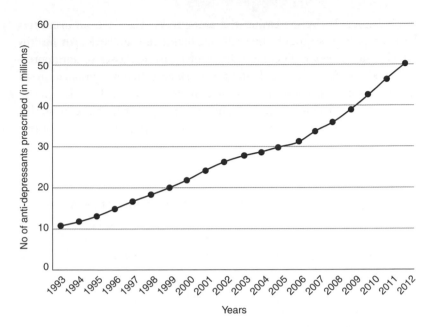

Figure 7.1 UK antidepressant prescribing between 1993 and 2012 (data taken from Office of National Statistics; http://www.ons.gov.uk/ons/index.html)

period of 18 years it has been estimated that there has been a 495% increase in antidepressant usage. The Health and Social Care Information Centre (HSCIC) estimated that in 2012 in the UK alone, 50.2 million antidepressant prescriptions were made, an increase of almost 4 million (or over 9%) from 2011. The graph (see Figure 7.1 above) highlights the continued, year-on-year increase of antidepressant prescriptions in the UK since 1993. In fact, there are now almost 40 million more antidepressant prescriptions per year than in 1993.

How do antidepressants work?

The most common explanation given for how antidepressants work is that they affect levels and functioning of certain types of neurotransmitters in the brain. In particular, many scientists suggest that antidepressants work by inhibiting the process of 'reuptake' of serotonin, norepinephrine and dopamine. As a result, these neurotransmitters remain in the synaptic gap longer than they did previously, and are then able to repeatedly trigger the receptors of the receiving neuron. As we know that the monoamine neurotransmitters play an important role in our emotions and behaviours (see Chapter 3), by increasing the amount of these neurotransmitters between cells it is thought that this facilitates re-stabilisation of healthy mood and behaviour. There are different types or classes of antidepressant medication, which are thought to work on different combinations of neurotransmitters. These are described in more detail in Box 7.1.

However, whilst many scientists and doctors feel that this explanation 'makes sense', it has been difficult to find *consistent*, categorical proof that

Box 7.1 Different classes of antidepressants

There are a number of different classes of antidepressants:

Selective serotonin reuptake inhibitors (SSRIs)

SSRIs are the most commonly prescribed antidepressant. Some examples of these are Fluoxetine (commonly known as Prozac), Citalopram and Sertraline. Whilst primarily prescribed for depression, SSRIs also work well for anxiety problems, so can be prescribed for certain phobias (e.g. social phobia, agoraphobia) and obsessive compulsive disorder (OCD).

As we discovered in Chapter 3, neurotransmitters play an important role in communication between neurons, and serotonin appears to be important in regulating things like our mood, feelings and sleep. Although there is disagreement about this process, some scientists suggest that SSRIs work by boosting the level of serotonin in the brain by stopping the brain from re-absorbing serotonin into the nerve terminals.

Serotonin and norepinephrine reuptake inhibitors (SNRIs)

SNRIs, such as Venlafaxine and Duloxetine, are frequently used in the treatment of depression. As with SSRIs, they are also prescribed for people with a number of anxiety disorders, and sometimes other health problems (e.g. those linked to some types of pain, such as fibromyalgia). It is thought SNRIs work by increasing two types of neurotransmitter – serotonin and norepinephrine – in the brain. However, they may also impact on other neurotransmitters, such as dopamine. Like SSRIs, it is thought that SNRIs work by blocking or inhibiting the re-absorption of these chemicals into neurons, thus increasing their levels in the brain over time.

Tricyclic antidepressants (TCAs)

TCAs are an older form of the antidepressants, discovered in the 1950s, although they are rarely prescribed as a firstline treatment due to the increased likelihood of adverse side-effects (e.g. dry mouth, constipation, sweating) and cardiac toxicity in overdose. It is thought that TCAs work by interfering with the reabsorption of serotonin and noradrenaline into brain cells. TCAs include Imipramine, Amitriptyline, Clomipramine and Lofepramine. Because of their side-effects, TCAs are more commonly used if other frontline antidepressants – such as SSRIs and SNRIs – have not been effective to begin with.

Monoamine oxidase inhibitors (MAOIs)

MAOIs are also an older class of antidepressants, which work by affecting the functioning of key neurotransmitters. In particular, they are thought to target monoamine oxidase – a type of enzyme that breaks down serotonin, noradrenaline and dopamine. Whilst taking MAOIs, people have to be very careful about the type of food and drink they have, particularly those that contain a substance called tyramine (e.g. some red wines, cheese, yoghurt). This is because, in combination with MAOIs, tyramine can lead to sudden and dangerously high blood pressure, which thus needs monitoring whilst on a prescription of MAOI. Because of this risk and the impact upon diet, MAOIs are sometimes prescribed if initial trials of SSRI or SNRI have been ineffective.

Other medications used to treat depression

There are a variety of other medications commonly used to treat depression. Some of these come from a group of medications called mood stabilisers, often used to treat bipolar affective disorder. A mood stabiliser sometimes used in depression is called Lithium. These are sometimes added to an existing antidepressant (a process known as 'augmenting').

these neurotransmitters work in the way they have been suggested to in depression, and by association, in antidepressant treatment. For example, whilst we can see desired changes on a cellular level between neurons relatively quickly after commencement of antidepressants, along with some changes in attention, it usually takes many further weeks before people start to *feel* better. This delay in the effect of antidepressants has caused many to question how they work (e.g. Harmer et al., 2009).

Moreover, as we will see below, whilst antidepressants are effective for many people, approximately 30–50% of people who take them do not experience clinically significant improvements. As Gitlin (2010) points out, the ways in which antidepressants lead to improved mood are still obscure, and that simply attributing this improvement to the impact of antidepressants upon neurotransmitters is 'naïve and likely to be incorrect'. Gitlin (2010) suggests that, alongside impacting on neurotransmitters directly, it may be that antidepressants also affect neurophysiological processes 'downstream'. What this means is that, rather than just impacting on levels of monoamine neurotransmitters (serotonin, norepinephrine or dopamine), antidepressants may work by impacting upon neurogenesis (the production of new neurons), which may in itself be involved in the alleviation of depression.

Some scientists suggest that antidepressants may work downstream by affecting the way genes in our brains work, whilst others feel they impact on the way we process information (i.e. reducing the negative emotional processing of information common in depression, and allowing a more 'positive' emotional processing of information instead; Harmer et al., 2009). At this time, whilst there are a variety of ideas for how antidepressants may work, we are lacking a more detailed, specific and nuanced understanding of the exact mechanisms through which they bring change.

How effective are antidepressant medications?

There has been a lot of research looking at the effectiveness of antidepressant medication. For example, in a large meta-analysis of the existing evidence base of 13 second-generation antidepressant effectiveness, Gartlehner et al. (2008) found that approximately 63% of people with depression displayed positive response to medication between 6 and 12 weeks, with 47% achieving remission. Although small statistical differences in effectiveness were found between different antidepressants, the authors felt these differences were so small in magnitude that they were unlikely to be clinically relevant. However, in other large studies of antidepressant effectiveness across multiple sites, remission rates for first use antidepressant were only 28% after a 14-week period (Trivedi et al., 2006).

Antidepressants take time to work. Although some suggest that their impact upon neurotransmitter levels is very fast (within a day), it is usually three weeks or so before people start to notice feeling better. In fact, for some types of depression, particularly those more complex and chronic in nature, people may need to be on an antidepressant for many months before they experience a positive difference to their mood. Even if a positive response occurs following initiation of antidepressants, due to high relapse rates with premature discontinuation of treatment, the **NICE guidelines** for depression (NICE, 2010) suggest that an individual should continue taking medication for at least six months after the remission of their symptoms. In general, antidepressant treatment can be broadly understood to occur in three phases:

- Acute phase – here, the aim is to reduce the symptoms of a current depression.
- Continuation phase – here, the depressive symptoms are in remission but antidepressants are used in order to minimise the chance of a relapse into the same episode of depression.
- Maintenance phase – this phase involves antidepressant use to minimise the possibility of a future (new) episode of depression.

Difficulties with evaluating effectiveness

There are a number of problems establishing evidence for the effectiveness of antidepressants, which tend to restrict our confidence in published results. There is now widespread acknowledgement of publication bias in scientific research, including medication trials. Here, journals have been found to be more likely to publish significant positive results and findings, rather than non-significant findings. Furthermore, researchers can also compound this problem by only submitting for publication results that show a positive effect, and choosing to not try and publish studies that did not find the results they were hoping for (this is known as 'cupboard drawer' studies – studies that remain in a drawer or filing cabinet rather than being submitted for publication).

Another problem arises from the nature of the trials conducted, and the populations recruited. In particular, researchers often recruit people with mild to moderate levels of depression symptoms, rather than those experiencing severe or chronic symptomatology. This may be for a number of reasons, including the hope that people with milder symptoms are more likely to engage in treatment and less likely to drop out of the trial early. Khan et al. (2002) pointed out that less severely depressed participants are more likely to improve 'spontaneously' with or without medication. This is a significant problem for studies as it can lead to difficulties in understanding the (potentially) different impact of antidepressants across depression severity levels. For example, Khan et al. (2005) found a correlation between antidepressant response and initial severity of depressive symptoms, with individuals more depressed at baseline having the greatest response to antidepressants, and those with milder symptoms the poorest.

A common way of conducting medication effectiveness research is though using **randomised control trials (RCTs)**. Here, the response of two groups of people (in our case, two groups of people with depression), both of whom are aware that they may be taking either an actual medication (e.g. an antidepressant) or a placebo pill, are compared. In general, a placebo is a pharmacologically ineffective or simulated medical treatment, and in drug trials, the pill usually contains an 'inert' sugar solution (see Box 7.2 for further discussion of **placebo effect**). Irving Kirsch and colleagues conducted a controversial yet high impacting study, which analysed the results of studies comparing the effectiveness of antidepressants against placebo pills. For many years, Kirsch had argued that antidepressants were often little better, if at all, than a placebo pill. In 2008, he conducted a meta-analysis (Kirsch et al., 2008) on data submitted to the US Food and Drug Administration (FDA – the US organisation that approves the safety and effectiveness of medications) of four commonly used antidepressants. Kirsch found that overall, whilst there were statistical differences between antidepressants and placebo, there were no significant *clinical differences* in the effectiveness of antidepressants over placebo in people with mild to moderate symptoms of depression. It was only at the more severe end of the symptom continuum that antidepressants produced a clinically significant improvement over the placebo. The authors argued this was due to the effectiveness of placebo falling off at this level of depression, rather than antidepressants becoming more effective. In fact, the authors concluded that there was little evidence for the prescription of antidepressants, unless people are severely depressed, postulating that approximately 80% of antidepressant effectiveness is through the placebo response.

It is likely that the debate about the clinical effectiveness of antidepressants will continue for some time. It should be noted that these findings do not suggest, per se, that antidepressants do not bring around change in symptoms in comparison with doing nothing (i.e. not taking any medication). Rather, they suggest that in comparison with taking a placebo pill, antidepressants may not lead to significant clinical improvements apart from people with severe depressive symptoms. It should be noted that although the sugar pills taken in placebo trials do not contain any active ingredient that might account for the documented improvement in depression symptoms the 'placebo effect' can be powerful in itself (see Box 7.2).

Box 7.2 What is the placebo effect, and how does it work?

The word 'placebo' comes from the Latin 'I shall please', and initially, was used to refer to a process in which patients were given a treatment that was based on pleasing them, rather than being the most effective intervention for them. Over time, the term 'placebo effect' has been used to refer to the response observed after someone is either deceived into thinking that a treatment (be it a drug, an injection or even an operation) they are receiving contains an active ingredient, whereas in reality it is inert or simulated, or they are not sure whether they are taking an active or inert agent (e.g. in a RCT trial).

Studying, and using, the placebo effect is very common within medical and health research, and there are a variety of studies supporting its effect. For example, Assefi and Garry (2003) found that a group of participants who were given non-alcoholic drinks but told they contained vodka subsequently performed worse on a memory task than participants who had not been told this. It should also be noted the Assefi and Garry came up with one of the best titles for a journal article I have ever seen (my italics added): *Absolut* memory distortions: alcohol placebos influence the misinformation effect.

There are a number of key ideas about how the placebo effect works (Stewart-Williams & Podd, 2004). One leading suggestion is that explicit, conscious belief of change, leads to actual change (sometimes known as 'expectancy theory'). For example, Irving Kirsch suggest that the belief (response expectancy) that one will feel better after taking an antidepressant leads one to feel better.

It is important to recognise that the placebo effect does not just occur with 'inert' substances or interventions. There are, of course, aspects of 'positive belief' that influence the results of active treatments like antidepressants and psychotherapy. Whilst some would argue that such phenomenon does not constitute a placebo effect, because the treatment is active rather than inert, the mind state that produces positive changes from the *belief* that a treatment will be helpful does indeed go across both inert and active treatments. For example, studies have found that when individuals were given an anxiolytic (anti-anxiety medication) but without knowing they had, they were likely to rate the reduction in their anxiety as smaller in comparison with when they were told that they had been treated with the medication.

A further difficulty in measuring antidepressant effectiveness relates to the type of change needed to be classified as 'effective'. As highlighted in the NICE guidelines for depression (2010), an antidepressant (but also any treatment in general) is defined as effective if it leads to a reduction in depression symptomology of 50%, as assessed by a depression rating scale. However, there is a difference between clinical effectiveness in research trials and real-life experience. For example, someone who meets the highest symptom levels on one of the commonly used depression measures in research studies (the Hamilton Rating Scale for Depression; HRSD) would score 52, which would place him/her in the 'severe' range. A 50% improvement for this person would translate to a score of 26 on the HRSD, which is still in the 'severe' category. So in this case we have a bit of a quandary; on one level, this individual would be counted as having made a 'response' to taking an antidepressant. However, in terms of symptomology, they are still suffering from depression symptoms that are characteristic of the 'severe' category range. Of course, 50% is an arbitrary, 'man made' decision about effectiveness. This could have easily been 40, 60 or 80%. Whilst a figure has to be set for the purpose of evaluating an intervention, it is always important to consider how we are measuring change and effectiveness.

Side-effects

As with any medication, antidepressants frequently have a variety of side-effects. In fact, some people have suggested that rather than calling them side-effects, we should just refer to them as 'effects', as these are as common as the designed effect (i.e. reducing depression symptoms).

The side-effects of antidepressants differ somewhat, and although there are some typical ones for each category (e.g. SSRI, TCA, etc.), there are also differences within the same class. In general, SSRIs and SNRIs can commonly trigger nausea, dry mouth, dizziness, blurred vision and lower libido (sex drive). For the TCAs, common side-effects include constipation, sweating, dry mouth and dizziness. For the MAOIs, side-effects include dizziness or light-headedness (particularly when standing up quickly), changes in appetite and weight gain, loss of libido, and high blood pressure. For the MAOIs, there are specific risks with certain types of food – particularly foods with tyramine such as cheese, cured meats, some pickled foods, wine and beer. Unfortunately, alongside using MAOI, this substance can lead to increased blood pressure and, in rare cases, death.

One of the most concerning side-effects of antidepressant medication is the potential they have for increasing suicidal thoughts, feelings and attempts in some people who take them. This seems to be particularly the case with children, adolescents and young adults. This issue became a major news story in the mid-2000s when evidence emerged that there was a small, yet consistent, link between antidepressant use and increased suicide thoughts (and therefore risk) in children. Subsequently, some of the large pharmaceutical companies also admitted to the potential risk of increased suicide in adults using antidepressants. The scandal related to the allegation that pharmaceutical companies seemed to have been aware of such risk but had not made this clear to the authorities or the general public. To date, it is unclear exactly why and how antidepressants may lead to increased suicidal thoughts and behaviour in some people, although there are ideas that rather than increasing levels of serotonin in the brain, antidepressants might actually lead to serotonin reduction in some people. Lower levels of serotonin in the brain can be associated with increased anger, aggressiveness and impulsivity, which could be, in turn, associated with certain types of suicidal thoughts and desires and, ultimately, attempts. It should be noted that overall, studies have generally found that antidepressants are associated with reductions in suicidal thoughts, behaviours and risk.

⊙ Non-pharmaceutical, biological and physiological treatments of depression

Whilst pharmaceutical treatments form the mainstay of biological interventions of depression, there are a variety of other important, non-pharmaceutical approaches to treating depression.

Light therapy

Light therapies are used to treat depression with a seasonal presentation, such as seasonal affective disorder (SAD). The intervention involves exposing individuals suffering from SAD to increased levels of natural or artificial sunlight. The use of light boxes is theorised to stimulate the same processes as actual sunlight, by altering circadian rhythms and the secretion of melatonin. A light box is an electronic device that emits certain levels of 'lux' (a measurement of luminance). Treatment involves having the light box at a certain distance from the face (eyes) for a set amount of time each day. The amount of time needed to use the box each day depends partly on the level of lux emitted by the box, and people are usually recommended to use the box in the early morning after waking.

In a meta-analytic review of RCTs (n=13) on bright light and dawn simulation for SAD, Golden et al. (2005) found that these interventions showed significant reductions in depression symptomology in seasonal and non-seasonal depression. They suggested that the size of symptom reduction was comparable to that found in antidepressant trials. These findings are interesting, particularly given that significant positive results were found for non-seasonal depressions as well as SAD. There has been a growing literature in the use of light therapy as a treatment for non-seasonal depressions. Although involving a small number of participants and no control group, a recent study by Naus et al. (2013) looking at response to light therapy in people with two different types of depression – melancholic (lack of mood reactivity, insomnia, decreased appetite or weight loss) and atypical (e.g. mood reactivity, increased appetite/weight gain, hypersomnia) – found that light therapy produced significant reductions of symptoms in both groups over a relatively short period of time (four weeks). A key finding of this study was that it was not just people with a seasonal depression that benefited from light treatment. In fact, after measuring and controlling for seasonal symptoms, the authors found that these did not significantly predict treatment response. One of the potential benefits of light therapy over other interventions (e.g. antidepressants and psychotherapy) is that it produces positive change in a shorter amount of time, with a considerable number of patients experiencing improvements as early as a week following treatment (Terman and Terman, 2005).

A review of light therapy by NICE guidelines for depression (NICE, 2010) suggested that it was difficult to evaluate the potential effects due to methodological issues of many of the studies (e.g. colour of light, dose and mixed participant characteristics), although in comparison with a waitlist control, their use was associated with significant reductions in symptomology. Importantly, this review showed no significant differences between light box treatment and a placebo (e.g. a light box that emitted low levels of lux hypothesised not to actively impact in the way that high lux counts would). In summary, NICE recommends that if light therapy is to be used, it should be at the level of 5,000 lux on a daily, morning basis throughout the winter months.

Electro-convulsive therapy (ECT)

ECT involves passing of an electrical current through the brain, which causes an induced neurological seizure. During the procedure – which is often repeated 6–12 times over a period of weeks – the patient is placed under general anaesthetic. Two electrodes are then placed on the same side of the forehead (unilaterally) or on either side of the forehead (bilaterally), and then an electrical current (the 'shock') is administered, causing a seizure in the brain. Before the procedure takes place, a variety of tests, such as an electrocardiogram (ECG; measuring heart function) and blood tests are carried out to ascertain physical health condition and check for any medical issues that may preclude the use of ECT.

Generally, ECT has been found to be an effective treatment for severe or treatment-resistant depression. For example, in a meta-analytic review of the literature, Pagnin et al. (2008) found that ECT produced significantly superior results than other treatment methods. Specifically it was found that ECT was five times more likely to bring around a positive result than placebo (a pill) or simulated ECT, and four times more likely to bring about a positive response than antidepressants. Whilst ECT can be a highly effective treatment, it is also controversial. For some people, the act of running electricity through an individual's brain is barbaric and inhumane, and some of the arguments against its use were led by the anti-psychiatry and political movement to bring change to the way that people with mental health problems were treated. It is important to note however that modern use of ECT is rather different from that conducted in the mid-twentieth century and simulated in films like 'One Flew over the Cuckoo's Nest' (http://www.youtube.com/watch?v=kHPdtWvL3Mk), when anaesthetic and muscle relaxants *weren't* given and the procedure could be quite dangerous. In fact, you can watch the process of modern day ECT online (http://www.youtube.com/watch?v=9L2-B-aluCE).

Whilst modern ECT is far removed from its unpleasant beginnings, it is still associated with a number of side-effects, in particular, short-term memory loss and cognitive impairment. Given this, it is advised that ECT should only be used in certain situations – when depression has been resistant to other treatments and when the condition is a threat to a person's life (e.g. via suicide or severe self-neglect, sometimes seen in catatonia).

Similar to antidepressants, scientists are not completely sure how ECT works. It may be that over the course of a number of ECT sessions, the balance of neurochemicals and transmitters in the brain changes, a bit like resetting the factory settings on a mobile phone. Recently, research has suggested that ECT may stimulate neuronal neurogenesis – that is, it may help the brain to develop new cells (neurons).

Diet

On a basic level, we can probably all appreciate that food has an impact on our mood. If, like me, you don't like Brussels sprouts, eating one will probably leave you feeling a little disgusted, and not very happy! If on the other hand, like me, you love beer, then having a pint of cold lager on a warm day is likely to give you feelings of pleasure and contentment! Of course, these experiences are highly transient with the feelings of disgust or pleasure only lasting *for a few moments*. However, is there any evidence that the food we eat is related to more lasting changes in mood, such as depression or positive well-being? Well, the answer is a 'maybe'.

Research has found that reduced consumption of foods high in Omega-3 polyunsaturated fatty acids – such as oily fish-like sardines, mackerel and salmon – may be linked to increased levels of depression. For example, in a study of older adults, Tiemeier et al. (2003) found lower levels of Omega-3 acids in the diets of depressed compared to non-depressed people. In a randomised, double-blind study of patients with depression, Su et al. (2003) gave half of the participants 9.6g of Omega-3 fatty acids a day and the other half a placebo, in addition to their usual treatment. Over an eight-week period, the authors found that those given Omega-3 fatty acids experienced a significant reduction in depression symptoms as measured by the HRSD. Although this study had a small number of participants, it suggests that Omega-3 may be a potentially important dietary supplement for people with depression. Other researchers have pointed out that certain types of diet (e.g. Mediterranean, characterised by high levels of fish, vegetables, fruits and pulses) may be protective against the development of depression.

As yet we do not have the quality of evidence to make any broader claims about the potential role of diet and depression. Moreover, one of the difficulties with studies looking at diet and depression is, of course, that a common symptom of depression is often changes in appetite, particularly the loss of appetite. This may be a confounding factor for the above studies, as it may be that depression itself causes changes in diet, which then may further exacerbate symptoms.

Exercise

Whilst some would describe exercise as a psychosocial intervention, we will discuss here how it may be used to bring specific physiological changes to the brain and body, and in doing so, alleviate depression. Studies looking at the effectiveness of exercise in depression have generally been quite favourable, although there appear to be a number of methodological problems with many of the studies conducted. For example, in a meta-analysis of published studies, Lawlor and Hopker (2001) found that exercise was associated with a significant improvement in depression scores, equivalent to those found in cognitive therapy. However, they found a number of problems with the standard of the studies they analysed, particularly that many did not adequately randomise or 'blind' their participants, or failed to provide appropriate follow-up measurements to ascertain maintenance of the initial benefits made. Craft and Perna (2004) analysed the results of Lawlor and Hopker's study and converted the outcomes into a score which showed that, on average, there was a 74% reduction in depression symptoms in the studies analysed by Lawlor and Hopker. They suggested that these figures highlight the potential powerful role exercise may have on depression, particularly given that medical 'significance' in reducing symptoms – as discussed above, based on NICE guidance, a symptom reduction of 50% or over is considered to indicate that an intervention is effective.

Does the type of exercise make a difference to levels of depression? Well, whilst many of the studies have looked at the impact of aerobic exercise (exercise that focuses on working the cardiovascular system, such as rowing, swimming and jogging), there have also been a few that examining the relationship between aerobic exercise and anaerobic exercise (linked to strength training such as lifting weights and explosive use of fast twitch muscles). Doyne et al. (1987) found that in comparison with a wait-list control group, women who engaged in regular aerobic (running) and anaerobic (weight lifting) activity over an eight-week period had significantly reduced depression symptomology scores. Moreover, they found no statistical difference between the two different types of exercise.

How about the amount and frequency of exercise? Does that make a difference to level of depression? In a study looking at the 'dose effect' of exercise on depression, Dunn et al. (2005) randomised participants to five different exercise groups, involving a combination of either 'suggested' (17.5kcal/kg/week) or 'low dose' (7kcal/kg/week) energy expenditure, either three or five times a week. The final group involved a placebo control of stretching exercises for 15–20 minutes, three times a week. They found that over a 12-week period, those in the higher energy expenditure group had a 47% response rate, a significantly higher rate of reduction than individuals in the lower energy expenditure group (30%), or the control/placebo group (29%). The frequency of exercise did not have a significant effect on reducing depression symptoms, suggesting that total energy expenditure rather than how often participants exercised over a week was more important in determining the effectiveness of exercise in targeting depression. These authors suggest that the rates of improvement found in this study are comparable to those found in trials of antidepressants and cognitive behavioural therapy.

These recent findings about the effectiveness of exercise have led to a scheme called 'exercise on prescription'. Here, a General Practitioner (GP; a primary care doctor) can refer a patient suffering with depression to a local centre which provides exercise facilities and a trainer who can work with the individual for a set amount of time. These schemes are often free or sometimes come at a highly subsidised rate, so as not to be prohibiting to those who cannot afford them.

Craft and Perna (2004) discuss a number of ideas about how exercise may be helpful for depression, many of which involve biological or neurophysiological explanations. They suggest that, like antidepressant medication, exercise may impact on the monoamine neurotransmitters (serotonin, dopamine and norepinephrine), although similar to antidepressants, there does not appear to be clear evidence for this yet. These researchers also suggest that exercise may impact on stimulating endorphins, which can leave us with a greater sense of calmness and well-being. Other scientists have suggested that exercise boosts brain-derived neurotrophic factor (BDNF) levels in the brain, and in particular, in the hippocampus area (Erickson et al., 2012). BDNF is a protein secreted in the brain, and may play an important role in the health of neurons and the birth of new neurons (a process known as neurogenisis). Thus, BDNF may help to protect neurons that come under threat through the affects of chronic stress response (e.g. cortisol).

Of course, there are likely to be a number of important psychological explanations for why exercise might be helpful. For example, someone with depression that I was working with recently said that learning to play tennis three times a week left them with a sense of achievement and mastery at developing a new skill. Moreover, they had met new people and spent more time developing social relationships, rather than their previous pattern of being stuck at home alone. Another client told me that it felt good to exercise (running) because, in those moments, he not only felt he was achieving something, but that this was also a time he was not focusing on his depression, hopelessness and negative thoughts. Instead he was trying to make sure he wasn't getting lost running the streets of London or falling down a pot-hole! For many of us (myself included!), doing exercise can lead to the loss of weight and increased sense of strength and satisfaction with our bodies, which can, again, be a boost to self-esteem. Of course, it is not just internal processes about exercise that are important – often when we exercise our friends and colleagues can praise us and express their positivity in us engaging in these type of behaviours (often as they are seen positively in our society). This, in itself, can leave us with an increased sense of social connectedness and well-being.

Interestingly, as Ströhle (2009) highlights, it may be that regular exercise is protective against developing depression, and that this could influence government policy about ways to prevent people from developing depression in the future. As pointed out in Chapter 1, depression has a significant impact on the economy of a country, and the treatment of depression itself is also very expensive. In comparison, exercise programmes are relatively inexpensive, and may provide a rather cost-effective way of preventing the development of depression in the future.

◉ Chapter summary

This chapter has explored a variety of biological and physiological treatments for depression. There appears to be emerging evidence for a variety of these treatments for depression, although most of the evidence gathered so far is for the effectiveness of antidepressants in treating depression.

This chapter has also highlighted that there are still a lot of 'unknowns' with regard to the biological and physiological treatments of depression. In particular, although there are some good suggestions, scientists still don't know for sure how antidepressants, ECT, diet or exercise actually work in alleviating depression. Furthermore, even the most successful of biological treatments only work for a certain number of people, and perhaps on certain types of symptoms.

Chapter 8

Psychological Interventions

Psychological interventions seek to find ways of bringing change to a variety of processes – thoughts, memories, feelings, behaviours and relationships – associated with depression. The most common and recognisable form of psychological intervention is through psychological therapy, often known as psychotherapy, which this chapter will predominantly focus on. Psychotherapy comes from two Greek words: *psyche* – spirit or soul and *therapia* – healing or treatment; so literally, the 'healing of the spirit'. The initial form of modern psychotherapy – Psychoanalysis – was described as the 'talking cure' by one of its first recipients. Psychological therapy involves helping someone through a process that emphasises talking and listening, and does not primarily use biological interventions (Feltham, 2013).

Although this chapter will focus on some of the main psychotherapies used to treat depression today, the core of psychotherapy – the offering of support, reassurance and talking-listening from one person to another – has likely existed since humans have walked this earth. It is probable that we have always communicated our concern and support to each other, just as we can see similar, non-verbal forms of caring in our ape and mammalian relatives. In a comprehensive review of the origins of psychotherapy, Ellenberger (1970) points out that whilst it is tempting to think that psychotherapy evolved relatively recently, in fact, it has existed in primitive forms for thousands of years. Historically, concerns with the psyche (soul) were thought to be caused by evil spirits, and dealing with this was mainly the domain of priests or shamans. Ellenberger suggests that in many cultures, concerns with loss of the soul, spirit intrusion or possession and, more broadly, disease and illness were often 'treated' with a variety of interventions, including hypnosis, 'healing' (both by 'magic' and in temples or places of worship), philosophical discussion, confession and 'gratification' of frustrated wishes.

In more structured and 'scientific' forms, a variety of psychological and psychotherapeutic approaches have existed for over 100 years. The emergence and predominance of modern science and medicine in the nineteenth century led to a shift in understanding and treatment of mental distress, including depression. In particular, it was in the late nineteenth century with the birth of psychoanalysis, built on the work of Joseph Brueur and his student, Sigmund Freud, that psychotherapy emerged in a more organised form. Since the early days of psychoanalysis in the 1880s, the field of psychotherapy has developed at a pace. A recent estimate suggested there were over 500 different psychological therapies, and clearly, there is not room to explore each one of these in this chapter. Rather, this chapter will explore the historical 'big three' psychological therapies for depression – psychodynamic, behavioural and cognitive-behavioural – which reflect interrelated but separate, developmental stages in the evolution of psychotherapy. We will also explore recent adaptations in each of these domains, and consider whether these different forms of psychological intervention are helpful in depression. We will also look at whether psychological interventions outside of formalised, structured psychotherapy (e.g. self-help books) may also be helpful in alleviating depression symptoms.

Psychodynamic therapy

Historical roots

Psychodynamic psychotherapy can be seen as a broad umbrella of approaches that grew out of Freudian psychoanalytic theory and practice. As described in Chapter 5, Freud trained as a neurologist, but became interested in finding a way to work with patients who were suffering with *neuroses* (meaning 'abnormal nerves', a type of distress without psychotic features) and *hysteria* (now known as 'conversion disorder', in which people experience physical health problems like seizures or paralysis without an identifiable physiological cause). Along with his mentor, physician Joseph Breuer, Freud began to develop a theory and treatment for these difficulties, which went on to be called psychoanalysis. Some of the key ideas of psychoanalysis are:

1 People's current distress was associated with unconscious experiences from the past.
2 Due to the painful nature of the unconscious feelings, patients use (often unconsciously) defence mechanisms to protect themselves from experiencing distressing thoughts, memories or fantasies (see Box 8.1).
3 Treatment should involve making 'the unconscious, conscious' following which there would be an alleviation of symptoms as people will be more likely to find healthier ways of coping with distress.

Box 8.1 Common defence mechanisms

In psychodynamic approaches, defence mechanisms are seen as individual attempts to (unconsciously) protect themselves from things that they find threatening. In depression, these defence mechanisms are seen as attempts to deal with powerful feelings (e.g. depression, sadness), and prevent the expression of these feelings to other people who are loved or valued in some way. From a psychodynamic perspective, unfortunately these defence mechanisms only exacerbate depressive symptoms and interpersonal difficulties.

Busch (2009) discusses a number of key defence mechanisms used in depression, including projection and passive aggression. These, and other key defence mechanisms in depression, are described below:

Passive Aggression – In passive aggression, the depressed person expresses their anger in an indirect manner. For example, they may withhold help, turn up late to a meeting or sit in silence during a meal with friends.
Repression – Here, an individual unconsciously blocks out of awareness distressing thoughts, feelings or memories. In depression, feelings of anger, rage, loss and sadness can be 'absent' in situations that you could imagine them being likely to surface.
Projection – This is when painful thoughts or feelings are attributed (projected) onto another person who does not have those thoughts or feelings. In someone suffering with depression, a common projection

involves suggesting that other people are being angry and hostile to us, whereas these are actually feelings they are feeling to other people. As projection involves a sense that others are angry with us, this can often lead to depressed people feeling rejected, uncared for and ultimately more depressed.

Reaction Formation – Here, an individual is fearful of experiencing and expressing negative feelings (e.g. disappointment or anger) towards others because in their early relationships such feelings were not allowed or punished. This person may defend against experiencing and expressing anger by becoming overly positive towards those they resent.

Displacement – Here, thoughts and feelings that are felt towards one person are instead redirected to another person. For example, a man who is angry with his wife for having an affair but is unable to express this due to fear that she will leave him directs these feelings instead to colleagues at work, arguing with them about things that he wouldn't normally be bothered about.

Psychodynamic treatment for depression

Traditional psychoanalysis was delivered in an unstructured way, based on frequent weekly meetings (typically, at least three times weekly), over a long time period (typically more than two years). In comparison, contemporary psychodynamic approaches are more structured, have a greater focus on depressive symptoms as well as early life and personality factors that have contributed to the person being depressed. Short-term dynamic psychotherapy (STDP) usually involves one session a week for a total of three to six months, whereas longer-term psychodynamic treatment can last up to two years.

Busch (2009) suggests that psychodynamic treatment of depression contains three phases. The first phase involves an assessment of the current depressive episode (e.g. triggers, symptoms), early life experiences and personality development, and what the quality of relationships with others are like. Here, the therapist focuses upon developing an understanding of common experiences in depression (e.g. loss, rejection), conflicted anger in response to losses or rejections (e.g. unexpressed anger to others and the presence of self-directed anger/criticism), guilt and shame, and the defences used to protect the self from painful memories, feelings or impulses (see Box 8.1 for a further discussion of defences in depression). Alongside this, the therapist focuses on developing a sound therapeutic alliance.

In the second phase of treatment, the therapist seeks to apply the understanding derived in the first phase to help to develop insight and a reduction of symptomology. Here, the therapist helps the depressed individual to focus upon issues highlighted in phase one, with a particular focus on how these play out in current relationships. The therapist also looks for how these dynamics are brought into the therapeutic work through *transference*. Transference involves the patient redirecting feelings, concerns or desires that have been (unconsciously) developed through experiences with other people as a child, on to the therapist. In turn, the therapist's reactions and responses to the client are known as 'counter transference'. By examining the therapeutic transference and counter transference, the therapist can help the client understand and work through past, hidden and recurring patterns (of feelings and desires) in the here-and-now.

The final phase of therapy involves the ending of treatment and the feelings associated with this. This might commonly involve the sense of loss that ending therapy – and contact with the therapist – may bring up, including feelings of anger towards the therapist for the sessions having to come to an end. These experiences are discussed in the context of the themes that were identified in the first phase of treatment and worked on in the second.

Busch (2009) suggests a number of goals of psychodynamic treatment of depression, including the reduction of vulnerability to loss, rejection and criticism from others, increased awareness, tolerance and healthy expression of anger, a reduction in self-directed anger, criticism and shame, and improved interpersonal relationships.

Evidence – Is psychodynamic therapy for depression effective?

Evidence for **psychodynamic therapy** for any mental health problem has been the source of much debate and controversy. Historically, some of this has had to do with ambivalence, indifference or at times, even hostility, from psychodynamic (and in particular, psychoanalytic) clinicians to conduct research on the effectiveness of their therapy. There were also methodological difficulties for researchers, as early psychoanalytic and dynamic therapies were rarely based on a structured approach, which made it difficult to make accurate comparisons about effectiveness with other treatments.

However, in recent years there have been increasing efforts to study the effectiveness of psychodynamic therapy. For example, in a robust defence of the evidence base for psychodynamic approaches, Shedler (2010) suggests that there is good evidence for psychodynamic approaches, and that for depression, the efficacy is equivalent to that found in cognitive behaviour therapy (CBT). Abbass and colleagues (Abbass et al., 2006) found evidence for the effectiveness of psychodynamic psychotherapy for depression in comparison with people on a waiting list for therapy.

However, in the UK recent NHS guidelines were less supportive of psychodynamic approaches for depression. In a review of the literature as part of the NICE guidelines for depression (NICE, 2010), ten RCT studies comparing short-term psychodynamic psychotherapy with wait-list control or antidepressants were evaluated. Overall, the authors found that there was a lack of quality studies (i.e. the methodology of the studies were flawed or lacking in various ways), which led to a number of contra-dictory findings on how helpful (if at all) psychodynamic therapy was in comparison with waitlist control, care as usual or other active treatments for depression. NICE (2010) therefore did not recommend the use of psychodynamic therapy (in this case, Short-Term Dynamic Psycho-therapy STDP) for depression in the NHS as a frontline treatment. Instead, they suggested that for those people with mild to moderate levels of depression who *declined* frontline treatments (antidepressant, CBT, interpersonal therapy, behavioural activation and behavioural couples therapy), STDP could be considered. Although NICE did not find strong support for STDP, the authors suggest that it is important to improve the research base for STDP. In particular, they suggest that given the 'patchy' provision of STDP throughout the NHS, and inconclusive evidence base, good RCTs are needed to compare effectiveness for moderate to severe depression, in comparison with antidepressants and **CBT**.

Criticisms of psychodynamic therapy for depression

There are a number of criticisms of psychodynamic therapy. Some of these relate to issues many people have about some of Freud's original ideas, rather than how psychodynamic therapy is practised today. For example, many people feel that Freud's original ideas were sexist and overly focused on sexual themes. Others feel that psychodynamic approaches and explanations lack empiricism (i.e. are unscientific with no way to 'prove' their existence). This view was propagated by the great twentieth century philosopher Karl Popper (1959), who suggested that psychoanalysis was unfalsifiable and therefore outside of scientific enquiry.

Other criticisms of psychodynamic therapy emerged and were key in the development of behavioural and cognitive approaches (see below, and Chapter 4 for further discussion). Both of these approaches disagree with aspects of psychodynamic theory (e.g. personality development) and the emphasis on unconscious processes, over those of observable behaviours or conscious experience. Both of these approaches suggest that change to depressive (and other) symptoms does not reliably emerge from gaining insight into certain aspects of mind alone (from 'simply' discovering previously unconscious desires, emotions or memories), and that instead, one must 'learn' and practise new, more helpful ways of thinking and behaving.

Recent adaptations

To a certain extent, STDP – in the sense that it is a *short-term* dynamic therapy – is a change from original conceptualisations of psychodynamic approaches, in which people would receive therapy multiple times a week, over a period of many years. However, there have also been adaptations of traditional psychodynamic approaches for working with depression. One such approach is known as Interpersonal Therapy (IPT). As Howard (2013) points out, IPT did not emerge out of a specific theoretical or psychotherapeutic approach (e.g. psychodynamic) as such, but rather emerged out of a pragmatic framework of deciding upon what the effective aspects of therapy for depression were, and then shaping a therapeutic structure around those factors. However, at the theoretical heart of IPT was the work of a variety of clinicians whose theories were in part psychodynamically orientated or influenced (e.g. John Bowlby and Harry Stack Sullivan). Howard (2013) suggests that IPT for depression highlights the importance of attachment needs, social relationships/roles and communication difficulties in the cause and maintenance of depression. However, unlike psychodynamic approaches, IPT focuses more on current relationships, and is more interested in interpersonal processes (relationships with other people) rather than intrapersonal processes (such as unconscious drives, defences and conflicts).

It may be that IPT offers some benefits that navigate some of the criticisms of psychodynamic approaches. For example, it makes great effort not to use 'psycho-jargon' which is sometimes off-putting and confusing for clients in psychodynamic approaches. Moreover, from the beginning, IPT focused on developing a solid research-base to support its efficacy in treating depression. In fact, the research literature for IPT for depression has been positive. For example, Elkin et al. (1989) found IPT was as effective as CBT and antidepressants in reducing levels of depression, and performed as well in reducing levels of relapse. As a testimony to the positive research findings, the NICE guidelines for depression endorsed the use of IPT for sub-threshold, mild, moderate and severe symptomology levels.

⊙ Behaviour therapy

Historical roots

As discussed in Chapter 4, behavioural approaches emerged out of a milieu of psychoanalytic critique, and developed with specific goals to understand behaviour in more scientific, observable ways. An early leader in British behaviourism, Hans Eysenck, was a vociferous critic of psychoanalytic ideas, and disputed that mental health problems were caused by unconscious conflicts (e.g. sexual). Eysenck (1960) suggested that rather than symptoms being a reflection of defences against an overwhelming, hidden unconscious distress (e.g. the fear of experiencing or expressing anger), the symptoms *were* the problem. Eysenck believed that symptoms were learned and therefore could be un-learned. For example, the loss of pleasurable feelings in depression could, through behavioural interventions, be un-learned, thus resolving the problem and lifting the 'depression'. He felt behaviourism offered coherent, testable ways of doing this.

Behavioural approaches to depression sought to understand depression in the context of classical and operant conditioning. They initially grew from Ferster's (1973) theory of depression, in which depression was linked to reduced opportunities (behaviour) for positive reinforcement, along with increased levels of escape and, crucially, avoidant behaviours. Lewinsohn (1974) suggested that depression occurs not only due to a reduction in positive reinforcers in the environment but also due to a person's inability to access (i.e. lack of skill) positive reinforcement (see Chapter 4 for a reminder of positive reinforcement). Using this, Lewinsohn and colleagues (Lewinsohn and Graf, 1973; Lewinsohn, 1974; Lewinsohn et al., 1974) conducted research on the association between activity levels, and the type of activity engaged in, and depression. They found that in comparison with non-depressed psychiatric patients and non-depressed control participants, people who were depressed engaged in fewer pleasant activities (Lewinsohn and Graf, 1973). Moreover, Lewinsohn et al. (1984) suggested that depression could result from an increased level of punishment/aversive experiences in the environment (e.g. criticism from others) or a decreased ability to cope/deal with these experiences.

Within a behavioural approach to depression, a person's behaviour is thought about in terms of its functions, and how this relates to patterns of reinforcement from the environment. For example, when depressed, individuals may initially receive more attention and care from others (positive reinforcement), which is likely to increase the depressed behaviour. They may also get away with not doing certain things they find aversive, such as going to work or doing housework. This is an example of negative reinforcement (the removal of an aversive experience) making the behaviour (e.g. low motivation) *more* likely. However, this means that over time depressed individuals are less likely to engage in behaviours and activities, such as completing a project at work or seeing friends for lunch, that lead to positive reinforcement, and consequentially, positive feelings. Moreover, these individuals may receive less positive reinforcement for active behaviours, and as a consequence, become increasingly passive. Coyne (1976) suggested that over time, rather than responding in positive, caring ways, other people may start to react in *negative* ways to the depressed person's behaviour - by becoming angry, critical or distant - and that this can compound the depression.

How does behaviour therapy aim to help people with depression?

Within **behaviour therapy (BT)**, treatment involves directly changing the factors that are hypothesised to cause depression. So, key aspects of the approach include:

- A functional analysis of the changes in environmental patterns of reinforcement and/or of deficits in social skills that prevent the person from accessing positive reinforcement or dealing with aversive events in the existing environment.

- Identifying the triggering (antecedent) events and subsequent consequences of the pattern of an individual's depressive behaviours.
- Measuring current levels of 'pleasant activities' using self-report questionnaires, and over a period of time, determining which behaviours are associated with lower levels of depression.
- Increase opportunities and motivation to engage in activities (known as activity scheduling) that are associated with sense of achievement and pleasure.
- Improving social skills so that the depressed individual may better access positive reinforcement in the environment and/or learn to manage aversive stimuli more successfully.

Evidence for behaviour therapy for depression

Initial research into the effectiveness of behaviour therapy for depression showed promising results. For example, in comparison with 'insight' orientated (psychodynamic) therapy, Gallagher and Thompson (1982) found that behavioural therapy was equally effective in reducing depression symptoms but led to greater improvement at one-year follow-up.

Other studies, comparing behavioural treatments for depression with cognitive therapy (see below), have generally found positive results for behaviour therapy. For example, Zeiss et al. (1979) found that in people with depression in the community, separate treatments focusing on developing (i) increased pleasant events in life, (ii) interpersonal skills or (iii) positive cognitions were equally effective in reducing depression symptoms. Similarly, in a review of the literature, Robinson et al. (1990) found that in comparison with cognitive and cognitive-behavioural therapy, standalone behaviour therapy produced a significant reduction in depression symptoms over waitlist control. Moreover, they also found that there was no discernable difference between the three types of therapy offered.

However, for many people, behavioural therapies fell out of favour during the late 1970s, 1980s and much of the 1990s. This was not so much because they did not have promising things to contribute to treating depression, but rather because of the emergence of cognitive therapy, and later, the absorption of behavioural approaches within cognitive behaviour therapy. It was only with the emergence of Behavioural Activation (BA; see below) that the behavioural model re-emerged as a popular and credible standalone treatment for depression.

Criticisms of behavioural therapy for depression

One of the main criticisms of BT for depression, and more generally as a psychotherapeutic approach, is that it tends to ignore the potential influence of other important factors, such as early life experiences or the role of cognition (thoughts) in contributing to emotion and behaviour. These criticisms were particularly aimed at 'radical behaviourists' who felt that mental health problems like depression and anxiety were completely the result of learning, and that with the right type of 'relearning', they could be eradicated. This was sometimes referred to as 'unqualified environmentalism', which basically meant that the environment was seen as the only influence upon the acquisition of behaviour.

Whilst there may have been some validity to this criticism, it only applies to some of the early and more radically held behavioural approaches to depression (e.g. those approaches that dismissed cognition as an unobservable, internal event) and therefore may be based on a caricature of the approach. The reality is that for many behaviourists working with depression, cognition was seen to play an important role in symptomology; in fact, within some behavioural models, cognition was understood as a type of behaviour that could be measured and changed. Moreover, many behaviourists ascribed to the importance of genes and heritability as factors influencing the acquisition of mental health problems.

Other criticisms of BT emerged out of the research literature. For example, some researchers found that increasing the number of positively reinforced activities did not improve level of depression symptomology (Dobson and Joffe, 1986). This of course is counter to what BT would suggest and led to arguments that there were other factors that were contributing towards depression and therefore other things in therapy that should be addressed to help depressed people.

Recent developments

Modern day behavioural approaches are still used frequently in clinical settings to help people with depression. One recent adaptation – or remodelling – of traditional behavioural approaches is known as

Behavioural Activation (BA). Behavioural Activation emerged in the mid-1990s after a period of time in which behavioural approaches for depression had languished behind the 'cognitive revolution'. Seminal to this re-emergence of behavioural approaches was the findings and work of Neil Jacobson and colleagues (Jacobson et al., 1996), who found that when they 'split' apart different aspects of Cognitive Behaviour Therapy (a process known as component analysis), behavioural activation as a standalone intervention produced as much change as a 'full package' of CBT. This was important, as it challenged the widely held belief that in CBT, cognitive change was primary in bringing about symptom improvement.

Building on the work of the initial pioneers of behavioural approaches for depression (e.g. Lewinsohn, 1974; Ferster, 1973), Jacobson and others went on to develop BA into a more comprehensive treatment for depression. Although similar to younger behaviour therapy approaches, BA took a more idiographic approach to treatment, targeting more specifically environmental events that may bring change to levels of positive reinforcement or punishment, and tailoring specific interventions to target change on an individual basis. Some of the features of BA are described in Box 8.2.

Box 8.2 Major therapeutic strategies and techniques of behaviour therapies

One of the main aims of BA for depression is to increase an individual's level of activity, bringing them in contact with more positive reinforcement and reducing the negative reinforcement of avoidance. O'Carroll (2013) suggested a number of therapeutic techniques by which BA can achieve this:

- *Activity Monitoring* – here, the therapist asks the depressed client to monitor their current level of activity and mood, providing a baseline and useful assessment of the 'current state of play'.
- *Assessment of Values* – this involves two processes: an initial exploration of the valued goals that give an individual direction in life (e.g. relationships with family or friends, work) and the identification of valued ways of behaving (e.g. behaving in the here-and-now in particular valued ways, such as with compassion, courage or honesty).
- *Activity Scheduling* – here, the therapist, using the information from the above techniques, works with the client to develop an activity plan in which activities are linked to positive reinforcement

- *Reducing Avoidance* – here, the therapist works with the client to identify examples of avoidance and escape behaviours (which, from a BA perspective, are kept in place by negative reinforcement). When these are identified, along with the context they arise in, the therapist works with the client to develop alternative ways of coping in these situations.
- *Skills training* – here, the therapist works with the client to identify how certain difficulties are related to deficits in specific skills (e.g. social communication) and then uses role-plays to help the client develop skills in this area.

There have been a number of RCT studies looking at BA in comparison with those not receiving any therapy, and also those receiving a particular type of therapy. In a meta-analysis summarising studies, Cuijpers et al. (2007) found that in comparison with no therapy, BA had a significant impact on reducing depression symptoms. However, in comparison with other active therapies there were no clinically significant differences in treatment effectiveness. In their guidelines for depression, NICE (2010) suggest that BA should be an option for treatment, but that patients should be offered 16–20 sessions, and that consideration should be given to patients having two sessions a week for the first three to four weeks of treatment. This is based on evidence that this is a more beneficial form of treatment than weekly sessions.

It is unclear as of yet exactly how BA may bring about a reduction of depression symptoms. Of course, the theory suggests that this is mainly via reducing levels of rumination and avoidance, and increasing behaviours that elicit positive reinforcement. However, like most psychotherapies, it is difficult for studies to actually test in a scientifically rigorous way whether this is indeed the case.

◉ Cognitive behaviour therapy (CBT)

History of CBT

There are many important stages in the historical development of CBT, although for our purpose, two are key. The first emerged in America in the 1950s and 1960s with the work of two trained and practising psychoanalysts – Aaron Beck and Albert Ellis – who over time, turned away from the core ideas and practice of psychoanalysis. Instead, they developed cognitive therapy and rational emotional behavioural therapy, respectively, and both approaches emphasised the seminal role of what they saw as 'faulty' or irrational cognition (or more broadly, faulty cognitive processing) in causing mental distress and disorder.

A second path to CBT emerged when practising behaviour therapists recognised the potential of Beck and Ellis' work, and started to integrate this into their treatment protocols. As Rachman (1997) points out, for some behaviourists this integration was linked with a feeling that progress with the development of behaviour therapy for depression had stalled. For others, this integration was due to decreased hostility and wariness towards cognitive ideas. The integration of behavioural and cognitive approaches went on to be referred to as CBT. Although there were differences, there were enough similarities between the approaches to bond them together. Both approaches emphasised a focus on the here-and-now experience, rather than prominently focusing on the past, and required therapist and patient to work collaboratively on a defined problem. Moreover, both approaches commonly used out-of-session tasks and practice to bring about change in depression symptoms. However, as others have pointed out (e.g. Gilbert, 2009), the integration proved difficult for many, and can still today create tensions between those who are more 'behavioural' in their approach and theorising, and those who are more 'cognitive' in their orientation.

CBT for depression

Beck's initial ideas emerged from working with people with depression and anxiety. In discussing his transition from psychoanalysis to the development of cognitive therapy, Beck highlighted how, in his psycho-analytic sessions, he became aware that his patients described a variety of pre-conscious, automatic thoughts that were distorted, making their interpretations about themselves and other people negatively biased. He found that these thoughts were often coloured by biases or distortions, such as generalising to the whole from just one event (known as *overgeneralising*, e.g. 'because I failed this test, I'll fail at everything in the future') or clustering information into distinct categories (known as *dichotomous thinking*, e.g. 'people always let you down'). Beck noticed that when he started to help his patients develop new, alterative and more accurate thoughts, their depressive symptoms improved. Over time, Beck began to merge existing behavioural treatments – such as activity scheduling – into cognitive therapy, particularly when working with depressed people who were experiencing anhedonia and low motivation.

Some of the specific interventions for treating depression in CBT are described in Box 8.3.

Box 8.3 Major therapeutic strategies and techniques of CBT

The major aim in CBT is the reduction in depression symptoms. The CB therapist attempts to do this via a number of key strategies and techniques:

- *Identify negative automatic thoughts (NATs)* – here the therapist teaches the client how to notice and record NATs, paying attention to the content of the thought itself but also to the context in which it occurred and the impact it had upon mood and behaviour.
- *Challenge NATs* – here, the therapist helps the client to learn skills to challenge and 'cognitively restructure' their NATs. This involves generating evidence for whether the negative thoughts are 'real', and more accurate alternatives that may leave the person feeling better.
- *Positive data log* – here the client is taught to notice and record positive experiences and examples which challenge the underlying negative thoughts.
- *Activity scheduling* – (see Box 8.2 for further information)
- *Behavioural Experiments* – these are used to 'test out' certain hypotheses that may be contributing or maintaining depression. For example, if a client expects not to enjoy or to fail a particular task, and therefore avoids it, he/she will be encouraged to engage in the task in order to test out the original prediction. The idea is that the outcome of the experiment will provide new, useful information which can 'update' the client's beliefs, and lead to positive behavioural changes, which will, in turn, lead to positive feelings.

CBT for depression is usually delivered in a structured manner of weekly sessions, over a relatively short period of time (for depression, typically between 10 and 16 sessions). The therapist and client work collaboratively to identify the difficulties they will work on (setting of an 'agenda'), and then structure sessions to focus upon these.

Evidence for CBT for depression

CBT has the largest evidence base of any psychotherapy. There have been many studies comparing CBT with a variety of other conditions, including waitlist control, antidepressants and other psychotherapies. In comparison with no specific treatment provision, CBT has consistently been found to be more effective in reducing depression symptoms. For example, Cuijpers et al. (2013) found that in comparison with waitlist control or treatment as usual, CBT produced a reduction of depression symptoms of a medium to large effect size. In comparison with antidepressants, a number of studies have found that CBT is equally effective in reducing symptoms. However, a number of studies have found some support for CBT over antidepressants. For example, at 12 months after discontinuation from a course of CBT or antidepressants, people who had CBT were more likely to have maintained the improvements they made in therapy than those who had taken antidepressants (Blackburn et al., 1997), and were less likely to have relapsed (Dimidjian et al., 2006). Interestingly, in their review of the data, NICE found that there was some evidence to suggest that a combined treatment of CBT and antidepressants was more effective than antidepressants alone.

In comparison with other types of psychotherapy – for example, short-term psychodynamic therapy (Shapiro, 1994), Gestalt psychotherapy (Rosner, 1999) and interpersonal therapy (IPT; Marshall et al., 2008) – CBT has been found to lead to broadly equivalent levels of effectiveness (see Cuijpers et al., 2013). Following their review of the literature, the NICE guidelines for depression (NICE, 2010) found sufficient evidence for the effectiveness of CBT for depression to suggest that it should be a treatment considered for all levels of depression severity.

Criticisms of CBT for depression?

There are a number of broad criticisms of CBT, that also relate to CBT for depression. One particular concern has been about the 'active' ingredient of the approach. Studies known as component analysis have tried to assess which parts of CBT actually 'do the work', that is, whether the 'C' (cognitive) or B (behavioural) component of the approach is the part that is helping people, or whether it is in the combination of the two that people derive most benefit. Recently, a number of studies have shown that the behavioural aspects of CBT treatment are as effective as the cognitive aspects (e.g. Jacobson et al., 2007; Longmore and Worrell, 1996). Another way of looking at these findings is in treating depression, changes in peoples' negative thoughts and beliefs (a central aspect of CBT model) are not necessary, but instead a behavioural focus (i.e. behaviour change) is effective in and of itself. In fact, Dimidjian et al. (2006) found that at severe levels of depression, behavioural activation was more effective than cognitive therapy.

These findings are interesting and bring to mind the 'Dodo bird verdict' (See Box 8.4) – that all therapies are broadly equivalent. However, they pose an important philosophical quandary for CBT, as they make us question which aspect of the theory and therapy is helpful to people. However, another way of looking at these findings is to consider the heterogeneous nature of depression; it may be that whilst CBT is helpful for people in general, certain types of depression may respond better to cognitive interventions, whereas others might respond better to behavioural components.

Box 8.4 The Dodo bird effect

One of the most heated arguments in psychology surrounds the effectiveness of different psychotherapies. Psychologists and psychotherapists aligned to different therapies – for example, psychodynamic or CBT – often argue that their approach is 'best', and put forward a variety of reasons, including studies that show that their therapy is most effective, to try and prove this. However, the publication of a number of large-scale studies suggested that there are no significant differences in effectiveness between different types of psychotherapy (e.g. Shapiro and Shapiro, 1982), which has led to the effectiveness of different forms of psychotherapy being referred to as the 'dodo-bird verdict'. The 'dodo-bird verdict' was first put forward in 1936 by psychologist Saul Rosenzweig as a metaphor, after finding that there were similar responses to both psychodynamic and behavioural approaches. He borrowed this term 'dodo-bird verdict' from Lewis Carroll's story of Alice in Wonderland. In *Alice's Adventures in Wonderland* (1865) a number of characters become wet and in order to dry themselves, a Dodo bird sets a competition, in which everyone would run around a lake until they were dry, although no limits were given to how far they should run for, nor for how long. When the characters asked the Dodo bird who won, it replies: 'Everybody has won and all must have prizes'. Rosenzweig saw in this phrase something similar in psychotherapy, in that whilst supposedly very different, all therapies appear to produce the same responses. This metaphor became widespread within psychotherapy literature following the research of psychologist Lester Luborsky in the US (Luborsky et al., 1975), who along with his colleagues, found that all therapies work equally well as each other.

However, a number of other researchers have criticised the evidence used here. For example, Budd and Hughes (2009) suggest flaws with the way that researchers have come to conclusions about therapy equivalence, particularly in using RCTs to do this. They suggest three features from the literature on therapy equivalence that cloud our capacity to get accurate results:

- The allegiance of psychotherapists to a particular model leads to improved effectiveness rating.
- The therapeutic relationship has been shown to be the most significant predictor of outcome, regardless of psychotherapy modality.
- Certain types of therapists have been found to be far more effective than others within the same therapeutic modality, thus creating doubt about reliability of findings from RCTs.

They suggest that instead of looking at the active ingredients of psychological therapies at the treatment package level, we should be looking at reciprocal individual differences at the level of the therapist and client. What they mean by this is that, because therapy is a reciprocal relationship between two people, we cannot treat type of therapy (e.g. CBT, psychodynamic) or, for that matter, diagnosis (e.g. depression, anxiety) as discrete independent variables.

Another enduring criticism of CBT for depression is that it overemphasises the 'here-and-now' difficulties and does not pay enough attention to a person's early life experiences, or difficult current social relationships and environments. For many, this goes alongside the concern that CBT overemphasises the importance of thinking and behaving, at the expense of emotions. In reality, this criticism is often dependent upon the 'form' of CBT. That is, in short-term CBT for mild depression, it may be that early life experiences are not discussed or emphasised much. However, for moderate to severe depression severity, CBT makes far greater use of understanding how early experiences have influenced current difficulties.

Recent adaptations to CBT – 'Third Wave CBT'

There have been a number of recent adaptations to traditional CBT. In a provocative but stimulating article, Hayes (2004) suggested that there were three waves of behavioural therapy. The first wave, behaviour therapy, was built upon the assumption that behavioural and emotional change occurred by altering opportunities for reinforcement, reducing avoidance and escape behaviour, and changing patterns of associated (conditioned) learning. The second wave – cognitive behavioural therapy – emerged with a reorganisation around the principle that psychological distress/pathology was due to, in one form or another, 'biased' or 'distorted' thinking, and that to bring about change, it was necessary to change one's thoughts about the self and others. Finally, Hayes suggested that we were currently in the wake of a third wave of CBT. He suggested that this wave marked a return to more explicit first wave behavioural principles, with a greater focus upon understanding the context and function of psychological processes, rather than the form or content of these processes (which cognitive therapy tended to do).

Hayes (2004) suggested that a number of factors brought about the third wave of behavioural therapy. These included anomalous findings that were emerging in the literature on cognitive behaviour therapy. For example, improvement in mood occurring before the implementation of cognitive strategies in therapy, and that changes in cognitive factors that were hypothesised to be causal of depression did not lead to any improvements. Moreover, Longmore and Worrell (2007) found that cognitive therapy interventions did not seem to add any additional effect above and beyond those of behavioural interventions. These findings suggested that the emphasis on change in the content of thinking might have been over-emphasised in second wave (cognitive) approaches.

A third wave approach that has emerged as an effective treatment for depression is mindfulness based cognitive therapy (MBCT). MBCT blends ideas and practices from Buddhist meditation with cognitive therapy. MBCT is an eight-week course, provided in a group format. MBCT teaches people to become more aware of their thoughts, emotions and physiological reactions (bodily sensations), and in particular, those that are related to depression symptomology. For example, people are taught how to notice depressive thought patterns (e.g. self-criticism and rumination), and rather than getting 'caught up' in them, they learn to de-centre from these, recognising that 'thoughts are just thoughts, not facts', and finding more helpful ways to direct attention. MBCT requires people to practise mindfulness meditation, which involves a daily practice of focusing attention. If you are interested to learn more about this approach, or try practising it yourself, you can have a look at www.freemindfulness. org and have a try at some of the exercises.

Research has suggested that MBCT is helpful in preventing relapse into depression, and in fact, the NICE guidelines for depression recommend it as a helpful therapy for people who have previously experienced depression, so that they are less likely to become depressed again (as you will remember from Chapter 2, the likelihood of repeated episodes of depression is high). For example, amongst people with recurrent depression, MBCT was found to lead to lower relapse compared to an antidepressant 'maintenance' dose approach, a commonly used and recommended way of reducing relapse in depression (Kuyken et al., 2008). There is also some emerging evidence that MBCT may be helpful for people who are currently depressed.

Finally, another approach that is sometimes classed as a 'third wave' psychotherapy is called Compassion Focused Therapy (CFT). CFT was developed by Psychologist Paul Gilbert (Gilbert, 2014, 2009; Gilbert and Irons, 2005) following recognition that many people with high levels of shame and self-criticism did not derive as much benefit from CBT and IPT as those people with low levels of shame and self-criticism. CFT roots itself in a broad scientific literature, including those relating to evolutionary psychology, neurobiology/physiology and the psychological sciences (e.g. social and developmental psychology). As we explored briefly in Chapter 4, low levels of compassion have been found to be associated with higher levels of depression symptomology, and CFT helps people to learn how to become more compassionate with themselves and their difficulties. Although a relatively 'young' psychotherapy, initial studies suggest that this may be helpful for people with a variety of difficulties, including depression (Gilbert, 2014).

⦿ Other psychological interventions for depression

Whilst this chapter has focused on psychological therapies for depression, there are a number of other psychological interventions used to treat depression, but that do not fit into a commonly accepted definitions of psychotherapy.

Self-help

Self-help for depression commonly comes in the form of books, and is also known as bibliography. Many self-help books come from a CBT perspective, and often provide a psycho-education about depression; explanation of the CBT model; reflection on types of thinking styles associated to depression, exercises on developing alternative, more helpful thoughts; and activity scheduling and behavioural activation practices.

NICE guidelines define 'guided self-help' as an intervention designed to alleviate depression that is 'self-administered' but facilitated by a healthcare professional that meets the depressed individual to monitor the use of the material and the individual's progress. NICE suggests that the healthcare professional will have between three and six contacts with the depressed person. In comparison, self-help (non-guided) is defined as the use of the same self-help material, but in the absence of professional guidance and monitoring.

Cuijpers et al. (2010) conducted a systematic review and meta-analysis of studies comparing CBT-orientated guided self-help and face-to-face psychotherapy for depression. For the purposes of their study, they defined guided self-help as:

- A treatment in which procedures or interventions were presented in written, audio or video format.
- Depressed patients had to work through these procedures and interventions relatively independently.
- The therapist gave support in guiding these procedures, although this was limited to a maximum of 12 contacts of up to 20 minutes for each contact.

The authors only compared studies in which the psychotherapy offered the same content as the guided self-help, but was given in traditional individual or group therapy format. When they analysed results, they found no significant differences in effectiveness between traditional face-to-face psychotherapy and guided self-help with minimal therapist contact for people with depression and/or anxiety. Unfortunately, the authors did not review studies of people with just depression, but rather, those people with depression and comorbid anxiety. Nonetheless, given the high overlap between depression and anxiety, these results are still helpful. As the authors point out, this study did not compare face-to-face psychotherapy to self-help in the absence of a therapist. From this, they postulate that the results suggest that a therapeutic relationship may be established with minimal contact between therapist and patient, and that minimal contact with a therapist may be enough to then translate to significant clinical improvements. However, as this study did not break down what were the active aspects of bringing change to depression, it is impossible to ascertain whether it was the therapeutic relationship – whether in small or large doses – that was transformative. The authors go on to cite evidence from previous studies that non-directed self-help has been found to be less effective than guided self-help (Spek et al., 2007).

Overall, research as part of NICE guidelines for depression (NICE, 2010) demonstrated that guided self-help was an effective treatment for persistent sub-threshold depression and for depression of mild to moderate severity. However, this was not the case for people with more severe levels of depression.

Problems with guided self-help

There are some obvious problems with self-help materials. The first is that currently, the majority of these come in the form of a book, or as a minimum, a readable printed booklet. This of course means that to get benefit from this, one needs to be able to read and must have a sufficiently high level of reading ability to take advantage of the material. Moreover, although self-help material has been translated into languages other than English, this work is patchy and materials are not always available in many common languages spoken in the UK. Furthermore, even if the material is available in the client's preferred language, for the 'guided' aspect to be implemented, a healthcare professional who speaks/reads the same language would have to be available. Meeting client needs by developing and delivering materials within a range of different languages, under the guidance of suitably trained professionals has presented a challenge to healthcare services. For example, in London, where I work and live, the 2011 UK Census data found that over 100 languages were spoken!

Finally, many people who are depressed, and certainly the majority of people who have more severe depression symptoms, find reading very difficult. This can be due to a number of factors, including difficulties with concentration, memory, motivation and energy. Whilst there may be ways to navigate this – such as using audio files of printed materials – similar challenges persist. To date we do not have detailed trials about the efficacy of different formats (e.g. printed, audio) of guided self-help.

Computer interventions

For a number of years, healthcare professionals have been using technology to help them deliver healthcare. In terms of treatment for depression and other common mental health problems, this has included delivering counselling and guided self-help via the telephone and, more recently, by email. The common form of computerised interventions today is known as Computerised Cognitive Behavioural Therapy (CCBT). This involves using a website or CDROM/DVD to deliver CBT. Usually, the form of CBT delivered is similar to face-to-face therapy, however with very little contact with a healthcare professional outside the initial introduction to CCBT material and intermittent monitoring of the person's progress.

Is CCBT effective?

There have been some mixed findings for the effectiveness CCBT. For example, in their summary of the literature, NICE found that for people with various levels of depression symptom severity, CCBT led to significant symptom reductions, compared to a control group. However, studies examining maintenance of such improvements showed no significant differences between CCBT and control groups at 12-month follow up (Spek et al., 2007). It is difficult to conclude therefore how effective CCBT might be in helping people to maintain any improvements made.

Problems with CCBT?

There are a variety of problems with CCBT. An obvious one is that by definition, a person would need to have access to a computer and know how to use it. To overcome this problem, some health centres provide computer facilities with CCBT access. However, these may still be difficult to access (e.g. the elderly or for people with disabilities, or for those who live in rural areas in which travelling to a health centre may include substantial amount of travel).

⦿ Chapter summary

This chapter has looked at psychological therapies for the treatment of depression. We have explored the background theory, clinical interventions and evidence base for each of the three main psychotherapeutic approaches of the last 100 years (psychodynamic, behavioural and cognitive behavioural), along with recent adaptations and changes. We have seen that whilst CBT and IPT are currently rated by NICE to have the largest evidence base for depression, the effectiveness of psychotherapy, and in particular, the relative effectiveness of different types of psychotherapies is a controversial area. As has been highlighted, a current lack of evidence does not mean that an approach is not effective. Moreover, conducting psychotherapy research continues to provide methodological challenges, with many studies suggesting equivalence of different therapies (the 'dodo bird verdict'), and others shedding little clarity as to why certain interventions may or may not be helpful for different people.

Binding all of these psychotherapeutic approaches together is the emphasis on the therapeutic alliance. Even in this area, however, we are not yet clear what aspects of the alliance are most helpful for people with depression, and how much of the apparent effectiveness of psychotherapy is attributable to these factors, rather than specific things (e.g. techniques or interventions) of the therapist or the model they are using. Adding to the complexity of this issue, there is also evidence that psychological interventions provided in the absence of a therapeutic alliance (i.e. a human being physically present), such as self-help books and computerised cognitive therapy, can be effective for some types of depression.

Overall, whilst there seems to be much hope for the potential helpful role of psychological therapies in treating depression, there is still much to discover and a series of controversies to make sense of. What appears clear is that there are likely to be a variety of psychological interventions that are helpful in depression. As my colleague Paul Gilbert wrote over

20 years ago: 'Basically, to treat depression you can't be a "one club golfer"' (Gilbert, 1992, p. 476).

Further reading

Busch, F. N. (2009) 'Anger and depression'. *Advances in Psychiatric Treatment*, 15, 271–278.

Rachman, S. (1997) 'The evolution of cognitive behaviour therapy'. In D.M. Clark and C. G. Fairburn (eds), *Science and Practice of Cognitive Behaviour Therapy*. Oxford: Oxford University Press.

Gilbert, P. (2007) *Psychotherapy and Counselling for Depression* (3rd edition). London: Sage.

| Chapter 9 |

Social Interventions

Whilst biological and psychological interventions for depression have formed the mainstay of treatment approaches in the UK and much of the Western world, in comparison social interventions have been relatively overlooked or ignored, and are sometimes criticised for overly involving the 'state' (government) in peoples' lives. However, although there may be less time, money and research investigating the impact of social interventions, this does not mean that they are not helpful or effective. As we discovered in Chapter 5, there are a variety of social and environmental factors that appear to impact upon the development and maintenance of depression. In this chapter, we will focus on four different types of social/environmental based interventions for depression:

- Improving access to social support and affiliative relationships, and improving relationships within families
- Increasing understanding, awareness and knowledge of depression
- Reducing stigma associated with depression
- Improving the standard of accommodation and local environment

<👁> Providing social support

As we explored in some of the previous chapters, different types of relationship difficulty can be associated with an increased likelihood of depression. Humans are the most social of species, and close, caring and supportive relationships can have an important role in regulating our threats and stresses in life. Unfortunately, disruptions to our affiliative relationships – whether through a lack of consistent warmth and support, or through the absence, or perceived absence, of others (e.g. loneliness; Cacioppo and Patrick, 2008) – have been found to be associated with higher levels of depression and an increased stress response. Although encompassing different interventions, one common approach in trying to reduce, and prevent, depression is through providing social support (peer and befriending) and by improving current familial relationships.

Peer support

Peer support has been described as a process in which support is provided by 'non-professionals' who have experienced difficulties, stress or similar health problems to those experienced by the person supported. Therefore, when working with depression, people providing peer support would have often experienced depression themselves. As Pfeiffer et al. (2011) suggest, peer support can be face-to-face, via the telephone or other forms of technology (email, Skype), and may involve one-to-one contact or groups.

There have been a number of studies looking at the potential benefits of peer support on depression. In a meta-analysis reviewing the effects of seven random control trials comparing peer support against 'treatment as usual', Pfeiffer et al. (2011) found that peer support had a significantly greater impact in reducing depressive symptomology than 'care as usual' did. The authors suggested that the magnitude of change in reduction of symptoms was broadly equivalent to those found in previous studies looking at the impact of psychotherapy and antidepressants upon depression symptomology. Pfeiffer et al. (2011) also reviewed seven RCT studies that compared peer support with CBT interventions. They found that there was no significant difference in the reduction of depression symptoms between these two types of interventions – that is, both approaches were equally as beneficial in reducing depression.

There have been a number of specific projects in the UK attempting to use peer support as a way of alleviating depression symptoms. For example, Gater et al. (2010) developed a social intervention for British Pakistani women who were suffering from depression, and measured outcomes of attending this group with a group of women just taking antidepressant medication and a combined treatment group (attendance at the social group and antidepressant medication). The social intervention included the forming of local weekly groups for a total of ten weeks.

These groups were led by a facilitator who had been given training and supervision by one of the researchers. Food was provided, and content of the activities were adapted to be sensitive of cultural values. The authors found that participants who had attended the social intervention group or had the combined treatment (social intervention and antidepressant medication) had significantly improved social functioning at follow-up (3 and 9 months) than the antidepressant group alone. They also found that depression symptomology scores were lower for the social intervention and combined intervention groups in comparison with antidepressants alone, although the magnitude of these differences did not reach statistical significance. Whilst the number of participants in this study were low, the findings suggest that helping depressed people to engage in greater social activity with peers may be helpful. Unfortunately, this study cannot delineate what the active mechanism of the social intervention group was; for example, it might be that social contact itself was important, or social contact with other people with depression, or social contact with other people from the same ethnic group with depression. Moreover, the weekly sessions involved different types of activities, and it is unclear whether these activities, rather than 'peer support', led to the benefits reported.

Befriending

Befriending has been defined as a relationship in which an individual, under the direction and monitoring by an organisation, attempts to develop a helpful and supportive relationship with a defined person (e.g. see Dean and Goodlad, 1998). Befriending commonly includes qualities such as respect, non-judgment and mutuality, with the intention of a commitment over a defined period of time. Mead et al. (2010) conducted a systematic review of published studies looking at the impact of befriending upon depression symptoms. The authors attempted to limit the studies examined to only those which provided non-directive emotional support, excluding studies that used non-directive counseling, self-help groups or mentors, as these were seen as more complex and directive interventions. They found that in comparison with treatment as usual or no treatment at all, befriending had a significant yet modest impact upon reducing depression symptoms. However, the authors found that in comparison with some more active treatments, such as CBT, befriending was less effective in reducing depression symptoms.

There are a variety of suggestions for how support, in the variety of forms it can take, may help to alleviate depression. For example:

1 Support may directly reduce isolation and feelings of aloneness, which as discussed in Chapter 5, appear to have a strong relationship with higher levels of depression.
2 Support may provide helpful ideas and information about things that might reduce depression symptoms.
3 Support may facilitate normalisation of the depressive experience (reducing shame and stigmatisation) and offer positive role modelling and hope (e.g. from someone who has managed to 'get through' depression).
4 Support may encourage increased levels of activity and reduce focus on negative thoughts and feelings.

It is likely that some of the above factors may interact and lead to some of the helpful benefits of social support. However, it seems clear that further research is needed to identify the exact mechanisms in which different types of social support (professional, peer, befriending) can be beneficial, and in particular, whether they impact upon depression in different ways.

Working with families

In Chapter 5 we explored how high expressed emotion, commonly measured through factors like hostility, emotional over-involvement and critical comments, may be associated with depression. We also saw how early experiences of neglect and abuse and the absence of consistent warmth, care and nurturance were also related to higher levels of depression. With this in mind, a variety of clinicians and researchers have tried to develop and evaluate the potential benefit of working with a depressed person's family in alleviating their depression.

In a review of the literature, Luciano et al. (2012) found that there were problems with the rigour of research methodology used to study family interventions in depression. However, in a number of studies they found that providing families with psychoeducation (teaching of information about depression, including about its cause, symptoms and treatment) and improving communication and problem-solving skills could lead to a number of benefits. Across four studies in particular, these improvements included increased understanding of difficulties, reduction in family burden (e.g. worry and tension), improved social functioning and reduction in relapses. Similarly, whilst the NICE guidelines for depression (2009) also highlight concerns with the quality of studies in this area, they suggest that family interventions should be considered for depression if there appears to be a significant element of family issues linked to the maintenance of depression.

There has also been some research looking at the potential of family interventions preventing depression developing in the first place. For example, Connell and Dishion (2008) compared two groups of 12- to 15-year-old adolescents who were identified as being 'at risk' of developing depression due to existing emotional and behavioural problems. One of the groups was given family interventions (these ranged from consultation and educational materials, through to specific sessions for parents about building positive relationships, communication and setting boundaries), whilst the other didn't receive anything. The researchers found that those in the family intervention condition were protected against developing depression in comparison with those in the control group.

Improving awareness of depression

Whilst we have spent time in the past two chapters, as well as above, exploring different ways to treat depression, it stands to reason that you can only really help to alleviate depression if you are aware that someone is suffering from it. Although it is difficult to identify how many people might be suffering from undetected depression, there are two important components here: (i) the individual suffering from depression, along with the people close to them in their life, do not understand that the symptoms they are experiencing are indicative of depression and (ii) at presentation to health services, the health professional does not detect that the patient is suffering from depression. There have been a number of interventions that have sought to improve both of these problems.

General public

A number of studies have assessed the outcome of national depression awareness campaigns upon general public awareness of this disorder. Jorm et al. (2005) reported on the impact of a depression awareness campaign in Australia called 'beyondblue'. Amongst other things, the researchers found that the programme led to a national-level increase in awareness and recognition of depression. beyondblue's own research suggested that since its launch in 2001, general public recognition of depression rose from 40% to 59% by 2008.

Dumesnil and Verger (2009) conducted a review of studies evaluating public campaigns aimed at increasing public awareness of depression and suicide. Their review included a total of 43 different studies, spanning 15 different awareness campaigns across eight different countries. The authors suggested that awareness campaigns attempted to reduce discrimination, counter misconceptions and enhance help-seeking behaviours, and could be classified into different categories:

- Short media campaigns, such as television programmes on depression, usually lasting a number of weeks. Gatekeeper training programmes that involve training of various people (health professionals, members of the general public) to have skills in understanding and helping people with depression.
- Long programmes involving repeated exposures (at both local and national level) – these interventions usually last for a number of years, and commonly utilise a variety of media outlets, including television, radio and advertising, along with other educational methods, such as lectures and conferences.

Dumesnil and Verger (2009) found that overall, the studies reviewed showed a modest impact of such campaigns upon improving public attitudes towards depression and suicide, although note that only three of reviewed studies found a significant improvement in professional help-seeking. Overall, the authors felt that having campaigns based on multiple methods – such as educational material along with training gatekeepers and media campaigns – are more effective than educational material alone, because they provide repeated exposure of relevant messages, and over longer periods of time. An example of a campaign to improve awareness and understanding of depression in the UK is described in Box 9.1.

Box 9.1 Example of a depression awareness campaign: The 'Black Dog Campaign'

In 2013, the UK charity called 'SANE' (http://www.sane.org.uk/what_ we_do/black_dog), whose goals are to reduce mental health stigma, unveiled their 'Black Dog' campaign to increase societal awareness of depression. The term 'black dog' has been used for many thousands of years as a metaphor for depression. In fact, the former British Prime Minister, Winston Churchill, who suffered from frequent and long lasting depressions, referred to his experience as 'the black dog', bringing to mind visions of a 'constant companion', that can at times be persistent, needy or scary, and if not properly put on a tight leash, can run amok. The World Health Organization (WHO) have an illuminating video which emphasises the metaphor of the black dog for depression, explaining what the experience of depression is like and how one can cope with it (http://www.youtube.com/watch?v=XiCrniLQGYc).

The SANE campaign set out to raise public awareness of depression. One of the ways they have done this is by designing different statues of 'black dogs', in an attempt to make visible a condition that is often invisible. Moreover, each dog is dressed with a 'collar of hope' and a brightly coloured coat designed by members of the public, including celebrities, some of whom have experienced depression themselves.

Health professionals

As we discussed in Chapters 1 and 2, a diagnosis of depression involves meeting certain criteria. However, identifying these criteria is not necessarily easy for health professionals, particularly if you remember that there are 227 different combinations of symptoms that can all lead to a diagnosis of depression. In fact, studies have shown that fewer than half of a representative sample of patients attending a clinic were diagnosed appropriately with depression (Simon et al., 1999).

In terms of addressing this problem, a number of social and policy interventions have attempted to increase awareness and knowledge of depression in health professionals. Rix et al. (1999) evaluated the impact of a campaign that ran in the UK between 1992 and 1997 called the 'Defeat Depression Campaign', which aimed to educate general practitioners

(GPs) in primary health settings. They found that almost 63% of GPs had heard of the campaign, and following this intervention, 40% of GPs reported that they had 'definitely' or 'possibly' made changes to their practice. Looking at the impact of the same campaign, Orrell et al. (1996) found those GPs who participated in the Defeat Depression Campaign tended to feel more confident in treating depression, continued prescribing antidepressant medications for longer (thus fitting with guidelines) and had greater awareness of potential psychological treatments for depression, compared to the practitioners who didn't get involved

◉ Reducing stigma of depression

As discussed in Chapter 5, stigma associated with depression can lead to a variety of negative outcomes, such as reduced help-seeking behaviour and discontinuation of treatment. With this in mind, a number of researchers have attempted to evaluate projects and interventions that specifically attempt to reduce the stigma associated with depression. For example, Barney et al. (2009) conducted research looking at the ways in which stigma about depression may be reduced. They conducted a series of focus groups with 23 people who had previously suffered from depression. They found that their participants had experienced a high degree of stigma, particularly linked to a sense that people with depression are somehow threatening or undesirable to be around, or are somehow responsible for their depression. Based on these findings, the authors suggest that stigma related to depression may be best targeted by focusing upon reducing the avoidance of people with depression, challenging internal attributions of 'blame' or responsibility and relabeling depression as a health condition, rather than calling it a mental illness.

Recently, a number of interventions have focused upon using technology – and in particular, the internet – to combat depression stigma. For example, Finkelstein and Lapshin (2007) recruited 42 staff and students from a university, and measured their attitudes towards depression in a variety of ways (e.g. self-report scale; response to a vignette on depression), before and after engaging in an internet-based education programme on depression. The measures assessed three components of stigma: *cognitive* (holding false beliefs, or lacking knowledge, of depression), *emotional* (emotions and feelings about people with depression) and *behaviour* (towards people with depression). The authors found that following the online education programme, levels of self-report stigma were significantly reduced, whilst knowledge increased. Although with a relatively small number of participants, and with a high level of education, this study suggests that a short, online education package could produce useful changes in the stigma people hold about depression. It would be interesting to explore whether reductions in stigma, following programmes such as the above, can affect how people subsequently treat others with depression, or respond to their own potential experience of depression.

Working with social difficulties – accommodation, homelessness and deprivation

Social interventions have also targeted working with difficult environments that are associated with increased levels of depression.

Improving the 'built environment'

In Chapter 5 we learnt that the quality of your 'built environment' was associated with levels of depression (e.g. Galea et al., 2005). Built environment was a term used to describe certain features both inside and outside a home. Galea et al. (2005) found that higher levels of internal disrepair in homes (such as percentage of homes with problems with toilets, lack of heating, or peeling wall plaster or paint), and external or street-level disrepair in a neighbourhood (such as percentage of buildings with a dilapidated appearance or percentage of unclean streets), was associated with increased levels of depression. There have been a variety of studies looking at how changes to the standard of housing and the local environment have an impact upon depression prevalence and symptomology.

In 2005, NICE conducted a review of the impact of housing on health ('Housing and public health: A review of reviews of interventions for improving health, 2005). This review found that whilst there was evidence for the effectiveness of rehousing people with depression and anxiety symptomology scores, in many other areas of housing, such as housing improvement or increased housing safety, there was no evidence to support these interventions having a positive impact on reducing depression symptoms. Whilst the lack of evidence for such an association does not mean that there is no link, the authors of this review make note of the paucity of good quality research in this area, that adequately tackles a variety of methodological issues. They suggest the need of further research to explore whether making changes to housing may lead to improved physical and mental health improvements. In the most recent large-scale attempt to look at this issue, Thomson et al. (2013) conducted a large systematic review of the literature looking at the relationship between housing improvements and health outcomes, which they published in the Cochrane database of systematic reviews (Cochrane Reviews are a database of systematic reviews and meta-analyses promoting evidence-based practice and made freely available to the public). Overall, Thompson et al. (2013) did not find a considerable amount of conclusive evidence for the impact of housing improvement upon health. Whilst the authors cited a number of studies that appear to show some improvement in mental health (including depression), these seemed to have been based on less rigorous research methods, and overall, yielded inconsistent results.

Homelessness

One particularly stressful social situation is homelessness. In fact, as discussed in Chapter 5, homelessness is associated with a high level of mental health problems, including depression (Weinreb et al., 2006). Karim et al. (2006) investigated the impact of rehousing families that were currently homeless into a hostel for homeless people, and subsequently, into an actual home. They assessed mental health, including depression, in 35 families, mostly consisting of a single parent (mother) and young children. Karim et al. (2006) did not find any significant reduction on measures of depression symptomology from being homeless to being placed either in a hostel or in a home. Interestingly, when they asked parents about their feelings following being rehoused after the hostel, the majority of parents commented positively on their mental health, feeling that their mood and stress levels had improved. The authors suggest that this contradiction between the quantitative and qualitative data may be due to the low sample size. However, it is also worth considering other factors that are likely to have influenced the outcomes. For example, unfortunately, many hostels and accommodations that people are placed in following homelessness can be quite stressful themselves, with poor physical conditions (e.g. poor built quality) and stressful environment. Moreover, it is likely that some of the other social stressors that may have initially led to the families becoming homeless (e.g. financial, occupational or relational problems) may still be present, therefore continuing to cause stress and maintain depression. A core issue with regard to the discrepancy between cross-sectional studies (showing a link between poor housing and increased depression/ill health) and intervention studies (failing to show consistent evidence for a link between improving housing reduced depression) is that it is difficult to control for the myriad of other social factors, such as employment, general poverty, existing (and often chronic) ill health and relational difficulties, which may also be contributing to depression.

Working in deprived communities

As discussed in Chapter 5, poor mental health, including increased rates of depression, appears to be linked to socioeconomic factors. Although well established, this link between poverty/social deprivation and negative health outcomes has been difficult to work with. In a study looking at deprivation and poverty, Kling et al. (2007) investigated the effects of a housing programme called 'Moving to Opportunity' (MTO) in five US cities. In this scheme, people living in public housing in areas characterised by high poverty were selected at random to move to safer and less poverty-stricken areas. Upon reviewing outcomes of this intervention 4–7 years later, Kling et al. (2007) found that this had had no significant impact in improving individuals' physical health or financial self-sufficiency. However, the authors did find that MTO had a significant positive impact on mental health, including level of depression symptomology. After conducting further research with people involved in this study, the authors suggest that it was the move away from an environment which was high in violence that might have been significant in bringing positive changes.

Although there have been a variety of initiatives attempting to improve health outcomes in deprived communities, it is unclear how successful these have been, as inequalities in health have persisted and even increased in places (e.g. Mackenbach et al., 2003). With this in mind, the 'Well London' programme was developed to try to work with deprived communities in a different way. Here, the approach involved community engagement and collaboration in developing and running community projects. The goal was to improve a variety of health outcomes, including depression and general well-being, in 20 neighbourhoods in London (UK) that suffered from the most socioeconomic deprivation. Well London involves a variety of social-based projects targeting mental health and wellbeing. These include:

- Changing Minds – here, local community members with experiences of mental health problems are recruited and trained to deliver awareness training to people about mental health problems. The aim of this project is to help people to understand mental health problems better, and reduce the stigma and fear associated with them.
- DIY Happiness – this project involves using knowledge from positive psychology, the arts and humour to help people understand the psychological consequences of stress, and develop skills to manage difficulties in life, and become more resilient.

Although as yet unpublished, the initial findings from this project are promising. For example, participants experienced a 35% reduction in depression symptoms, a 33% increase in number of people engaged in high-level physical activity and a 17% increase in the number of people eating five pieces of fruit and vegetables a day (see http://www.biglot-teryfund.org.uk/research/health-and-well-being/evaluating-well-being for details). As this project is ongoing it is difficult to know what limitations there may to these findings, or how robust they are under closer methodological scrutiny. However, they provide initial evidence for the potential power of community-based interventions for mental and physical health in deprived areas.

◉ Chapter summary

This chapter has explored a variety of social interventions for depression. Many of these may provide helpful ways of either directly reducing depression symptoms or contribute to preventing depression arising in the first place. Social interventions cover a broad expanse – from making improvements to housing and the local environment, to offering greater social support or befriending – and can provide benefits in reducing depression. However, overall, the available research examining the role of social interventions in depression appears to be less substantial and rigorous compared to studies looking at biological and psychological interventions. It may be that this reflects researchers' and policy maker's bias in locating depression in the individual, rather than focussing on a systemic level and examining such things as the environment or social realm. Interestingly, none of the above social interventions are suggested by NICE guidelines for depression, although this is likely to be partly linked to the scope of the NICE project. It is therefore understandable that, particularly in Western countries, available treatments of mental illness tend to target the individual. It may be that in future years, greater funding and interest can be generated for studying the role of working at the social and systemic level in treating depression. Social interventions are closely related to social policy, which of course ties in with political agendas. This brings in to question issues of priority and funding, but also difficulties in gathering accurate data on how changes in social policy may be linked to reductions in levels of depression in millions of people.

Further reading

www.depressionalliance.org

NICE (2005) Housing and public health: A review of reviews of interventions for improving health.

Glossary

amygdala An almond-shaped structure of cells in the brain (one in each hemisphere) that plays an important role in threat detection, emotion and memory. In depression, a number of studies have found altered functioning and size of the amygdala.

anhedonia The inability to experience pleasure from activities that would usually be pleasurable. A core symptom of depression.

antidepressant A type of medication used to treat depression, or help to prevent depression from returning. Common antidepressants include tricyclics (TCAs), monoamine oxidase inhibitors (MAOIs), selective serotonin reuptake inhibitors (SSRIs) and serotonin and noradrenaline reuptake inhibitors (SNRIs).

attachment theory A theory developed by British psychiatrist John Bowlby which suggests that infants are born with an innate, biological need to seek out proximity to their parent (or other main carer), and use the parent as a source of reducing distress, and as a point from which to explore the world. The theory suggests that the manner in which the parent (or other primary carer) responds to the child's care-seeking behaviour (i.e. the extent to which the carer is available, responsive, consistent and nurturing) affects how the child's attachment system develops, and more broadly, their psychological development and well-being.

behaviourism An approach in psychology initially led by psychologist John Watson (1878–1958) that is interested in the study of the measurement and prediction of behaviour that can be observed. Behaviourism suggests the behaviour is learnt through the process of conditioning.

behaviour therapy The psychotherapeutic approach that emerged out of behaviourism, using classical and operant conditioning principles.

biopsychosocial approach A way of understanding and accounting for emotional and mental health difficulties (such as depression) by considering the interaction between biological, psychological and social factors.

classical conditioning A form of learning first identified by Russian physiologist Ivan Pavlov. Involves a process of associative learning in which an initial, automatic response can be linked to new stimuli.

cognitive behavioural therapy (CBT) CBT helps people to become more aware of how their thoughts and beliefs about something can influence the way they feel and behave. It then seeks to help people change unhelpful styles of thinking and behaving by learning more helpful patterns of thinking and behaving.

cognitive psychology A school or branch of psychology relating to cognition, the mental activity that is involved in the processing information. Cognitive psychology is interested in processes such as attention, learning, thinking, memory and problem solving.

cognitive therapy A type of psychological intervention developed by American Psychiatrist Aaron Beck. Attempts to alleviate difficulties by helping people to become aware of and then change unhelpful, negative thinking patterns.

comorbidity When one or more disorder exists alongside a primary disorder. For example, someone might have a primary diagnosis of depression, but over time, after struggling to have motivation to leave their home, start to feel anxious about going out, which may lead to an additional diagnosis of agoraphobia (a fear of being in outside spaces in which escape might be hard).

diagnostic and statistical manual of mental disorders (DSM) A classification system of mental health disorders. Currently this is in its fifth edition – DSM-5.

dopamine A neurotransmitter related to motivation, pleasure and reward. It is thought to be involved in (amongst others) the anhedonic component of some types of depression.

drive A motivational force that moves animals towards a goal or resource that is important. This is often highly and adversely affected in depression.

dysthymia A mild but persistent (chronic) form of low mood that does not meet criteria for a diagnosis of major depressive disorder.

electroconvulsive therapy (ECT) A treatment for depression used when other, less invasive treatments have failed. It involves the passing of electrical current through the brain, causing convulsions. It can be effective in alleviating symptoms of some depressions but may also be associated with a number of negative side-effects.

epidemiology The study of the causes, distribution, effects and control of diseases and disorders in defined populations.

evolutionary psychology An approach to psychology that is interested in human experience (e.g. thinking, emotion, behaviour) in the context of its evolved function and adaptiveness.

functional magnetic resonance imaging (fMRI) A method of examining brain activity by generating a picture of oxygen metabolisation (a measure of neuron activity) whilst a person engages in a particular functional mental task or activity.

genotype The genetic 'make-up', or the specific genes, an organism has that in interaction with the environment, impacts upon how the individual will develop certain characteristics (phenotypes).

hippocampus A part of the brain that plays an important role in emotion and memory. Studies have found that this area of the brain is sensitive to chronic stress, and may be adversely affected in depression.

hormone A chemical secreted by an endocrine gland into the blood stream, and transported to another part of the body in which it exerts a particular effect. A key hormone in depression is cortisol.

hypothalamic–pituitary–adrenal (HPA) axis The HPA axis involves an interconnected process in which, under stress, the hypothalamus releases hormones that stimulate the pituitary gland. When stimulated, the pituitary releases another hormone into the blood stream that travels to the adrenal glands (located near to the kidneys) which produce cortisol, a hormone that plays a key role in the immune response and in maintaining blood glucose levels.

immune response The bodily response to the presence of a pathogen (a disease-producing agent such as a virus), in which antibodies travel within the bloodstream to the site of infection.

International Statistical Classification of Diseases and Related Health Problems (ICD) A system of classifying mental health problems endorsed by the World Health Organisation (WHO) and used by health professionals in the UK and many other countries internationally. This is currently in its tenth edition: ICD–10.

major depressive disorder A diagnostic term based on DSM criteria (DSM-5) which is given to an individual if, over at least the past two weeks, he/she has experienced at least five symptoms of depression, including either depressed mood (most of the day, almost every day) or a clear loss of interest or pleasure in most, if not all, activities.

monoamine oxidase inhibitor (MAOIs) An older group of antidepressant medications that impact on neurotransmitters thought to be important in depression.

negative affect A state in which a person experiences negative mood or emotions, such as anxiety, anger, sadness or shame.

neurotransmitters Chemicals in the brain through which neurons 'communicate' with one another. In depression, a type of neurotransmitter known as monoamine neurotransmitter seems to play an important role. Three types of monoamine have been identified as key in depression – serotonin, norepinephrine and dopamine.

NICE guidelines NICE stands for National Institute for Clinical Excellence. It is a body of professionals created by the British Government to consider the effectiveness of interventions for a variety of illnesses, including mental and physical health problems. The guidelines are based on a review of the evidence from published studies in a particular area, and make recommendations on what treatments should be available on the National Health Service (NHS) for particular illnesses.

operant conditioning A type of learning in which the consequences that follow a behaviour, whether positive or negative, impact upon how likely that behaviour is to occur again in the future. Also known as learning by consequences.

phenotype The observable characteristics of an organism that are the result of an interplay between their genotype (genetic makeup) and environmental factors. In humans, these may include various physical characteristics (e.g. height) and psychological traits, such as attachment style.

placebo effect A physiological or psychological effect following an intervention (e.g. taking a pill or injection) in which the recipient believes that the intervention contained an active substance when in reality the intervention contained only an inert substance.

positive affect A state in which an individual experiences positively based emotions, such as happiness, joy or excitement.

prevalence The total number of cases of a particular disorder or disease as a proportion of a population (usually per 100,000 people) at a particular time.

psychoanalysis A form of psychotherapy developed initially by Sigmund Freud, which suggests that unconscious mental processes (thoughts, emotions, fantasies), and the way in which an individual defends against internal conflict stemming from these, can lead to a variety of emotional and mental health problems, including depression.

psychodynamic therapy An umbrella term used to describe talking therapies that emerged from Freudian Psychoanalysis, and which focus on unconscious processes (feelings, thoughts, fantasies, dreams), and an individual's way of relating to self and others.

psychotherapy The treatment of psychological and mental health problems primarily via psychological means, and often through a process of talking therapy between a therapist and the individual suffering with a difficulty. There are many different forms of psychotherapy, including psychodynamic therapy, behaviour therapy and cognitive behaviour therapy (CBT).

randomised control trial (RCT) A type of experimental research methodology to test the effectiveness of a particular intervention (e.g. medication, therapy). In a RCT, participants are randomly assigned to either the active treatment group, or a control or placebo group.

reinforcement A term used in operant conditioning, in which a stimulus presented or removed shortly after a behaviour increases or decreases the likelihood of that behaviour occurring again in the future.

remission A period of time in which the symptoms of an illness or disorder are reduced or are no longer present.

relapse The recurrence of an illness or disorder.

selective serotonin reuptake inhibitor (SSRI) The most commonly prescribed antidepressant. It is thought to work by affecting levels of the neurotransmitter serotonin.

serotonin A neurotransmitter that is thought to play an important role in the regulation of mood. It is suggested to play an important role in depression.

socioeconomic status (SES) A measure of an individual's social and economic standing based upon a variety of factors, including education, occupation and income.

stress or stress response A psychological or physiological reaction to the presence of a stressor.

stressor Any situation or event that may destabilise the body's ability to maintain homeostasis (metabolic balance).

References

Abbass, A.A., Hancock, J.T., Henderson, J. and Kisely, S. (2006) 'Short-term psychodynamic psychotherapies for common mental disorders', *Cochrane Database of Systemic Reviews*, Issue 4, Article No. CD004687.

Abramson, L.Y., Seligman, M.E.P. and Teasdale, J.D. (1978) 'Learned helplessness in humans: Critique and reformulation', *Journal of Abnormal Psychology*, 87, 49-74.

Adler, D.A., McLaughlin, T.J., Rogers, W.H., Chang, H., Lapitsky, L. and Lerner, D. (2006) 'Job performance deficits due to depression', *American Journal of Psychiatry*, 163, 1569–1576.

Ahmed, K. and Bhurga, D. (2006) 'Diagnosis and management of depression across cultures', *Psychiatry*, 5, 417–419.

Ainsworth, M.D.S., Blehar, M., Waters, E. and Wall, S. (1978) *Patterns of Attachment.* New Jersey: Erlbaum.

Allan, S. and Gilbert, P. (1995) 'A social comparison scale: Psychometric properties and relationship to psychopathology', *Personality and Individual Differences*, 19 (3), 293–299.

Almond, S. and Healey, A. (2003) 'Mental health and absence from work: New evidence from the UK quarterly labour force survey', *Work, Employment and Society*.

American Psychiatric Association (2000) *Diagnostic and Statistical Manual of Mental Disorders* (4th edition). Washington D.C.

Andrade, L., Caraveo-Anduaga, J.J., Berglund, P., Bijl, R.V., de Graaf, R., Vollebergh, W., Dragomirecka, E., Kohn, R., Keller, M., Kessler, R.C., Kawakami, N., Kilic, C., Offord, D., Ustun, T.B. and Wittchen, H.U. (2003) 'The epidemiology of major depressive episodes: Results from the International Consortium of Psychiatric

Epidemiology (ICPE) surveys', *International Journal of Methods in Psychiatric Research*, 12, 3–21.

Andrews, B. (1995) 'Bodily shame as a mediator between abusive experiences and depression', *Journal of Abnormal Psychology*, 104 (2), 277.

Andrews, B. and Hunter, E. (1997) 'Shame, early abuse, and course of depression in a clinical sample: A preliminary study', *Cognition & Emotion*, 11 (4), 373–381.

Andrews, B. and Wilding, J.M. (2004) 'The relation of depression and anxiety to life-stress and achievement in students', *British Journal of Psychology*, 95, 509–521.

Argyropoulos, S.V. and Nutt, D.J. (2013) 'Anhedonia revisited: Is there a role for dopamine-targeting drugs for depression?', *Journal of Psychopharmacology*, 27, 869–877.

Assefi, S.L. and Garry, M. (2003) 'Absolut memory distortions: Alcohol placebos influence the misinformation effect', *Psychological Science*, 14, 77–80.

Barney, L.J., Griffiths, K.M., Christensen and Jorm, A.F. (2009) 'Exploring the nature of stigmatising beliefs about depression and help-seeking: Implications for reducing stigma', *BMC Public Health*, 9, 61.

Bartholomew, K. and Horowitz, L. M. (1991) 'Attachment styles among young adults: A test of a four-category model', *Journal of Personality and Social Psychology*, 61 (2), 226.

Beck, A.T. (1976) *Cognitive Therapy and the Emotional Disorders.* New York: New American library.

Beck, J. S. (2005) *Cognitive Therapy for Challenging Problems: What to Do When the Basics Don't Work.* New York: Guilford.

Beck, A.T., Steer, R.A. and Brown, G.K. (1996) *Manual for the BDI-II.* San Antonio, TX: Psychological Corporation.

Beck, A.T., Brown, G., Eidelson, J.I., Steer, R.A. and Riskind, J.H. (1987) 'Differentiating anxiety and depression: A test of the cognitive content-specificity hypothesis', *Journal of Abnormal Psychology*, 96, 179–183.

Berman, A.L. (2010) 'Depression and suicide'. In I.H. Gotlib and C.L. Hammen (eds), *Handbook of Depression* (2nd edition), New York: The Guildford Press.

Bifulco, A., Moran, P. M., Ball, C. and Bernazzani, O. (2002) 'Adult attachment style. I: Its relationship to clinical depression', *Social Psychiatry and Psychiatric Epidemiology*, 37 (2), 50–59.

Bifulco, A., Brown, G. W. and Harris, T. O. (1994) 'Childhood experience of care and abuse (CECA): A retrospective interview measure', *Journal of Child Psychology and Psychiatry*, 35 (8), 1419–1435.

Björkqvist, K. (2001) 'Social defeat as a stressor in humans', *Physiology & Behavior*, 73 (3), 435–442.

Blackburn, I. M. and Moore, R. G. (1997) 'Controlled acute and follow-up trial of cognitive therapy and pharmacotherapy in out-patients with recurrent depression', *The British Journal of Psychiatry*, 171 (4), 328–334.

Blackburn, I.M., Euson, K. and Bishop, S. (1986) 'A two-year naturalistic follow-up of depressed patients treated with cognitive therapy, pharmacotherapy and a combination of both', *Journal of Affective Disorders*, 10, 67–75.

Blatt, S. J. and Homann, E. (1992) 'Parent–child interaction in the etiology of dependent and self-critical depression', *Clinical Psychology Review*, 12 (1), 47–91.

Blatt, S.J. and Zuroff, D.C. (1992) 'Interpersonal relatedness and self-definition: Two prototypes for depression', *Clinical Psychology Review*, 12, 527–562.

Boland, R.J. and Keller, M.B. (2010) 'Course and outcome of depression'. In I.H. Gotlib and C.L. Hammen (eds), *Handbook of Depression* (2nd edition). New York: The Guildford Press.

Bowlby, J. (1969) *Attachment. Attachment and Loss, Vol. 1*. London: Hogarth Press.

Bowlby, J. (1973) *Attachment and Loss, Vol. 2: Separation: Anxiety and Anger*. London: Hogarth Press.

Bowlby, J. (1980). *Attachment and Loss: Vol. 3: Sadness and Depression*. London: Hogarth Press.

Brampton, S. (2008). *Shoot the Damn Dog: A Memoir of Depression*. London: Bloomsbury Publishing PLC.

Brennan, K. A., Clark, C. L. and Shaver, P. R. (1998) 'Self-report measurement of adult attachment', *Attachment Theory and Close Relationships*, 46–76.

Brewin, C.R., Andrews, B. and Gotlib, I.H. (1993) 'Psychopathology and early experience: A reappraisal of retrospective reports', *Psychological Bulletin*, 113, 82–98.

Bright, J.I., Baker, K.D. and Neimeyer, R.A. (1999) 'Professional and paraprofessional group treatments for depression: A comparison of cognitive-behavioral and mutual support interventions', *Journal of Consulting and Clinical Psychology*, 67, 491–501.

Brody, C.L., Haaga, D.A.F., Lindsey, K. and Solomon, A. (1999) 'Experiences of anger in people who have recovered from depression and never-depressed people', *Journal of Nervous and Mental Disease*, 187, 400–405.

Bromet, E., Andrade, L.H., Hwang, I., Sampson, N.A., Alonso, J., de Girolamos, G., de Graaf, R., Kostyuchenko, S., Lépine, J.P., Levinson, D., Matschinger, H., Mora, M.E.M., Browne, M.O., Posada-Villa, J., Viana, M.C., Williams, D.R. and Kessler, R.C. (2011) 'Cross-national epidemiology of DSM-IV major depressive episode', *BMC Medicine*, 9, 90–105.

Brown, G.W. and Harris, T.O. (1978) *Social Origins of Depression*. London: Free Press.

Brown, G.W. and Harris, T.O. (1989) 'Depression'. In G.W. Brown and T.O. Harris (pp. 49–93), *Life Events and Illness*. New York: Guilford.

Brown, G.W. and Moran, P. (1994) 'Clinical and psychosocial origins of chronic depressive episodes. I: A community survey', *The British Journal of Psychiatry*, 165, 447–456.

Brown, G. W., Harris, T. O. and Hepworth, C. (1995) 'Loss, humiliation and entrapment among women developing depression: A patient and non-patient comparison', *Psychological Medicine*, 25 (1), 7–22.

Budd, R. and Hughes, I. (2009) 'The dodo bird verdict – Controversy, inevitable and important: A commentary on 30 years of meta-analysis', *Clinical Psychology and Psychotherapy*, 16, 510–522.

Busch, F.N. (2009) 'Anger and depression', *Advances in Psychiatric Treatment*, 15, 271–278.

Bush, G., Luu, P. and Posner, M.I. (2000) 'Cognitive and emotional influences in anterior cingulated cortex', *Trends in Cognitive Sciences*, 4, 215–222.

Buss, D.M. (2012) *Evolutionary Psychology: The New Science of the Mind* (4th ed.) Boston: Allyn & Bacon.

Butzlaff, R.L. and Hooley, J.M. (1998) 'Expressed emotion and psychiatric relapse: A meta-analysis', *Archives of General Psychiatry*, 55, 547–552.

Cacioppo, J.T. and Patrick, W. (2008) *Loneliness: Human Nature and the Need for Social Connection*. New York: W.W. Norton & Company, Inc.

Cacioppo, J. T., Hughes, M. E., Waite, L. J., Hawkley, L. C. and Thisted, R. A. (2006) 'Loneliness as a specific risk factor for depressive symptoms: Cross-sectional and longitudinal analyses', *Psychology and Aging*, 21 (1), 140.

Calev, A. (1996) 'Affect and memory in depression: Evidence of better delayed recall of positive than negative affect words', *Psychopathology*, 29, 71–76.

Campbell, S., Marriott, M., Nahmias, C. and MacQueen, G.M. (2004) 'Lower hippocampal volume in patients suffering from depression: A meta-analysis', *American Journal of Psychiatry*, 161, 598–607.

Caspi, A., Sugden, K., Moffitt, T.W., Taylor, T.E., Taylor, A., Craig, I.W., Harrington, H.L., McClay, J., Mill, J., Martin, J., Braithwaite, A. and Poulton, R. (2003) 'Influence of life stress on depression: Moderation by a polymorphism in the 5-HTT gene', *Science*, 301, 386–389.

Chen, L., Lawlor, D.A., Lewis, S.J., Yuan, W., Abdollahi, M.R., Timpson, N.J., Day, I.N.M., Ebrahim, S., Smith, G.D. and Shugart, Y.Y. (2008) 'Genetic association study of BDNF in depression: Finding from two cohort studies and a meta-analysis', *American Journal of Medical Genetics Part B: Neuropsychiatric Genetics*, 147, 814–821.

Cheung, M. P., Gilbert, P. and Irons, C. (2004) 'An exploration of shame, social rank and rumination in relation to depression', *Personality and Individual Differences*, 36 (5), 1143–1153.

Chentsove-Dutton, Y.E. and Tsai, J.L. (2009) 'Understanding depression across cultures'. In I.H. Gotlib and C.L. Hammen (eds), *Handbook of Depression* (2nd edition), New York: The Guildford Press.

Clark, D.A., Beck, A.T. and Brown, G. (1989) 'Cognitive mediation in general psychiatric outpatients: A test of the cognitive content-specificity hypothesis', *Journal of Personality and Social Psychology*, 56, 958–964.

Clark, C., Ryan, L., Kawachi, I., Canner, M.J., Berkman, L. and Wright, R.J. (2007) Witnessing community violence in residential neighborhoods: A mental health hazard for urban women', *Journal of Urban Health: Bulletin of the New York Academy of Medicine*, 85, 22–38.

Cohen, S. and Wills, T.A. (1985) 'Stress, social support and the buffering hypothesis', *Psychological Bulletin*, 98, 310–357.

Connell, A.M. and Dishion, T.J. (2008) 'Reducing depression among at-risk early adolescents: Three-year effects of a family-centered intervention embedded within schools', *Journal of Family Psychology*, 22, 574–585.

Costantini, A., Braun, J.R., Davis, J. and Iervolino, A. (1973) 'Personality and mood correlates of schedule of recent experience scores', *Psychological Reports*, 32, 1143–1150.

Cournoyer, D. E. and Rohner, R.P. (1996) 'Reliability of retrospective reports of perceived maternal acceptance-rejection in childhood', *Psychological Reports*, 78, 147–150.

Coyne, J.C. (1976) 'Depression and the response of others', *Journal of Abnormal Psychology*, 85, 186.

Cozolino, L. (2006) *The Neuroscience of Human Relationships: Attachment and the Developing Social Brain*. WW Norton & Co.

Craft, L.L. and Perna, F.M. (2004) 'The benefits of exercise for the clinically depressed', *Primary Care Companion to the Journal of Clinical Psychiatry*, 6, 104.

Cryan, J.F. and Slattery, D.A. (2007) 'Animal models of mood disorders: Recent developments', *Current Opinion in Psychiatry*, 20, 1–7.

Cuijpers, P., van Straten, A. and Warmerdam, L. (2007) 'Behavioral activation treatments of depression: A meta-analysis', *Clinical Psychology Review*, 27, 318–326.

Cuijpers, P., Donker, T., Van Straten, A., Li, J. and Andersson, G. (2010) 'Is guided self-help as effective as face-to-face psychotherapy for depression and anxiety disorders? A systematic review and meta-analysis of comparative outcome studies', *Psychological medicine*, 40, 1943.

Cuijpers, P., Sijbrandij, M., Koole, S. L., Andersson, G., Beekman, A. T. and Reynolds, C. F. (2013) 'The efficacy of psychotherapy and pharmacotherapy in treating depressive and anxiety disorders: A meta-analysis of direct comparisons', *World Psychiatry*, 12 (2), 137–148.

Davidson, R. J., Pizzagalli, D. A. and Nitschke, J. B. (2009) 'Representation and regulation of emotion in depression', in I. H. Gotlib and C. L. Hammen (eds), *Handbook of Depression* (2nd ed.). New York: The Guildford Press.

Dean, J. and Goodlad, R. (1998) *Supporting Community Participation: The Role and Impact of Befriending*. Pavillion.

Dhabhar, F.S. (2009) 'Enhancing versus suppressive effects of stress on immune function: Implications for immunoprotective and immunopathology', *Neuroimmunomodulation*, 16, 300–317.

Diagnostic and Statistical Manual of Mental Disorders, Fifth Edition (DSM-5) (2013), American Psychiatric Association.

Diala, C.C., Muntaner, C., Walrath, C., Nickerson, K., LaVeist, T. and Leaf, P. (2001) 'Racial/ethnic differences in attitudes toward seeking professional mental health services', *American Journal of Public Health*, 91, 805–807.

Dimidjian, S., Hollon, S.D., Dobson, K.S., Schmaling, K.B., Kohlenberg, R.J., Addis, M. E. and Jacobson, N. S. (2006) 'Randomized trial of behavioral activation, cognitive therapy, and antidepressant medication in the acute treatment of adults with major depression', *Journal of Consulting and Clinical Psychology*, 74, 658.

Dobson, K.S. and Joffe, R. (1986) 'The role of activity level and cognition in depressed mood in a university sample', *Journal of Clinical Psychology*, 42, 264–271.

Doyne, E.J., Ossip-Klein, D.J., Bowman, E.D., Osborn, K.M., McDougall-Wilson, I.B. and Neimeyer, R.A. (1987) 'Running versus weight lifting in the treatment of depression', *Journal of Consulting and Clinical Psychology*, 55, 748–754.

Drevets, W.C., Savitz, J. and Trimble, M. (2008) 'The subgenual anterior cingulate cortex in mood disorders', *National Institute of Health: Public Access*, 13, 663–681.

Due, P., Damsgaard, M.T., Lund, R. and Holstein, B.E. (2009) 'Is bullying equally harmful for rich and poor children? A study of bulling and depression from age 15 to 27', *European Journal of Public Health*, 19, 464–469.

Dumesnil, H. and Verger, P. (2009) 'Public awareness campaigns about depression and suicide: A review', *Psychiatric Services*, 60, 1203–1213.

Dunlop, D.D., Song, J., Lyons, J.S., Manheim, L.M. and Chang, R.W. (2003) 'Racial/ethnic differences in rates of depression among preretirement adults', *American Journal of Public Health*, 93, 1945–1952.

Dunn, A.L., Trivedi, M.H., Kampert, J.B., Clark, C.G. and Chambliss, H.O. (2005) 'Exercise treatment for depression: Efficacy and dose response', *American Journal of Preventative Medicine*, 28, 1–8.

Egger, H.L. and Angold, A. (2006) 'Common emotional and behavioral disorders in preschool children: Presentation, nosology, and epidemiology', *Journal of Child Psychology and Psychiatry*, 47, 313–337.

Eisenberg, D., Golberstein, E. and Hunt, J.B. (2009) 'Mental health and academic success in college', *The B.E. Journal of Economic Analysis and Policy*, 9, Article 40.

Elkin, I., Shea, T., Watkins, J.T., Imber, S.D., Sotsky, S.M., Collings, J.F., Glass, D.R., Pilkonis, P.A., Leber, W.R., Docherty, J.P., Fiester, S.J. and Parloff, M.B. (1989) 'National Institute of Mental Health Treatment of Depression Collaborative Research Program: General effectiveness of treatments', *Archives of General Psychiatry*, 46, 971–982.

Ellenberger, H.F. (1970) *The Discovery of the Unconscious: The History and Evolution of Dynamic Psychiatry*. New York: Basic Books.

Erickson, K.I., Miller, D.L. and Roecklein, K.A. (2012) 'The aging hippocampus: Interactions between exercise, depression and BDNF", *Neuroscientist*, 18, 82–97.

Eysenck, H.J. (ed.) (1960) *Behaviour Therapy and the Neuroses*. New York: Pergamon Press.

Feltham, C. (2013) 'The cultural context of British psychotherapy'. In W. Dryden and A. Reeves (eds), *The Handbook of Individual Therapy* (6th edition). London: Sage.

Ferdowsian, H.R., Durham, D.L., Kimwele, C., Kranendonk, G., Otali, E., Akugizibwe, T., Mulcahy, J.B., Ajarova, L. and Johnson, C.M. (2011) 'Signs of mood and anxiety disorders in chimpanzees', *PLoS ONE*, 6, e19855.

Fergusson, D.M. and Woodward, L.J. (2002) 'Mental health, educational and social role outcomes of adolescents with depression', *Journal of the American Medical Association*, 59, 225–231.

Ferster, C.B. (1973) 'A functional analysis of depression', *American Psychologist*, 28, 857–870.

Finkelstein, J. and Lapshin, O. (2007) 'Reducing depression stigma using a web-based program', *International Journal of Medical Informatics*, 76, 726–734.

Freedland, K.E. and Carney, R.M. (2010) 'Depression and medical illness'. In I.H. Gotlib and C.L. Hammen (eds), *Handbook of Depression* (2nd edition). New York: The Guildford Press.

Freud, S. (1917/2001) 'Mourning and melancholia'. In James Strachey (ed. and trans.), *The Standard Edition of the Complete Psychological Works of Sigmund Freud*, 19, 3–66, London: Hogarth Press, (Original work published in 1923).

Freud, S. (1961/2001), 'The ego and the id'. In J. Strachey (ed. and trans.), *The Standard Edition of the Complete Psychological Works of Sigmund Freud*, 19, 3–66, London: Hogarth Press, (Original work published in 1923).

Galea, S., Ahern, J., Rudenstine, S., Wallace, Z. and Vlahov, D. (2005) 'Urban built environment and depression: A multilevel analysis', *Journal of Epidemiology and Community Health*, 59, 822–827.

Galea, S., Ahern, J., Nandi, A., Tracy, M., Beard, J. and Vlahov, D. (2007) 'Urban neighborhood poverty and the incidence of depression in a population-based cohort study', *Annals of Epidemiology*, 17, 171–179.

Gallagher, D.E. and Thompson, L.W. (1982) 'Treatment of major depressive disorder in older adult outpatients with brief psychotherapies', *Psychotherapy: Theory, Research & Practice*, 19, 482–490.

Garber, J., Gallerani, C.M. and Frankel, S.A. (2010) 'Depression in children'. In I.H. Gotlib and C.L. Hammen (eds), *Handbook of Depression* (2nd edition), New York: The Guildford Press.

Gartlehner, G., Hansen, R.A., Morgan, L.C., Thaler, K., Lux, L., Van Noord, M., Mager, U., Thieda, P., Gaynes, B.N., Wilkins, T., Strobelberger, M., Lloyd., S., Reichenpfader, U. and Lohr, K.N. (2011) 'Comparative benefits and harms of second-generation antidepressants for treating major depressive disorder: An updated meta-analysis', *Annals of Internal Medicine*, 155, 772–785.

Gater, R., Waheed, W., Husain, N., Tomenson, B., Aseem, S. and Creed, F. (2010) 'Social intervention for British Pakistani women with depression: Randomised controlled trial', *The British Journal of Psychiatry*, 197, 227–233.

George, L.K., Blazer, D.G., Hughes, D.C. and Fowler, N. (1989) 'Social support and the outcome of major depression', *British Journal of Psychiatry*, 154, 478–485.

Gerlsma, C., Das, J. and Emmelkamp, P.M.G. (1993) 'Depressed patients' parental representations: Stability across changes in depressed mood and specificity across diagnoses', *Journal of Affective Disorders*, 27, 173–181.

Gilbert, P. (1992) *Depression: The Evolution of Powerlessness*. Hove: Lawrence Erlbaum Associates & New York: Guilford.

Gilbert, P. (1998) 'The evolved basis and adaptive functions of cognitive distortions', *British Journal of Medical Psychology*, 71, 447–464.

Gilbert, P. (2000) 'Varieties of submissive behaviour as forms of social defence: Their evolution and role in depression'. In L. Sloman and P. Gilbert (eds), *Subordination and Defeat: An Evolutionary Approach to Mood Disorders and their Treatment*, pp. 3–45, Mahwah, NJ: Lawrence Erlbaum Associates.

Gilbert, P. (2001) 'Depression and stress: A biopsychosocial exploration of evolved functions and mechanisms', *Stress: The International Journal of the Biology of Stress*, 4, 121–135.

Gilbert, P. (2005) 'Evolution and depression: Issues and implications', *Psychological Medicine*, 36, 287–297.

Gilbert, P. (2009) 'Introducing compassion-focussed therapy', *Advances in Psychiatric Treatment*, 15, 199–208.

Gilbert, P. (2013) 'Depression: The challenges of an integrative, biopsychosocial evolutionary approach'. In M. Power (ed), *The Wiley-Blackwell Handbook of Mood Disorders* (2nd edition, pp. 229–288), Chichester, UK: J. Wiley.

Gilbert, P. (2014) 'The origins and nature of compassion focused therapy', *British Journal of Clinical Psychology*, 53, 6–41.

Gilbert, P. and Allan, S. (1994) 'Assertiveness, submissive behaviour and social comparison', *British Journal of Clinical Psychology*, 33 (3), 295–306.

Gilbert, P. and Allan, S. (1998) 'The role of defeat and entrapment (arrested flight) in depression: An exploration of an evolutionary view', *Psychological Medicine*, 28, 585–598.

Gilbert, P. and Irons, C. (2005) 'Focused therapies and compassionate mind training for shame and self-attacking', *Compassion: Conceptualisations, Research and Use in Psychotherapy*, 263–325.

Gilbert, P., Gilbert, J. and Irons, C. (2004) 'Life events, entrapments and arrested anger in depression', *Journal of Affective Disorders*, 79, 149–160.

Gilbert, P., Allan, S., Brough, S., Melley, S. and Miles, J. (2002) 'Relationship of anhedonia and anxiety to social rank, defeat, and entrapment', *Journal of Affective Disorders*, 71, 141–151.

Gilbert, P., Clarke, M., Hempel, S., Miles, J.N.V. and Irons, C. (2004) 'Criticising and reassuring oneself: An exploration of forms, styles and reasons in female students', *British Journal of Clinical Psychology*, 43, 31–50.

Gilbert, P., McEwan, K., Matos, M. and Rivis, A. (2011) 'Fears of compassion: Development of three self-report measures', *Psychology and Psychotherapy: Theory, Research and Practice*, 84 (3), 239–255.

Gilbert, P., McEwan, K., Catarino, F., Baiao, R. and Palmeira, L. (2013) 'Fears of happiness and compassion in relationship with depression, alexithymia, and attachment security in a depressed sample', *British Journal of Clinical Psychology*, doi: 10.1111/bjc.12037.

Gilbert, P., McEwan, K., Gibbons, L., Chotai, S., Duarte, J. and Matos, M. (2012) 'Fears of compassion and happiness in relation to alexithymia, mindfulness, and self-criticism', *Psychology and Psychotherapy*, 85, 374–390.

Gilbert, P., Price, J. and Allan, S. (1995) 'Social comparison, social attractiveness and evolution: How might they be related?', *New Ideas in Psychology*, 13 (2), 149–165.

Gitlin, M.J. (2020) 'Pharmacotherapy and other somatic treatments for depression', in I. H. Gotlib and C. L. Hammen (eds), *Handbook of Depression* (2nd ed.). New York: The Guildford Press.

Golden, R.N., Gaynes, B.N., Ekstrom, D.R., Hamer, R.M., Jacobsen, F.M., Suppes, T., Wisner, K.L. and Nemeroff, C.B. (2005) 'The efficacy of light therapy in the treatment of mood disorders: A review and meta-analysis of the evidence', *American Journal of Psychiatry*, 162, 656–662.

Goldman, L. and Haaga, D.A. (1995) 'Depression and the experience and expression of anger in marital and other relationships', *Journal of Nervous and Mental Disorders*, 183, 505–509.

Gonzalez, H.M., Tarraf, W., Whitfield, K.E. and Vega, W.A. (2010) 'The epidemiology of major depression and ethnicity in the United States', *Journal of Psychiatric Research*, 44, 1043–1051.

Griffiths, K.M., Christensen, H. and Jorm, A.F. (2008) 'Predictors of depression stigma', *BMC Psychiatry*, 8, 25.

Gusmão, R., Quintão, S., McDaid, D., Arensman, E., Van Audenhove, C., Coffey, C., Värnik, A., Värnik, P., Coyne, J. and Hegerl, U. (2013) 'Antidepressant utilization and suicide in Europe: An ecological multi-national study', *PloS one*, 8, e66455.

Haaga, D. A., Dyck, M. J., & Ernst, D. (1991). Empirical status of cognitive theory of depression. *Psychological bulletin*, *110*(2), 215.

Hamilton, E.W. and Abramson, L.Y. (1983) 'Cognitive patterns and major depressive disorder: A longitudinal study in a hospital setting', *Journal of Abnormal Psychology*, 92, 173–184.

Hammen, C. (2005) 'Stress and depression', *Annual Review of Clinical Psychology*, 1, 293–319.

Harlow, H. (1958) 'The nature of love', *American Psychologist*, 13, 673–685.

Harmer, C.J., Goodwin, G.M. and Cowen, P.J. (2009) 'Why do antidepressants take so long to work? A cognitive neuropsychological model of antidepressant drug action', *The British Journal of Psychiatry*, 195 (2), 102–108.

Hawthorne, G., Goldney, R. and Taylor, A.W. (2008) 'Depression prevalence: Is it really increasing?', *Australian and New Zealand Journal of Psychiatry*, 42, 606–616.

Hayes, S.C. (2004) 'Acceptance and commitment therapy, relational frame theory, and the third wave of behavioral and cognitive therapies', *Behavior Therapy*, 35, 639–665.

Henkel, V., Mergl, R., Kohnen, R., Maier, W., Moller, H-J. and Hegerl, U. (2003) 'Identifying depression in primary care: A comparison of different methods in a prospective cohort study', *British Medical Journal*, 326, 200–201.

Holmes, T.H. and Rahe, R.H. (1967) 'The social readjustment rating scale', *Journal of Psychosomatic Research*, 11, 213–218.

Hooley, J.M., Orley, J. and Teasdale, J.D. (1986) 'Levels of expressed emotion and relapse in depressed patients', *The British Journal of Psychiatry*, 148, 642–647.

Howard, S. (2013) 'Interpersonal therapy'. In W. Dryden and A. Reeves (eds), *The Handbook of Individual Therapy* (6th edition), London: Sage.

Ingram, R.E. and Siegle, G.J. (2010). 'Methodology issues in the study of depression'. In I.H. Gotlib and C.L. Hammen (eds), *Handbook of Depression* (2nd edition), New York: The Guildford Press.

International Statistical Classification of Diseases and Related Health Problems 10th revision (ICD-10) (1992). World Health Organisation.

Irons, C. and Gilbert, P. (2005) 'Evolved mechanisms in adolescent anxiety and depression symptoms: The role of the attachment and social rank systems', *Journal of Adolescence*, 28 (3), 325–341.

Jacobson, N.S., Dobson, K.S., Truax, P.A., Addis, M.E., Koerner, K., Gollan, J.K., Gortner, E. and Prince, S.E. (1996) 'A component analysis of cognitive-behavioral treatment for depression', *Journal of Consulting and Clinical Psychology*, 64, 295–304.

Jacobson, N.S., Dobson, K.S., Truax, P.A., Addis, M.E., Koerner, K., Gollan, J.K., Gortner, E. and Prince, S.E. (1996) 'A component analysis of cognitive-behavior treatment for depression', *Journal of Consulting and Clinical Psychology*, 64, 295–304.

Jamison, K.R. (2011) *An Unquiet Mind: A Memoir of Moods and Madness.* New York: Vintage Books.

Jaycox, L.H., Stein, B.D., Paddock, S., Miles, J.N.V., Chandra, A., Meredith, L.S., Tanielian, T., Hickey, S. and Burnam, M.A. (2009)

'Impact of teen depression on academic, social and physical functioning', *Pediatrics*, 124, 596–605.

Jorm, A.F., Christensen, H. and Griffiths, K.M. (2005) 'The impact of beyondblue: The national depression initiative on the Australian public's recognition of depression and beliefs about treatments', *Australian and New Zealand Journal of Psychiatry*, 39, 248–254.

Kaufman, G. (1996) *The Psychology of Shame: Theory and Treatment of Shame-based Syndromes*. New York: Springer Publishing Company.

Karam, E.G., Howard. D.B., Karam, A.N., Ashkar, A., Shaaya, M., Melhem, N. and El-Khoury, N. (1998). Major depression and external stressors: The Lebanon Wars. *European Archives of Psychiatry and Clinical Neuroscience*, 248, 225–230.

Karim, K., Tischler, V., Gregory, P. and Vostanis, P. (2006) 'Homeless children and parents: Short-term mental health outcome', *International Journal of Social Psychiatry*, 52, 447–458.

Katon, W.J. (2011) 'Epidemiology and treatment of depression in patients with chronic medical illness', *Dialogues of Clinical Neuroscience*, 13, 7–23.

Keedwell, P. (2008) *How Sadness Survived: The Evolutionary Basis of Depression*. Oxford: Radcliff Publishing.

Keeney, A., Jessop, D.S., Harbuz, M,S., Marsden, C.A., Hogg, S. and Blackburn-Munro, R.E. (2006) 'Differential effects of acute and chronic social defeat stress on hypothalamic–pituitary–adrenal axis function and hippocampal serotonin release in mice', *Journal of Neuroendocrinology*, 18, 330–338.

Keller, M. C. and Nesse, R. M. (2005) 'Is low mood an adaptation? Evidence for subtypes with symptoms that match precipitants', *Journal of Affective Disorders*, 86 (1), 27–35.

Kessler, R.C. and Walters, E.E. (1998) 'Epidemiology of DSM-III-R major depression and minor depression among adolescents and young adults in the national comorbidity survey', *Anxiety and Depression*, 7, 3–14.

Kessler, R.C., Berglund, P., Demler, O., Jin, R., Koretz, D., Merikangas, K.R., Rush, A.J., Walters, E.E. and Wang, P.S. (2003) 'The epidemiology of major depressive disorder: Results from the National Comorbidity Survey Replication (NCS-R)', *Journal of the American Medical Association*, 289, 3095–3105.

Kessler, R.C., Berglund, P., Demler, O., Jin, R., Merikangas, K.R. and Walters, E.E. (2005a) 'Lifetime prevalence and age-of-onset distributions of DSM-IV disorders in the National Comorbidity Survey Replication', *Archives of General Psychiatry*, 62, 593–602.

Kessler, R.C., Chiu, W.T., Demler, O. and Walters, E.E. (2005b) 'Prevalence, severity and comorbidity of twelve-month DSM-IV disorders in the National Comorbidity Survey Replication (NCS-R)', *Archives of General Psychiatry*, 62, 617–627.

Kessler, R.C., McLaughlin, K.A., Green, J.G., Gruber, M.J., Sampson, N.A., Zaslavsky, A.M., Aguilar-Gaxiola, S., Alhamzawi, A.O., Alonso, J., Angermeyer, M., Benjet, C., Bromet, E., Chatterji, S., de Girolamo, G., Demyttenaere, K., Fayyad, J., Florescu, S., Gal, G., Gureje, O., Haro, J.M., Hu, C.Y., Karam, E.G., Kawakami, N., Lee, S., Lepine, J.P., Ormel, J. Posada-Villa, J., Sagar, R., Tsang, A., Ustun, T.B., Vassilev, S., Viana, M.C. and Williams, D.R. (2010) 'Childhood adversities and adult psychopathology in the WHO World Mental Health Surveys', *British Journal of Psychiatry*, 197, 378–385.

Khan, A., Leventhal, R.M., Khan, S.R. and Brown, W.A. (2002) 'Severity of depression and response to antidepressants and placebo: An analysis of the Food and Drug Administration database', *Journal of Clinical Psychopharmacology*, 22, 40–45.

Khan, A., Brodhead, A.E., Kolts, R.L. and Brown, W.A. (2005) 'Severity of depressive symptoms and response to antidepressants and placebo in antidepressant trials', *Journal of Psychiatric Research*, 39, 145–150.

Kirsch, I., Deacon, B.J, Huedo-Medina, T.B., Scoboria, A., Moore, T.J. and Johnson, B.T. (2008) 'Initial severity and antidepressant benefits: A meta-analysis of data submitted to the food and drug administration', *PLoS Med*, 5(2): e45. Doi:10.1371/journal.pmed.0050045.

Kling, J.R., Liebman, J.B. and Katz, L.F. (2007) 'Experimental analysis of neighborhood effects', *Econometrica*, 75, 83–119.

Klinger, E. (1975) 'Consequences of commitment to and disengagement from incentives', *Psychological Review*, 82 (1), 1.

Klomek, A.B., Marrocco, F., Kleinman, M., Schonfeld, I.S. and Gould, M.S. (2007) 'Bullying, depression and suicidality in adolescents', *Journal of the American Academy of Child & Adolescent Psychiatry*, 46, 40–49.

Kosidou, K., Dalman, C., Lundberg, M., Hallqvist, J., Isacsson, G. and Magnusson, C. (2011) 'Socioeconomic status and risk of psychological distress and depression in the Stockholm Public Health Cohort: A population-based study', *Journal of Affective Disorders*, 134, 160–167.

Krieger, T., Altenstein, D., Baettig, I., Doerig, N. and Holtforth, M. G. (2013) 'Self-compassion in depression: Associations with depressive symptoms, rumination, and avoidance in depressed outpatients', *Behavior Therapy*, 44 (3), 501–513.

Kroenke, K, Spitzer, R.L. and Williams, J.B. (2001) 'The PHQ-9: Validity of a brief depression severity measure', *Journal of General Internal Medicine*, 16, 606–613.

Kronmuller, K-T., Backenstrass, M., Victor, D., Postelnicu, I., Schenkenback, C., Joest, K., Fiedler, P. and Mundt, C. (2008) 'Expressed emotion, perceived criticism and 10-year outcome of depression', *Psychiatry Research*, 159, 50–55.

Kung, S., Alarcon, R.D., Williams, M.D., Poppe, K.A., Moore, M.J. and Frye, A. (2013) 'Comparing the Beck Depression Inventory-II (BDI-II) and Patient Health Questionnaire (PHQ-9) depression measures in an integrated mood disorders practice', *Journal of Affective Disorders*, 145, 341–343.

Kuyken, W., Byford, S., Taylor, R.S., Watkins, E., Holden, E., White, K., Barrett, B., Bng, R., Evans, A., Mullan, E. and Teasdale, J.D. (2008) 'Mindfulness-based cognitive therapy to prevent relapse in recurrent depression', *Journal of Consulting and Clinical Psychology*, 76, 966–978.

Lara, M.E., Klein, D.N. and Kasch, K.L. (2000) 'Psychosocial predictors of the short-term course and outcome of major depression: A longitudinal study of a nonclinical sample with recent-onset episodes', *Journal of Abnormal Psychology*, 109, 644–650.

Lawlor, D.A. and Hopker, S.W. (2001) 'The effectiveness of exercise as an intervention in the management of depression: Systematic review and meta-regression analysis of randomised controlled trials', *British Medical Journal*, 322, 763.

LeDoux J.E. (2000) 'Emotion circuits in the brain', *Annual Review of Neuroscience*, 23, 155–184.

Leff, J.P. and Vaughn, C.E. (1985) *Expressed Emotion in Families*. New York: Guildford Press.

Lerner, D., Adler, D.A., Rogers, W.H., Chang, H., Lapitsky, L., McLaughlin, T. and Reed, J. (2010) 'Work performance of employees with depression: The impact of work stressors', *American Journal of Health Promotion*, 24, 205–213.

Lewinsohn, P.M. (1974) 'A behavioural approach to depression'. In R.M. Friedman and M.M. Katz (eds), *The Psychology of Depression: Contemporary Theory and Research*, New York: Wiley.

Lewinsohn, P.M. and Graf, M. (1973) 'Pleasant activities and depression', *Journal of Consulting and Clinical Psychology*, 41, 261–268.

Lewinsohn, P.M. and Rosenbaum, M. (1987) 'Recall of parental behaviour by acute depressives, remitted depressives and nondepressives', *Journal of Personality and Social Psychology*, 52, 611–619.

Lewinsohn, P.M., Biglan, A. and Zeiss, A.S. (1976) 'Behavioural treatment of depression'. In P.O. Davidson (ed.), *The Behavioural Management Of Anxiety, Depression and Pain* (pp. 91–146), New York: Brunner/Mazel.

Lewinsohn, P. M., Hoberman, H. M. and Rosenbaum, M. (1988) 'A prospective study of risk factors for unipolar depression', *Journal of Abnormal Psychology*, 97 (3), 251.

Lewinsohn, P.M., Antonuccio, D.O., Steinmetz, J.L. and Teri, L. (1984) *The Coping with Depression Course: A Psychoeducational Intervention for Unipolar Depression.* Eugene, OR: Castalia.

Lewinsohn, P.M., Steinmetz, J.L., Larson, D.W. and Franklin, J. (1981) 'Depression-related cognitions: Antecedents or consequences?', *Journal of Abnormal Psychology*, 90, 213–219.

Lohoff, F.W. (2010) 'Overview of the genetics of major depressive disorder', *Current Psychiatry Reports*, 12, 539–546.

Longmore, R. and Worrell, M. (2007) 'Do we need to challenge thoughts in cognitive behaviour therapy?', *Clinical Psychology Review*, 27, 173–187.

Lopez-Leon, S., Croes, E.A., Sayed-Tabatabaei, F.A., Claes, S., Van Broeckhoven, C. and van Dujin, C.M. (2005) 'The dopamine D4 receptor gene 48-base-pair-repeat polymorphisms and mood disorders: A meta-analysis', *Biological Psychiatry*, 57, 999–1003.

Luborsky, L., Singer, B. and Luborsky, L. (1975) 'Comparative studies of psychotherapies: Is it true that "everyone has won and all must have prizes?"', *Archives of General Psychiatry*, 32, 995.

Luciano, M., Del Vecchio, V., Giacco, D., De Rosa, C., Malangone, C. and Fiorillo, A. (2012) 'A "family affair"? The impact of family psychoeducational interventions on depression', *Expert Review of Neurotherapeutics*, 12, 83–92.

Luscher, B., Shen, Q. and Sahir, N. (2011) 'The GAPAergic deficit hypothesis of major depressive disorder', *Molecular Psychiatry*, 16, 383–406.

MacBeth, A. and Gumley, A. (2012) 'Exploring compassion: A meta-analysis of the association between self-compassion and psychopathology', *Clinical Psychology Review*, 32, 545–552.

Mackenbach, J.P. and Bakker, M. (2003) 'Tackling socioeconomic inequalities in health: Analysis of European experiences', *The Lancet*, 362, 1409–1414.

MacLean, P.D. (1990) *The Triune Brain in Evolution: Role in Paleocerebral Functions.*

Magnusson, A. (2000) 'An overview of epidemiological studies on seasonal affective disorder', *Acta Psychiatrica Scandinavica*, 101, 176–184.

Magnusson, A. (2009) 'Seasonal affective disorder: An update', *Scandinavian Neuropsychopharmacology*, 2.

Main, M. and Cassidy, J. (1988) 'Categories of response to reunion with the parent at age 6: Predictable from infant attachment classifications and stable over a 1-month period', *Developmental Psychology*, 24 (3), 415.

Main, M. and Solomon, J. (1990) 'Procedures for identifying infants as disorganized/disoriented during the Ainsworth Strange Situation', *Attachment in the Preschool Years: Theory, Research, and Intervention*, 1, 121–160.

Main, M. and Weston, D. R. (1981) 'The quality of the toddler's relationship to mother and to father: Related to conflict behavior and the readiness to establish new relationships', *Child Development*.

Mair, C., Diez Roux, A.V. and Galea, S. (2008) 'Are neighbourhood characteristics associated with depressive symptoms? A review of evidence', *Journal of Epidemiology and Community Health*, 62, 940–946.

Marganska, A., Gallagher, M. and Miranda, R. (2013) 'Adult attachment, emotion dysregulation, and symptoms of depression and generalised anxiety disorder', *American Journal of Orthopsychiatry*, 83, 131–141.

Marmot, G., Davey Smith, G., Stansfeld, S.A., Patel, C., North, F., Head, J., White, I., Brunner, E.J. and Feeney, A. (1991) 'Health inequalities among British civil servants: The Whitehall II study', *Lancet*, 337, 1387–1393.

Marshall, M.B., Zuroff, D.C., McBride, C. and Bagby, R.M. (2008) 'Self-criticism predicts differential response to treatment for major depression', *Journal of Clinical Psychology*, 64, 231–244.

Mazure, C.M. (1998) 'Life stressors as risk factors in depression', *Clinical Psychology: Science and Practice*, 5, 291–313.

McDougall, F.A., Matthews, F.E., Kvaal, K., Dewey, M.E. and Brayne, C. (2007) 'Prevalence and symptomatology of depression in older people living in institutions in England and Wales', *Age and Ageing*, 36, 562–568.

McFarland, C. and Buehler, R. (1998) 'The impact of negative affect on autobiographical memory: The role of self-focused attention to moods', *Journal of Personality and Social Psychology*, 75, 1424–1440.

Mcquaid, J.R., Monroe, S.M., Roberts, J.E., Kupfer, D.J. and Frank, E. (2000) 'A comparison of two life stress assessment approaches: Prospective prediction of treatment outcome in recurrent depression', *Journal of Abnormal Psychology*, 109, 787–791.

Mead, N., Lester, H., Chew-Graham, C. and Gask, L. (2010) 'Effects of befriending on depressive symptoms and distress: Systematic review and meta-analysis', *The British Journal of Psychiatry*, 196, 96–101.

Merikangas, K.R., Ames, M., Cui, L., Stang, P.E., Ustun, T.B., von Korff, M. and Kessler, R.C. (2007) 'The impact of comorbidity of mental and physical conditions on role disability in the US adult household population', *Archives of General Psychiatry*, 64, 1180–1188.

Mersch, P.P.A., Middendorp, H.M., Bouhuys, A.L., Beersma, D.G.M. and van den Hoofdakker, R.H. (1999) 'Seasonal affective disorder and latitude: A review of the literature', *Journal of Affective Disorders*, 53, 35–48.

Mickelson, K.D., Kessler, R.C. and Shaver, P.R. (1997) 'Adult attachment in a nationally representative sample', *Journal of Personality and Social Psychology*, 73, 1092–1106.

Miranda, J. and Gross, J.J. (1997) 'cognitive vulnerability, depression, and the moodstate dependent hypothesis: I out of sight out of mind?', *Cognition & Emotion*, 11 (5–6), 585–605.

Miranda, J., Persons, J.B. and Byers, C.N. (1990) 'Endorsement of dysfunctional depends on current mood state', *Journal of Abnormal Psychology*, 97, 237–241.

Mitchell, A.J. and de Santiago, A.I. (2009) 'Prognosis of depression in the elderly in comparison with adult age. Is there a significant clinical difference?', *Actas Espanolas de Psiquiatria*, 37, 289–296.

Monroe, S.M. and Harkness, K.L. (2005) 'Life stress, the "kindling" hypothesis, and the recurrence of depression: Considerations from a life stress perspective', *Psychological Review*, 112, 417–445.

Monroe, S.M., Slavich, G.M. and Georgiades, K. (2010) 'The social environment and life stress in depression'. In I.H. Gotlib and C.L. Hammen (eds), *Handbook of Depression* (2nd edition). New York: The Guildford Press.

Moore, R.G. and Garland, A. (2004). *Cognitive Therapy for Chronic and Persistent Depression*. Chichester: John Wiley & Sons.

Moos, R.H. and Cronkite, R.C. (1999) 'Symptom-based predictors of a 10-year chronic course of treated depression', *The Journal of Nervous and Mental Disease*, 187, 360–368.

Morrow, J. and Nolen-Hoeksema, S. (1990) 'Effects of responses to depression on the remediation of depressive affect', *Journal of Personality and Social Psychology*, 58, 519–527.

Mueller, T.I., Kohn, R., Leventhal, N., Leon, A.C., Solomon, D., Coryell, W., Endicott, J., Alexopoulos, G.S. and Keller, M.B. (2004) 'The course of depression in elderly patients', *American Journal of Geriatric Psychiatry*, 12, 22–29.

Murphy, B. and Bates, G.W. (1997) 'Adult attachment style and vulnerability to depression', *Personality and Individual Differences*, 22, 835–844.

Murphy, J.M., Laird, N.M., Monson, R.R., Sobol, A.M. and Leighton, A.H. (2000) 'A 40-year perspective on the prevalence of depression: The Stirling County study', *Archives of General Psychiatry*, 57, 209–215.

Murphy, J.M., Nierenberg, A.A., Monson, R.R., Laird, N.M., Sobol, A.M. and Leighton, A.H. (2002) 'Self disparagement as a feature and forerunner of depression: Findings from the Stirling County study', *Comprehensive Psychiatry*, 43, 13–21.

Murthy, R.S. and Lakshminarayana, R. (2006) 'Mental health consequences of war: A brief review of research findings', *World Psychiatry*, 5, 25–30.

Muskin, P.R. (2010) 'Major depressive disorder and other medical illness: A two-way street', *American Academy of Clinical Psychiatrists*, 22 (4 Suppl 3), S15–20.

Meyer, J.H., McNeely, H.E., Sagrati, S., Boovariwala, A., Martin, K., Verhoeff, N.P., Wilson, A.A. and Houle, S. (2006) 'Elevated putamen D(2) receptor binding potential in major depression with motor retardation: An [11C]raclopride positron emission study', *American Journal of Psychiatry*, 163, 1594–1602.

Nanni, V., Uher, R. and Danese, A. (2012) 'Childhood maltreatment predicts unfavourable course of illness and treatment outcome in depression: A meta-analysis', *The American Journal of Psychiatry*, 169, 141–151.

Naus, T., Burger, A., Malkoc, A., Molendijk, M. and Haffmans, J. (2013) 'Is there a difference in clinical efficacy of bright light therapy for different types of depression? A pilot study', *Journal of Affective Disorders*, 151, 1135–1137.

Nesse, R. M. (2000) 'Is depression an adaptation?', *Archives of General Psychiatry*, 57 (1), 14–20.

Nestler, E.J. and Carlezon, W.A. (2005) 'The mesolimbic dopamine reward circuit in depression', *Biological Psychiatry*, 59, 1151–1159.

NICE (2004) *Depression: Management of Depression in Primary and Secondary Care.* Clinical Guideline 23. London: NICE.

NICE (2005) 'Housing and public health: a review of reviews of interventions for improving health', *Evidence briefing Summary*.

NICE (2007) *Depression: Management of Depression in Primary and Secondary Care.* Clinical Guideline 23 (amended). London: NICE.

NICE (2009) *Depression in Adults with a Chronic Physical Health Problem: Treatment and Management.* Clinical Guideline 91. London: NICE.

NICE (2010) *Depression: The Treatment and Management of Depression in Adults* (updated version). National Clinical Practice Guideline 90. London: NICE.

Nielsen, M.B. and Einarsen, S. (2012) 'Outcomes of exposure to workplace bullying: A meta-analytic review', *Work and Stress: An International Journal of Work, Health and Organisations*, 26, 309–332.

Nolan-Hoeksema, S. (2000) 'The role of rumination in depressive disorders and mixed anxiety/depressive symptoms', *Journal of Abnormal Psychology*, 109, 504–511.

Nolan-Hoeksema, S. and Hilt, L.M. (2010) 'Gender differences in depression'. In I.H. Gotlib and C.L. Hammen (eds), *Handbook of Depression* (2nd edition). New York: The Guildford Press.

Nolan-Hoeksema, S. and Morrow, J. (1991) 'A prospective study of depression and post-traumatic stress symptoms after a natural disaster: The 1989 Loma Prieta earthquake', *Journal of Personality and Social Psychology*, 61, 115–121.

Nunn, K., Hanstock, T. and Lask, B. (2008) *The Who's Who Of The Brain: A Guide To Its Inhabitants, Where They Live And What They Do.* London: Jessica Kingsley.

O'Carroll, P. J. (2013) 'Behavioural Activation', in Dryden, W. and Reeves, A. (eds) *Dryden's Handbook of Individual Therapy*. London: Sage.

O'Connor, L. E., Berry, J. W., Weiss, J. and Gilbert, P. (2002) 'Guilt, fear, submission, and empathy in depression', *Journal of Affective Disorders*, 71 (1), 19–27.

Orrell, M. W., Baldwin, B., Collins, E. and Katona, C. (1996) 'The impact of the Defeat Depression campaign', *Psychiatric Bulletin*, 20, 50–51.

Oquendo, M.A., Echavarria, G., Galfalvy, H.C., Grunebaum, M.F., Burke, A., Barrera, A., Cooper, T.B., Malone, K.M. and Mann, J.J. (2003) 'Lower cortisol levels in depressed patients with comorbid post-traumatic stress disorder', *Neuropsychopharmacology*, 28, 591–598.

Overmier, J. B. and Seligman, M.E.P. (1967) 'Effects of inescapable shock upon subsequent escape and avoidance responding', *Journal of Comparative and Physiological Psychology*, 63, 28–33.

Ozsoy, S., Esel, E. and Kula, M. (2009) 'Serum oxytocin levels in patients with depression and the effects of gender and antidepressant treatment', *Psychiatry Research*, 169, 249–252.

Pagnin, D., Queiroz, V.D., Pini, S. and Cassano, G.B. (2008) 'Efficacy of ECT in depression: A meta-analytic review', *Focus*, 6, 155–162.

Parker, G. (1981) 'Parental representations of patients with anxiety neurosis', *Acta Psychiatrica Scandinavica*, 63, 33–36.

Parker, K.J., Kenna, H.A., Zeitzer, J.M., Keller, J., Blascy, C.M., Amico, J.A. and Schatzberg, A.F. (2010) 'Preliminary evidence that plasma oxytocin levels are elevated in major depression', *Psychiatry Research*, 178, 359–362.

Paul, K.I. and Moser, K. (2009) 'Unemployment impairs mental health: Meta-analyses', *Journal of Vocational Behavior*, 74, 264–282.

Peen, J., Schoevers, R.A., Beekman, A.T. and Dekker, J. (2010) 'The current status of urban-rural differences in psychiatric disorders', *Acta Psychiatrica Scandinavica*, 121, 84–93.

Perris, C., Arrindell, W.A., Perris, H., Eisemann, M., Van Der End, J. and Von Knorring, L. (1986) 'Perceived depriving parental rearing and depression', *British Journal of Psychiatry*, 148, 170–175.

Pfeiffer, M.D., Heisler, M., Piette, J.D., Rogers, M.A.M. and Valenstein, M. (2011) 'Efficacy of peer support interventions for depression: A meta-analysis', *General Hospital Psychiatry*, 33, 29–36.

Pizzagalli, D.A., Holmes, A.J., Dillon, D.G., Goetz, E.L., Jeffrey, L.B., Bogdan, R., Dougherty, D.D., Iosifescu, D.V., Scott, L.R. and Fava, M. (2009) 'Reduced caudate and nucleus accumbens response to rewards in unmedicated individuals with major depressive disorder', *American Journal of Psychiatry*, 166, 702–710.

Popper, K.R. (1959) *Logic of Scientific Discovery*. Basic Books.

Post, R. (1992) 'Transduction of psychosocial stress into the neurobiology of recurrent affective disorder', *American Journal of Psychiatry*, 149, 999–1010.

Potts, M.K., Burnam, M.A. and Wells, K.B. (1991) 'Gender differences in depression detection: A comparison of clinician diagnosis and standardized assessment', *Psychological Assessment: A Journal of Consulting and Clinical Psychology*, 3, 609–615.

Price, J. (1967) 'The dominance hierarchy and the evolution of mental illness', *The Lancet*, 290 (7509), 243–246.

Price, J., Sloman, L., Gardner, R., Gilbert, P. and Rohde, P. (1994) 'The social competition hypothesis of depression', *The British Journal of Psychiatry*, 164 (3), 309–315.

Rachman, S. (1997) 'The evolution of cognitive behaviour therapy'. In D.M. Clark and C. G. Fairburn (eds), *Science and Practice of Cognitive Behaviour Therapy*. Oxford: Oxford University Press.

Raes, F. (2010) 'Rumination and worry as mediators of the relationship between self-compassion and depression and anxiety', *Personality and Individual Differences*, 48 (6), 757–761.

Rahe, R.H. (1979) 'Life change events and mental illness: An overview', *Journal of Human Stress*, 5, 2–10.

Raikkonen, K., Matthews, K.A. and Kuller, L.H. (2007) 'Depressive symptoms and stressful life events predict metabolic syndrome among middle-aged women: A comparison of World Health Organisation, Adult Treatment Panel III, and International Diabetes Foundation definitions', *Diabetes Care*, 30, 872–877.

Raison, C.L. and Miller, A.H. (2013) 'Role of inflammation in depression: Implications for phenomenology, pathophysiology and treatment', *Pharmacopsychiatry*, 38, 33–48.

Rao, U., Hammen, C. and Daley, S. (1999) 'Continuity of depression during the transition to adulthood: A 5-year longitudinal study of young women', *Journal of the American Academy of Child and Adolescent Psychiatry*, 38, 908–915.

Riley, W.T., Treiver, F. and Woods, M.G.M.S. (1989) 'Anger and hostility in depression', *The Journal of Nervous and Mental Disease*, 177, 668–674.

Riolo, S.A., Nguyen, T.A., Greden, J.F. and King, C.A. (2005) 'Prevalence of depression by race/ethnicity: Findings from the national health and nutrition examination survey III, *American Journal of Public Health*, 95, 998–1000.

Ritchey, F.J., Gory, M.L., Fitzpatrick, K.M. and Mullis, J. (1990) 'A comparison of homeless, community-wide and selected distressed samples on the CES-depression scale', *American Journal of Public Health*, 80, 1384–1386.

Ritsher, J.E.B., Warner, V., Johson, J.G. and Dohrenwend, B.P. (2001) 'Inter-generational longitudinal study of social class and depression: A test of social causation and social selection models', *The British Journal of Psychiatry*, 178, 84–90.

Rix, S., Paykel, E.S., Lelliott, P., Tylee, A., Freeling, P., Gask, L. and Hart, D. (1999) 'Impact of a national campaign on GP education: An evaluation of the Defeat Depression Campaign', *British Journal of General Practice*, 49, 99–102.

Roberts, J.E., Gotlib, I.H. and Kassel, J.D. (1996) 'Adult attachment security and symptoms of depression: The mediating roles of dysfunctional attitude and low self-esteem', *Journal of Personality and Social Psychology*, 70, 310–320.

Robinson, L.A., Herman, J.S. and Neimeyer, R.A. (1990) 'Psychotherapy for the treatment of depression: A comprehensive review of controlled outcome research', *Psychological Bulletin*, 108, 30–49.

Rohde, P., Noell, J., Ochs, L. and Seeley, J.R. (2001) 'Depression, suicidal ideation and STD-related risk in homeless older adolescents', *Journal of Adolescence*, 24, 447–460.

Rojo-Moreno, L., Livianos-Aldana, L., Cervera-Martinez, G., Dominquez-Carabantes, J.A. and Reig-Cerbrian, M.J. (2002) 'The role of stress in the onset of depressive disorders: A controlled study in a Spanish clinical sample', *Social Psychiatry and Psychiatric Epidemiology*, 37, 592–598.

Rosenbaum, M., Lewinsohn, P. M. and Gotlib, I. H. (1996) 'Distinguishing between state-dependent and non-state-dependent depression-related psychosocial variables', *British Journal of Clinical Psychology*, 35 (3), 341–358.

Rosenfarb, I.S., Becker, J. and Khan, A. (1994) 'Perceptions of parental and peer attachments by women with mood disorders', *Journal of Abnormal Psychology*, 103, 637–644.

Rosenthal, N.E., Sack, D.A., Gillin, J.C., Lewy, A.J., Goodwin, F.K., Davenport, Y., Mueller, P.S., Newsome, D.A. and Wehr, T.A. (1984) 'Seasonal affective disorder: A description of the syndrome and preliminary findings with light therapy', *Archives of General Psychiatry*, 41, 72–80.

Rush, A.J., Kraemer, H.C., Sackeim, H.A., Fava, M., Trivedi, M.H., Frank, E., Ninan, P.T., Thase, M.E., Gelenberg, A.J., Kupfer, D.J., Regier, D.A., Rosenbaum, J.F., Ray, O. and Schatzberg, A.F. (2006) 'Report by the ACNP Task Force on response and remission in major depressive disorder', *Neuropsychopharmacology*, 31, 1841–1853.

Rygula, R., Abumaria, N., Flugge, G., Fuchs, E., Ruther, E. and Havemann-Reinecke, U. (2005) 'Anhedonia and motivational deficits in rats: Impact of chronic social stress', *Behavioural Brain Research*, 162, 127–134.

Sadowski, H., Ugarte, B., Kolvin, I., Kaplan, C. and Barnes, J. (1999) 'Early life family disadvantages and major depression in adulthood', *British Journal of Psychiatry*, 174, 112–120.

Sapolsky, R. M. (1989) 'Hypercortisolism among Socially Subordinate Wild Baboons Originates at the CNS Level', *Archives of General Psychiatry*, 46 (11), 1047–1051.

Sapolsky, R. (2004) *Why Zebras Don't Get Ulcers* (3rd edition). New York: St Martin's Press.

Scantamburlo, G., Hansenne, M., Fuchs, S., Pitchot, W., Marechal, P., Pequeux, C., Asseau, M. and Legros, J.J. (2007) 'Plasma oxytocin levels and anxiety in patients with major depression', *Psychoneuroendocrinology*, 32, 407–410.

Scher, C.D., Ingram, R.E. and Segal, Z.V. (2005) 'Cognitive reactivity and vulnerability: Empirical evaluation of construct activation and cognitive diatheses in unipolar depression', *Clinical Psychology Review*, 25, 487–510.

Seligman, M.E.P. and Maier, S.F. (1967) 'Failure to escape traumatic shock', *Journal of Experimental Psychology*, 74, 1–9.

Selye, H. (1965) 'The stress syndrome', *The American Journal of Nursing*, 65, 97–99.

Shapiro, D. A. and Shapiro, D. (1982) 'Meta-analysis of comparative therapy outcome studies: A replication and refinement', *Psychological Bulletin*, 92, 581.

Shapiro, D. A., Barkham, M., Rees, A., Hardy, G. E., Reynolds, S. and Startup, M. (1994) 'Effects of treatment duration and severity of depression on the effectiveness of cognitive-behavioral and psychodynamic-interpersonal psychotherapy', *Journal of Consulting and Clinical Psychology*, 62 (3), 522.

Shaw, C.M., Creed, F. Tomenson, B., Riste, L. and Cruickshank, J.K. (1999) 'Prevalence of anxiety and depressive illness and help seeking behaviour in African Caribbean and white Europeans: Two phase general population survey', *British Medical Journal*, 318, 302–306.

Shedler, J. (2010) 'The efficacy of psychodynamic psychotherapy', *American Psychologist*, 65, 98.

Shively, C.A. (1999) 'Social subordination stress, behavior, and central monoaminergic function in cynomolgus monkeys', *Biological Psychiatry*, 44, 882–891.

Simon, G.E., Goldberg, S.D., Tiemens, B.G. and Ustun, T.B. (1999) 'Outcomes of recognized and unrecognized depression in international primary care study', *General Hospital Psychiatry*, 21, 97–105.

Singh-Manoux, A., Adler, N.E. and Marmot, M.G. (2003) 'Subjective social status: Its determinants and its association with measures of ill-health in the Whitehall II study', *Social Science and Medicine*, 56, 1321–1333.

Sirey, J.A., Bruce, M.L., Alexopoulos, G.S., Perlick, D.A., Raue, P., Friedman, S.J. and Meyers, B.S. (2001) 'Perceived stigma as a predictor of treatment discontinuation in young and older outpatients with depression', *American Journal Psychiatry*, 158, 479–481.

Skinner, B.F. (1953) *Science and Human Behavior*. New York: Macmillan.

Slavich, G.M., Thornton, T., Torres, L.D., Monroe, S.M. and Gotlib, I.H. (2009) 'Targeted rejection predicts hastened onset of major depression', *Journal of Social Clinical Psychology*, 28, 223–243.

Slopen, N., Fitzmaurice, G.M., Williams, D.R. and Gilman, S.E. (2012) 'Common patterns of violence experiences and depression and anxiety among adolescents', *Social Psychiatry and Psychiatric Epidemiology*, 47, 1591–1605.

Smith, J.P. and Smith, G.C. (2010) 'Long-term economic costs of psychological problems during childhood', *Social Science and Medicine*, 71, 110–115.

Sloman, L., Gilbert, P. and Hasey, G. (2003) 'Evolved mechanisms in depression: The role and interaction of attachment and social rank in depression', *Journal of Affective Disorders*, 74 (2), 107–121.

Solomon, D.A., Keller, M.C., Leon, A.C. Mueller, T.I., Lavori, P.W., Shea, M.T., et al. (2000) 'Multiple recurrences of major depressive disorder', *American Journal of Psychiatry*, 157, 229–233.

Spek, V., Cuijpers, P.I.M., Nyklícek, I., Riper, H., Keyzer, J. and Pop, V. (2007) 'Internet-based cognitive behaviour therapy for symptoms of depression and anxiety: A meta-analysis', *Psychological Medicine*, 37, 319–328.

Spijker, J., de Graaf, R., Bijl, R.B., Beekman, A.T.F., Ormel, J. and Nolen, W.A. (2002) 'Duration of major depressive episodes in the general population: Results from the Netherlands mental health survey and incidence study (NEMESIS)', *British Journal of Psychiatry*, 181, 208–213.

Stewart-Williams, S. and Podd, J. (2004) 'The placebo effect: Dissolving the expectancy versus conditioning debate', *Psychological Bulletin*, 130, 324–340.

Ströhle, A. (2009) 'Physical activity, exercise, depression and anxiety disorders', *Journal of Neural Transmission*, 116, 777–784.

Su, K-P., Huang, S-Y., Chiu, C-C. and Shen, W.W. (2003) 'Omega-3 fatty acids in major depressive disorder: A preliminary double-blind, placebo-controlled trial', *European Neuropsychopharmacology*, 4, 267–271.

Sullivan, P.F., Neale, M.C. and Kendler, K.S. (2000) 'Genetic epidemiology of major depression: Review and meta-analysis', *American Journal of Psychiatry*, 157, 1552–1562.

Surtees, P.G., Wainwright, N.W., Willis-Owen, S.A., Sandhu, M.S., Luben, R., Day, N.E. and Flint, J. (2007) 'No association between the BDNF Val66Met polymorphism and mood status in a non-clinical community sample of 7,389 older adults', *Journal of Psychiatric Research*, 41, 404–409.

Sweeney, P.D., Anderson, K. and Scott, B. (1986) 'Attributional style in depression: A meta-analytic review', *Journal of Personality and Social Psychology*, 50, 974–991.

Taylor, P.J., Gooding, P., Wood, A.M. and Tarrier, N. (2011) 'The role of defeat and entrapment in depression, anxiety and suicide', *Psychological Bulletin*, 137, 391–420.

Tanney, M.R., Naar-King, S. and MacDonnel, K. (2012) 'Depression and stigma in high-risk youth living with HIV: A multi-site study', *Journal of Pediatric Health Care*, 26, 300–305.

Terman, M. and Terman, J.S. (2005) 'Light therapy for seasonal and nonseasonal depression: Efficacy, protocol, safety and side effects', *CNS Spectrums*, 10, 647–663.

Thase, M.E. (2010) 'Neurobiological aspects of depression'. In I.H. Gotlib and C.L. Hammen (eds), *Handbook of Depression* (2nd edition), New York: The Guildford Press.

Thomas, C.M. and Morris, S. (2003) 'Cost of depression among adults in England in 2000', *British Journal of Psychiatry*, 183, 514–519.

Thomson, H., Thomas, S., Sellstrom, E. and Petticrew, M. (2013) 'Housing improvements for health and associated socio-economic outcomes', *Cochrane Database of Systematic Reviews (Online)*, 2 (2).

Thorndike, E.L. (1898) 'Animal intelligence: An experimental study of the associative processes in animals', *Psychological Monographs: General and Applied*, 2, i–109.

Tiemeier, H., van Tuijl, H.R., Hofman, A., Kiliaan, A.J. and Breteler, M.M. (2003) 'Plasma fatty acid composition and depression are associated in the elderly: The Rotterdam study', *The American Journal of Clinical Nutrition*, 78, 40–46.

Torres, S.J. and Nowson, C.A. (2007) 'Relationship between stress, eating behaviour and obesity', *Nutrition*, 23, 887–894.

Trivedi, M.H., Rush, A.J., Wisniewski, S.R., Nierenberg, A.A., Warden, D., Ritz, L., Norquist, G., Howland, R.H., Lebowitz, B., McGrath, P.J., Shores-Wilson, K., Biggs, M.M., Balasubramani, G.K. and Fava, M. (2006) 'Evaluation of outcomes with citalpram for depression using measurement-based care in STAR*D: Implications for clinical practice', *American Journal of Psychiatry*, 163, 28–40.

van IJzendoorn, M. H., Sagi, A. and Lambermon, M. W. (1992) 'The multiple caretaker paradox: Data from Holland and Israel', *New Directions for Child and Adolescent Development*, 1992 (57), 5–24.

Videbech, P. and Ravnkilde, B. (2004) 'Hippocampal volume and depression: A meta-analysis of MRI studies', *American Journal of Psychiatry*, 161, 1957–1966.

Wang, J.L. (2004) 'Rural–urban difference in the prevalence of major depression and associated impairment', *Social Psychiatry and Psychiatric Epidemiology*, 39, 19–25.

Wang, J., Iannotti, R.J. and Nansel, T.R. (2009) 'School bullying among US adolescents: Physical, verbal, relational and cyber', *Journal of Adolescent Health*, 45, 368-375.

Warren, J.R. (2009) 'Socioeconomic status and health across the life course: A test of the social causation and health selection hypotheses', *Social Forces*, 87, 2125–2154.

Watson, J.B. (1913) 'Psychology as the behaviorist views it', *Psychological Review*, 20, 158–177.

Watson, J.B. and Rayner, R. (1920) 'Conditioned emotional reactions', *Journal of Experimental Psychology*, 3, 1–14.

Weinreb, L.F., Buckner, J.C., Williams, V. and Nicholson, J. (2006) 'A comparison of the health and mental health status of homeless mothers in Worcester, Mass: 1993 and 2003', *American Journal of Public Health*, 96, 1444–1448.

Weissman, M.M., Bland, R.C., Canino, G.J., Greenwald, S., Hwu, G.G., Joyce, P.R., Karam, E.G., Lee, C.-K., Lellouch, J., Lepine, J.-P., Newman, S.C., Rubio-Stipec, M., Wells, J.E., Wickramartne, P.J., Wittchen, H.-U. and Yeh, E.-K. (1999) 'Prevalence of suicide ideation and suicide attempts in nine countries', *Psychological Medicine*, 29, 9–17.

Whelton, W.J. and Greenberg, L.S. (2005) 'Emotion in self-criticism', *Personality and Individual Differences*, 38, 1583–1595.

Whisman, M.A. (2001) 'The association between depression and marital dissatisfaction'. In S.R.H. Beach (ed.), *Marital and Family Processes in Depression: A Scientific Foundation for Clinical Practice* (pp. 3–24), Washington, D.C.: American Psychological Association.

Wilhelm, K. and Parker, G. (1990) 'Reliability of the parental bonding instrument and intimate bond measure scales', *Australian and New Zealand Journal of Psychiatry*, 24, 199–202.

Wilkinson, R.G. and Pickett, K.E. (2006) *Social Science and Medicine*, 62, 1768–1784.

Wilkinson, R. and Pickett, K. (2010) *The Spirit Level: Why Equality Is Better for Everyone*. London: Penguin.

Williams, M. (1997) 'Depression'. In D.M. Clark and C.G. Fairburn (eds), *Science and Practice of Cognitive Behaviour Therapy*. Oxford: Oxford University Press.

Willner, P. and Goldstein, R. C. (2001) 'Mediation of depression by perceptions of defeat and entrapment in high-stress mothers', *British Journal of Medical Psychology*, 74 (4), 473–485.

Wolpe, L. (1971) 'Neurotic depression: Experimental analogue, clinical syndromes and treatment', *American Journal of Psychotherapy*, 25, 365–361.

Wolpe, L. (1979) 'The experimental model and treatment of neurotic depression', *Behaviour Research and Therapy*, 17, 555–565.

Wolport, L. (2001) 'Stigma of depression – a personal view', *British Medical Bulletin*, 57, 221-224.

Zeiss, A.M., Lewinsohn, P.M. and Munoz, R.F. (1979) 'Nonspecific improvements in depression using interpersonal skills training, pleasant activity schedules, or cognitive training', *Journal of Consulting and Clinical Psychology*, 47, 427–439.

Zuroff, D.C., Santor, D. and Mongrain, M. (2005) 'Dependency, self-criticism, and maladjustment', *Relatedness, Self-definition and Mental Representation. Essays in Honour of Sidney J. Blatt*, 75–90.

Index